T0330170

Bridging the Prosperity Gap in the EU

Bridging the Prosperity Gap in the EU

The Social Challenge Ahead

Edited by

Ulf Bernitz

Professor of European Law, Stockholm University, Sweden

Moa Mårtensson

PhD, Researcher, Department of Government, Uppsala University, Sweden

Lars Oxelheim

Professor of International Business and Finance, School of Business and Law, University of Agder (UiA), Kristiansand, Norway, Research Institute of Industrial Economics (IFN), Stockholm and Lund University School of Economics and Management (LUSEM), Lund, Sweden

Thomas Persson

Associate Professor, Department of Government, Uppsala University, Sweden

Cheltenham, UK • Northampton, MA, USA

Published by
Edward Elgar Publishing Limited
The Lypiatts
15 Lansdown Road
Cheltenham
Glos GL50 2JA
UK

Edward Elgar Publishing, Inc.
William Pratt House
9 Dewey Court
Northampton
Massachusetts 01060
USA

A catalogue record for this book
is available from the British Library

Library of Congress Control Number: 2017950479

This book is available electronically in the **Elgar**online
Social and Political Science subject collection
DOI 10.4337/9781786436672

ISBN 978 1 78643 666 5 (cased)
ISBN 978 1 78643 667 2 (eBook)

Typeset by Servis Filmsetting Ltd, Stockport, Cheshire
Printed and bound in Great Britain by TJ International Ltd, Padstow

Contents

Figures

Tables

Contributors

Ulf Bernitz is Professor of European Law at Stockholm University, Visiting Professor of Örebro University and Senior Research Fellow at St Hilda's College, University of Oxford.

Nicholas Charron is Senior Lecturer and Associate Professor at the Department of Political Science and a research fellow at the Quality of Government Institute, University of Gothenburg.

Jenny Julén Votinius is Associate Professor and Senior Lecturer at the Department of Law, Lund University.

Ann-Cathrine Jungar is Associate Professor and Senior Lecturer in Political Science at the School of Social Sciences and the Centre for Baltic and East European Studies (CBEES), Södertörn University.

Anna-Sara Lind is Professor of Public Law at the Faculty of Law, Uppsala University.

Martin Ljunge, PhD, is a research fellow at the Research Institute of Industrial Economics (IFN), Stockholm, and an affiliated researcher at SITE at the Stockholm School of Economics.

Lars Magnusson is Professor in Economic History, Prefect of the Department of Economic History and Dean of Faculty of the Social Sciences, Uppsala University.

Moa Mårtensson, PhD, is a researcher in political science at the Department of Government, Uppsala University and a former coordinator of the Swedish Network for European Studies in Political Science.

Sofia Murhem is Associate Professor and Senior Lecturer in Economic History at the Department of Economic History, Uppsala University.

Pär Nyman, PhD, is a post-doctoral researcher at the Department of Government, Uppsala University, and affiliated with the Uppsala Center for Labor Studies (UCLS).

Lars Oxelheim is Professor of International Business and Finance at the School of Business and Law, University of Agder (UiA), Kristiansand, Norway, Research Institute of Industrial Economics (IFN), Stockholm and Lund University School of Economics and Management (LUSEM), Lund, Sweden.

Jaan Paju, is Associate Professor and Senior Lecturer in Public Law at the Faculty of Law, Stockholm University.

Thomas Persson is Associate Professor and Senior Lecturer in Political Science at the Department of Government, Uppsala University, and former Chairman of the Swedish Network for European Studies in Political Science.

Bo Rothstein is Professor of Political Science and holds the August Röhss Chair in Political Science at the University of Gothenburg. Since 2012 he has been a member of the Royal Swedish Academy of Sciences.

Joakim Ruist, PhD, is a researcher at the Department of Economics, University of Gothenburg.

Preface

The European Union (EU) is currently facing its biggest challenge since the signing of the Rome Treaty some 60 years ago. What started out as economic cooperation among six founding countries has developed over the decades into a union of 28 – soon 27 – member states, with in-depth cooperation in virtually all conceivable areas. Yet, despite its success, recurrent crises have revealed significant social and economic inequalities in the wake of European integration. The gap between the more fortunate and the least became apparent in the aftermath of the Great Recession, as certain countries teetered on the brink of national bankruptcy while others continued to prosper. The large gap between the 'winners' and 'losers' of integration has favoured political forces that want to roll back integration and which prefer national solutions to European ones. The wave of Euroscepticism grew and became particularly evident during the migration crisis and culminated in the referendum on Brexit.

What these intertwined crises show is that the construction of the Union is incomplete. It is not designed to help the worst-off countries, let alone the individuals in greatest need. Above all, the crises demonstrate the increasing imbalance in the Union between far-reaching market integration on the one hand, and minimal economic and social redistribution on the other. To remedy the growing economic and social inequalities, and to ensure fairness and social justice in Europe, the European Commission has taken several steps recently. It has launched a 'European Pillar of Social Rights' initiative, started an inquiry on the 'social acquis' and begun a debate on how to achieve greater social convergence within the Union. But will these measures lead to a stronger emphasis on social issues, or help diminish inequalities in Europe? This book addresses the great social challenge the EU currently faces, as a multifaceted problem that requires interdisciplinary analysis. What can be done to bridge the prosperity gap in Europe?

The impetus for writing this book came from Swedish scholars with a special interest in understanding the major challenges facing the EU. Since 1998, Swedish universities have cooperated within a national network structure for European studies. This structure consists of networks for political science, economics and law. Special resources are made available for this purpose by the Swedish parliament (*Sveriges Riksdag*). The present book represents a joint effort by the three networks.

We greatly appreciate the efforts made by all of our contributors in putting this volume together. We are also grateful to the patient and supportive commissioning editors at Edward Elgar Publishing. A special thanks also to Peter Mayers for polishing up the English in the larger part of the manuscript, and for translating certain portions of it from Swedish into English.

Ulf Bernitz, Moa Mårtensson, Lars Oxelheim and Thomas Persson
Stockholm, Lund and Uppsala, 28 April 2017

1. Analysing the prosperity gap: the economic, legal, and political challenges facing the EU

Ulf Bernitz, Moa Mårtensson, Lars Oxelheim, and Thomas Persson

INTRODUCTION

The European Union (EU) is currently experiencing its greatest existential crisis since it came into being in the aftermath of World War II. The origins of the current challenges are to be found in three intertwined developments.

First, the global financial and economic crisis – often referred to as the Great Recession – posed a serious threat to the common currency, and it has rapidly widened the gap between rich and poor citizens in many European countries (Keeley 2015; EU SPC 2016). Moreover, the austerity policies prescribed for the countries most affected by the crisis – primarily in the Balkans and southern Europe – have increased the gap between richer and poorer member states (Raitano 2016). A growing prosperity gap has developed within the EU, giving rise to new doubts that the ideas of 'solidarity' and 'Europe' can be combined (cf. Ferrera 2005).

Second, the global refugee crisis has sparked further political debate over questions of solidarity and shared responsibility within the Union. National responses to the challenge have diverged widely. Sharp disagreements have arisen between the so-called Visegrad countries on the one hand, and the main refugee-receiving countries on the other. The former – Hungary, Poland, the Czech Republic, and Slovakia – oppose the European Commission's scheme to redistribute refugees among the member states. The latter – Germany, Sweden, and such southern member states as Italy and Greece – consider migration to be a shared responsibility (Greenhill 2016).

Last but not least, the unexpected decision of the United Kingdom to leave the EU has highlighted the legitimacy deficit of the latter, by exposing the unwillingness of many citizens to accept EU policies on migration and free movement (Portes 2016; Thielemann and Schade 2016). The

Brexit decision clearly involved a cultural backlash against values such as cosmopolitanism and multiculturalism (Inglehart and Norris 2016). It also revealed growing centre–periphery tensions in matters relating to European integration and global capitalism. Cities and regions in the United Kingdom that have benefitted the most from immigration and trade voted most strongly in favour of remaining, while peripheral regions, characterized by scepticism towards globalization and migration, voted to leave (Arnorsson and Zoega 2016; Streeck 2016).

In the wake of these three intertwined European and global developments, and in view of the severe splits they have caused both within and among the member states, a collapse of the Union can no longer be ruled out. However, if we merely point out the self-interested behaviour of many of the member states in these various crises, we risk overlooking the rootedness of such behaviour in the basic conditions on which European integration builds. The EU, that is to say, is an asymmetric union (Gustavsson 1998; Scharpf 2002). As the three intertwined crises demonstrate, the Union was not primarily designed to help the member states which are worst off. Nor was its purpose to help the citizens who are in greatest need.

Above all, the three crises lay bare the fundamental imbalance that obtains between the economic and social dimensions of European integration. Within the framework of the nation-state, as Scharpf notes (2002, p. 665), economic policy on the one hand and social policy on the other developed historically alongside one another. Conducted as they were at the same level, they could be continuously balanced against each other. But European integration separates the two, creating an asymmetric relationship between (Europeanized) economic policies and (national) systems for social sharing:

> [T]he course of European integration from the 1950s onward has created a fundamental asymmetry between policies promoting market efficiencies and those promoting social protection and equality. In the nation-state, both types of policy had been in political competition at the same constitutional level. In the process of European integration, however, the relationship has become asymmetric as economic policies have been progressively Europeanized, while social-protection policies remained at the national level.

Social policy remains essentially a national competence within the EU, as does fiscal policy. This sets strict limits on redistribution and social investment on a larger, European scale. To a degree, in fact, the treaties even prevent the member states from helping each other out. This is most evident in the so-called *no-bailout clause*, which makes it illegal for EU member states to assume one another's debts (Article 125 of the Treaty on the Functioning of the European Union; Castillo Ortiz 2017).

Despite this, the EU has gradually developed a social dimension. This involves a set of instruments in the social field such as financial support, European legislation, and mechanisms for coordinating national policies – making it possible to speak of a 'Social Europe' (Ferrera 2005, 2014; Martinsen and Vollaard 2014; Fernandes and Rinaldi 2016).

Following the election of Jean-Claude Juncker as its president in 2014, the European Commission has taken further steps in this direction. In a speech to the European Parliament (EP) upon his election, Juncker launched the idea that the EU should aim for a 'social triple-A' rating (European Commission 2014a). This commitment subsequently resulted in a European Pillar of Social Rights (European Commission 2016a, 2017), an inquiry into the EU's so-called social acquis (European Commission 2016b), and a massive investment plan for jobs and inclusive growth (European Commission 2014b). But will these measures suffice to map out a new and socially more sustainable line of development for the EU?

This book addresses the great social challenge the EU currently faces. This is a multifaceted problem, requiring interdisciplinary analysis. What can be done to bridge the prosperity gap in Europe? We have asked innovative researchers in economics, law, and political science to tackle this question and to seek out new solutions within their respective fields of expertise.

Several chapters in the book cover crucial policy challenges: What can be done to tackle youth unemployment? How can national social insurance systems be made to work together within the Union? Can austerity policies be made more balanced and sustainable? Is there a better way to implement European social rights?

Other chapters analyse fundamental mechanisms or developments that limit or condition the evolution of a European social dimension: What are the economic costs and benefits of free movement? What are the factors underlying differing levels of trust in countries and regions within the EU? How do radical-right parties make use of the EP as a political arena? Can the social dialogue between trade unions and employer organizations help solve the EU's problems with legitimacy?

We must stress at the outset that no simple solutions to Europe's current dilemmas appear to be available. Nevertheless, the chapters that follow propose measures that may help gradually restore the balance between market integration and social protection in the EU.

Our purpose in this introduction is to do four things, thereby paving the way for discussions in greater depth. First, in the section that follows, we briefly describe the social dimension and its historical development. Second, we identify the new social challenges the Union faces in the wake of the Great Recession, the ongoing refugee crisis, and the Brexit referendum.

Third, we propose an analytical point of departure for examining these challenges – an interdisciplinary approach that pinpoints a number of overarching problems and possibilities associated with the social dimension of European integration. Fourth and finally, we introduce each of the book's chapters, and the key policy recommendations provided therein.

THE EU'S SOCIAL AGENDA – A BRIEF HISTORY

The idea of a social dimension in European integration was present as early as 1957, in the Treaty of Rome. But social progress was not a priority for the European Economic Community (EEC). It was expected simply to result, rather, from the economic prosperity brought about by the creation of the common market. Following World War II, far-reaching structural rationalization had hit the coal and steel industries in Europe very hard. To be sure, a common European market promised to open up economic opportunities and to boost trade among the participating states. At the same time, there was an early realization that the costs and benefits of economic integration could end up being unevenly distributed. Certain groups would risk marginalization as a result of economic restructuring. With this danger in mind, the European Social Fund – the very first Structural Fund – was created. Its mandate was to increase the mobility of workers and to enhance their ability to find work in the common market (Majone 1993, p. 153). Those struck by unemployment would be given the opportunity to retrain, or would be helped to move to parts of Europe where new jobs could be found.

The design of the European Social Fund illustrates the level of ambition that has been present from the start. The primary object of the fund has been to reduce economic and social disparities among the countries and regions of the Union. Some support can certainly be provided to particularly vulnerable persons – young people, immigrants, the long-term unemployed – but the Union's aid is mainly aimed at the weakest European regions. The idea is that, by enhancing competitiveness and expanding employment in disadvantaged *regions* – rather than by targeting assistance directly on vulnerable individuals – the EU's efforts in this area will serve to enhance social cohesion.

Moreover, the redistribution that takes place through the European Social Fund is vanishingly small compared to that which results from the social expenditures of the member states themselves. The Union's budget comes to about 155 billion euros a year (2016), with each country contributing about 1 per cent of its gross national income (GNI) and about 0.3 per cent of its VAT revenues. Of the total EU budget, the European Social

Fund accounts for some 8 per cent. A much larger portion of the budget goes to agriculture, rural development, and the environment, as well as to regional support through the other Structural Funds. The budgets of the member states taken together are some 50 times larger than the EU budget, and each country on its own spends much greater sums on social welfare (the average expenditure on social protection relative to gross domestic product, GDP, being about 30 per cent, although the variation is considerable).

The imbalance between market integration and social protection is also apparent in the design of the Economic and Monetary Union (EMU), as set out in the Maastricht Treaty of 1993. The so-called Delors Committee, made up of the governors of the central banks of the member states and chaired by the president of the European Commission, Jacques Delors, was responsible for the original outline of the EMU project (Committee for the Study of Economic and Monetary Union 1989). The fundamental idea behind the EMU was that the participating countries would coordinate their economic policies, but never proceed to the next step: a common fiscal union and redistribution (Gustavsson 2002; Jabko 2006). The responsibility for monetary policy would be transferred to an independent central bank for Europe, while fiscal policies would remain in the hands of the member states themselves. Only a limited degree of redistribution would take place through a regional policy based on the annual membership fees paid by the member countries.

But when, in 2008, the crisis struck Europe after the bankruptcy of Lehman Brothers, the US investment bank, ad hoc solutions to save the countries hit by crisis were instead the order of the day. These involved making citizens in the member states (especially those using the euro) fork out hundreds of billions of euros in emergency loans to the worst-hit countries. Meanwhile, central parts of the welfare system in the crisis-struck countries have been dismantled, with growing inequalities as a consequence. It took the global economic and financial crisis to bring the weaknesses of this construction abruptly to light (Scharpf 2012).

Would another course of development have been possible? In certain periods, ambitions for the social dimension of European integration have been much higher. When Jacques Delors took on the role of president of the European Commission in 1985, an intensive phase in the history of the EU began. The Single European Act entered into force on 1 July 1987. In addition to pointing the way to the realization of a single market for goods, services, capital, and labour, this new treaty introduced certain provisions for a common social policy, above all in connection with questions of health and safety at work. It contained, moreover, a new treaty title: that of Economic and Social Cohesion. A common policy to help less developed regions and member states meet the challenges associated with the single market began thereby to take shape, with the aim of ensuring economic and social cohesion. In the following year, 1988, the financial resources allocated to the Structural Funds were doubled.

The extension of Community powers for which the Single European Act provided, and the reform of European institutions to which it gave rise, also provided the basis for the economic and monetary union that would be established by the Treaty of Maastricht.

Parallel with negotiations on the Single European Act, moreover, Delors convened a meeting with the social partners: the European Trade Union Confederation (ETUC) and the Union of Industrial and Employers' Confederations of Europe (UNICE, now known as BusinessEurope). This was the start of the so-called Social Dialogue. A 'social Europe', Delors declared, was a precondition for further integration. In step with the opening up of various sectors of the European economy to competition (including the public sector), the social partners needed to discuss the conditions that would apply in the single market. The work that began with the Social Dialogue eventually led to the Community Charter of Fundamental Social Rights of Workers in 1989, and to the Social Protocol annexed to the Maastricht Treaty in 1992. The Amsterdam Treaty of 1997, finally, incorporated the Social Protocol directly.

The Union's social ambitions were further broadened in the year 2000, when it embraced the so-called Lisbon Strategy. The aim was to make Europe the most competitive economy in the world, while at the same time ensuring that growth is sustainable and social cohesion is not jeopardized. The method chosen for realizing these lofty ambitions – the Open Method of Coordination (OMC) – is based essentially on voluntary or 'soft' coordination, rather than on mandatory rules and legislation (Scharpf 2002). By comparing their different pension and social security schemes, for instance, member states would be able to learn from each other. The legal basis for social rights was also expanded, with the EU's adoption of the Charter of Fundamental Rights in 2001. The proposed treaty establishing a Constitution for Europe included the Charter, which was then adopted in modified form along with the Lisbon Treaty in 2009. The Lisbon Treaty also declared the Union's economic model to be that of a social market economy.

At the time of writing, in the wake of the economic crisis of recent years, the fight against poverty and social exclusion is once again said to be a top EU priority. Through the Europe 2020 strategy – the successor to the Lisbon Strategy – the EU aims to help at least 20 million people out of poverty and social exclusion (European Commission 2010). Furthermore, 75 per cent of the population aged 20–64 are to have a job by 2020 at the latest. The flagship initiatives of the Europe 2020 strategy, including the 'platform against poverty and social exclusion' and the 'agenda for new skills and jobs', are intended to help achieve these goals. Moreover, with the Commission's Social Investment Package, member states now receive advice on how to reform their welfare systems and to make social investments (European Commission 2013a). The European Semester, one of the most important reforms introduced after the crisis, furnishes the framework for supervising and monitoring the various economic and social reforms introduced by the member states for achieving the Europe 2020 objectives. The Commission proposes solutions to the different countries' problems in its country-specific recommendations.

Despite these efforts, the EU's social deficit has become more glaring. It is true that the Union, with its Europe 2020 strategy, has put the fight against poverty and social exclusion among the top items on its agenda. All the same, the development on the ground has been in the opposite direction. Economic disparities within the crisis-struck countries have gotten worse, as has the prosperity gap between the different member states. Let us therefore turn to the challenges ahead.

THE CHALLENGES AHEAD

According to the latest summary from the EU's own statistical agency, Eurostat (2016), around 120 million EU citizens suffer from poverty or social exclusion, or run the risk of falling into such a condition. This represents almost one in four EU citizens (24 per cent). And the differences between the member states are great. The situation is worst in Bulgaria, Romania, and Greece. By contrast, citizens of the Czech Republic, Finland, the Netherlands, and Sweden run a significantly lower risk of falling into poverty or social exclusion (Eurostat 2016). The Great Recession reversed a previous trend towards increased economic and social convergence among the member states. Prior to 2008, most social and employment indicators were moving in the same direction across the Union. Since 2008, by contrast, the trend has been towards a lasting polarization between the southern and peripheral member states on the one hand, and the northern and central member states on the other (European Commission 2013b).

But the prosperity gap within the EU is not just between countries; it is within them as well. Cross-national differences in levels of economic development covary with income inequalities within countries. In the states hardest hit by the economic crisis, unemployment became one of the key drivers behind growing income inequality (European Commission 2013b; EU SPC 2016). Approximately 21 million Europeans are currently out of work. But while unemployment in Greece and Spain is somewhere between one fourth and one fifth of the labour force, Germany and the Czech Republic have a rate of just 4 per cent (Eurostat 2016). Income inequality as measured by the quintile ratio – the ratio of the average income of the wealthiest 20 per cent of the population to that of the poorest 20 per cent – increased significantly between 2008 and 2014 in the southern member states of Cyprus, Greece, Italy, and Spain, as in the similarly crisis-struck countries of Estonia, Hungary, and Ireland. With the notable exceptions of Germany, Luxemburg, Slovakia, Slovenia, and Sweden, countries that fared better during the financial crisis saw declining or stable rates of income inequality during those years (EU SPC 2016, p. 72).

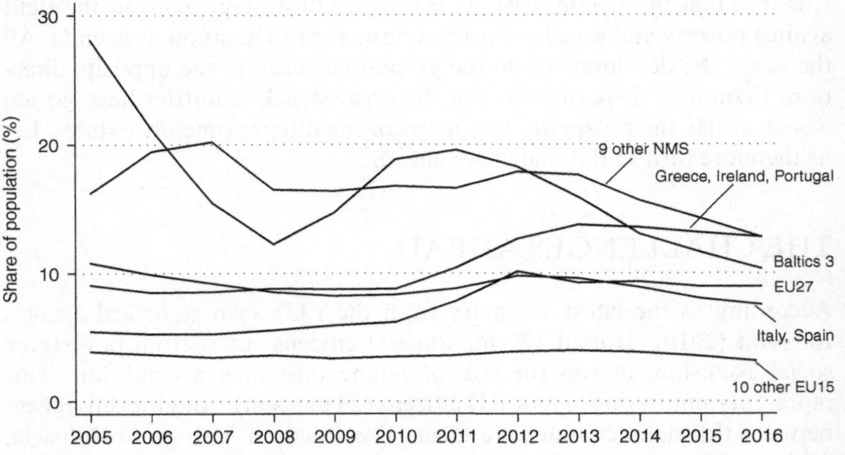

Note: Data for 2016 are estimates. The rate of severe material deprivation represents the proportion of people living in households that cannot afford at least four of the following nine items: (1) mortgage or rent payments, utility bills, hire purchase instalments, or other loan payments; (2) one week's holiday away from home; (3) a meal with meat, chicken, fish, or vegetarian equivalent every second day; (4) unexpected financial expenses; (5) a telephone (including mobile telephone); (6) a colour TV; (7) a washing machine; (8) a car; and (9) heating to keep the home adequately warm. The group '9 other NMS' includes all 'new' EU member states except the Baltic countries. Bulgaria was only included in this country group from 2006, Romania from 2007, and Croatia from 2010. The inclusion of Bulgaria and Romania explains the increasing rate of severe material deprivation in the group between 2005 and 2007. The group '10 other EU15' includes all 'old' EU member states except Greece, Ireland, Italy, Portugal, and Spain.

Source: Eurostat 2017, http://ec.europa.eu/eurostat/web/income-and-living-conditions. The country groupings follow those in Darvas and Wolff (2016).

Figure 1.1 The rate of severe material deprivation in six groups of EU member states, 2005–2016

Looking at the most suitable indicator of poverty in the EU member states (the rate of severe material deprivation), a similar pattern of growing polarization can be observed. The rate of severe material deprivation represents the share of the population in each country that cannot afford things considered by most people to be necessary to live a viable life: to pay rent or utility bills; to keep one's home adequately warm; to eat meat, fish, or a protein equivalent regularly; and so on. As shown in Figure 1.1, Greece, Ireland, Portugal, and the three Baltic countries saw a sharp rise in the rate of severe material deprivation during the economic crisis. The Baltic states have returned to a rate comparable to that before the economic crisis, but the situation in Greece, Ireland, and Portugal continued to deteriorate until 2013, and since then it has only improved marginally. Thus, the rate of severe material deprivation in the EU spanned a wide range in 2016: averaging 3.2 per cent in the group of ten 'old' member states that fared better through the economic crisis, and 12.8 per cent both in the crisis-hit group made up of Greece, Ireland, and Portugal, and in the group of nine 'new' member states, excluding the Baltic countries.

A lasting prosperity gap, then, has established itself between Europe's wealthier countries and those which have lagged behind. As can be seen in Table 1.1, moreover, little overall progress has been made towards the employment and poverty targets set out in the Europe 2020 strategy. The employment rate in the Union as a whole was only slightly higher in 2016 than in 2008 (the baseline year for the 2020 targets), and the number of people at risk of falling into poverty has grown quite substantially.

In sum, the social challenge the EU now faces is colossal. The crisis has exposed the Union's inability to act effectively in the social field. Taxes and social welfare lie in all essentials beyond the ambit of Union decision making, as do most measures for the labour market. The social consequences of recent attempts to cope with the crisis – large-scale unemployment, widespread poverty, and increasingly threadbare social security systems – are thus left more or less to the member states themselves to deal with.

ADDRESSING THE PROSPERITY GAP: AN INTERDISCIPLINARY APPROACH

This book explores different ways of dealing with the social challenge facing Europe. Our point of departure is a broad and interdisciplinary understanding of what this challenge entails (for a similar approach to the EU's role in fighting global imbalances, see Bakardjieva Engelbrekt et al.

Table 1.1 Progress towards the EU 2020 employment and poverty targets

	2008	2014	2015	2016	2020 Target
Employment rate (% of the population aged 20–64)	70.3	69.2	70.1	71.1	75.0
People at risk of poverty or social exclusion (million people)	115.9	120.7	117.8	116.8	96.2

Note: People at risk of poverty or social exclusion are (1) at risk of poverty after social transfers, or (2) severely materially deprived, or (3) living in a household with very low work intensity. Due to data availability, the poverty target is only evaluated for the EU27 and the figure for 2016 is an estimate. The employment target is evaluated for the EU28. Monitoring of the Europe 2020 indicators takes data from 2008 as a baseline year.

Source: Eurostat 2017, http://ec.europa.eu/eurostat/web/europe-2020-indicators.

2015). What economic, legal, and political measures are required to bridge the growing prosperity gap between the EU's member states?

From an economic perspective, it is essential to understand why cross-national differences in levels of economic development and prosperity increased so dramatically during the years of the Great Recession, along with income inequalities within some countries. It is also vital to analyse how public finances and national welfare systems are affected by market deregulation and the free movement of people within the Union. The EU has primarily sought to level out inequalities between its member states, by directing development aid and regional support to poorer areas. Indeed, the Union has been quite successful historically at reducing cross-national economic differences; but the Great Recession broke this trend (Beckfield 2009). An economic perspective is thus crucial for pointing out possible ways of bridging the prosperity gap in Europe.

From a legal perspective, it is important to understand the 'social acquis' of the EU. This involves 'hard law' measures such as EU primary law (the treaties), the EU Charter, social rights, principles of EU secondary law, and the case law of the European Court of Justice (ECJ). While the EU's main goal has been to promote economic and political integration, the ECJ has ruled on many cases involving social rights. It is of key importance to analyse the balance which it strikes between market rules and the social rights of EU citizens. In addition, moreover, to the EU's legally binding instruments, there are 'soft law' measures for coordinating the social and fiscal policies of the member states (European Commission 2016b). More recently, in an effort to ameliorate the social consequences of the Great Recession, the Commission has taken new initiatives in the area of social policy, including a European Pillar of Social Rights aimed at identifying a number of essential principles for all states in the eurozone in the field of employment and social policy (European Commission 2016a; 2017). The social pillar builds on and complements the 'social acquis' of the existing legal framework, and seeks to promote fair and well-functioning labour markets and welfare systems (European Commission 2016b).

The political perspective is crucial for understanding how governments and political actors can promote social cohesion in Europe, and how the challenge from populist parties sets limits on what can be done. The EU is currently struggling to cope with intensified conflict between winners and losers from market integration (Kriesi et al. 2006, 2012; Kriesi 2014). National welfare states are economically and legally constrained by European laws promoting economic integration, liberalization, and competition. At the same time, common social policies have proven hard to enact at the European level. When they have been enacted at that level, moreover, they have proven hard to carry out domestically, due to the diversity of national welfare systems. Not only do levels of economic development and prosperity vary among the member states (making for differing capacities to provide social transfers and services); there are also significant differences in terms of political aspirations to provide social welfare (Scharpf 2002).

Overall, European integration has led to an ever-increasing imbalance between market integration and social cohesion (Scharpf 2010). Economic, legal, and political mechanisms built into the EU system are fuelling a growing prosperity gap. Examining this gap from a range of disciplines, the authors in this book seek to deepen our understanding of its nature, and to propose measures whereby we can bridge it.

OUTLINE OF THE BOOK

The following nine chapters in this book seek to assess the EU's social challenge from the standpoints of economics, law, and political science. In Chapter 2 of the book, Anna-Sara Lind describes how the social rights which, according to the treaties, EU citizens possess – such as the right to social assistance, to health, and to work – find expression in a Union which is suffering not just from an economic crisis, but from a crisis of confidence as well. Lind argues that the confidence crisis itself puts limits on the prospects for realizing these rights, and undermines the solidarity between member states articulated in the Union's basic treaties. New wording in the Lisbon Treaty sought to consolidate the EU as a social market economy with clearly specified social rights, but this has not had the impact that might have been expected. As Lind's analysis in the chapter makes clear, the member states have taken a cautious line on the question of European social rights. Furthermore, the ECJ has found this to be a tricky and difficult area, and has hesitated to enter it. In this area of conflicting interpretations, political decisions have been transferred de facto to a judicial body.

It is therefore crucial, Lind contends, that the member states themselves take the next step now. Within a framework of mutual cooperation, they must actively interpret and utilize the basic rules which have a bearing on social rights. This way, the ECJ too may dare to break new ground – to interpret and apply the rules actively, and to take the step towards yet another paradigm shift in EU law. Lind underlines how essential it is for a well-functioning society and constitutional state that in challenging times it is possible to foresee – and to rely upon – the utmost provisions of the law. Perhaps – if the fundamental rights of citizens had been highlighted – greater trust could have been generated for the measures taken to combat the economic crisis. Lind's overarching conclusion is that the policies for meeting the crisis could have been justified and explained in a new way, and also given a different content, if the fundamental rights of EU citizens had been taken into account. She stresses the importance of social rights for counteracting economic imbalances, both between member states and between citizens.

In Chapter 3, Ann-Cathrine Jungar asks whether Europe's right-wing populist parties pose a threat to freedom of movement and to the Union's fundamental values. Jungar's analysis shows that right-wing populist parties contribute to a better congruence of opinion between voters and parties in European party systems: as a result of their presence, the diverse preferences of voters on questions of immigration and the Union are reflected more fully. Jungar concludes from this that these parties have come into being and grown because there is a demand among certain groups of voters for their critical line on immigration and the EU. The classic political conflict between left and right on socio-economic issues continues to be the most relevant one for the majority of voters in Europe, but conflicts relating to socio-cultural issues – immigration and multiculturalism, equality between men and women, the position of sexual minorities, and so on – have gained greater relevance. This trend is closely connected to large-scale changes like globalization, European integration, and the growing denationalization of both economics and politics.

Jungar thus contends that right-wing populist parties put forward pertinent questions about the legitimacy of the EU, as well as about the limits of national, European, and global solidarity in the distribution of economic and social resources. Can this group of parties in some way provide a corrective, thereby helping to make European integration more relevant and credible for those European citizens who distrust it most? Jungar concludes, however, that these parties have little ability – notwithstanding their success in the last EP elections, in 2014 – to affect political decisions in the Union directly. Their indirect influence via national governments in the Council of Ministers has been strengthened, but their potential for exerting influence lies less in their own hands than in those of the other parties. The challenge for the established parties is to formulate answers, on the basis of their own ideologies and visions, to the questions that supporters of the right-wing populist parties ask. Among the central issues here, of course, is the degree of solidarity and redistribution to be effected between the EU member states.

In Chapter 4 of the book, Joakim Ruist looks at how the prosperity gap between the member states is affected by the EU's free movement of labour. The purpose of this free movement is to even out economic imbalances between countries in the Union. As these imbalances have increased over the last decade, however, freedom of movement within the Union has been questioned more and more. This reflects a fear that people from poorer parts of the Union will seek out the more generous welfare systems in the richer parts. Ruist argues, however, that both the hopes and the fears in this matter are exaggerated. In reality, differences in economic development lead only in small measure to labour migration among EU countries. Mobility in the Union is too low to make any significant contribution to economic equalization between the member states. A partial exception here is the movement of workers that has taken place from the new to the old member states since the EU's enlargement in 2004 and 2007. But contrary to what is often feared, migrants from the new member states have not entailed any net cost for welfare systems in the old member states. In fact Ruist shows that migrants contribute somewhat more to the public purse than they cost.

Ruist concludes that the Union and its member states should strive to uphold the free movement of labour, although it has never been challenged as much as it is today. He contends that the free movement of labour – while less extensive than might be desired – has brought with it a number of positive effects. Although it does not bring about a high degree of economic equalization between EU states, it does indeed raise the living standards of hundreds of thousands of Europeans, namely those of the workers who move from lower-income to higher-income countries. Ruist demonstrates, furthermore, that the free movement of labour has no significant negative consequences for welfare systems anywhere. In view of this, he concludes, there is no persuasive reason to restrict it.

In Chapter 5, Pär Nyman analyses how the tension between fiscal discipline and responsiveness to popular demands contributes to widening the prosperity gap in Europe. On the one hand, he argues, the countries most affected by the Great Recession still have a pressing need to strengthen their budget balances and to reduce their debt levels. If they fail to improve fiscal discipline, they will remain vulnerable to economic crises in future. On the other hand, austerity is often met by public resistance, and the political consequences of going against voters' preferences can be dramatic. These consequences, Nyman finds, are not limited to the electoral performance of parties in power. A lack of responsiveness can also reduce trust in government more generally, and thereby pave the way for populist parties.

Nyman argues that if governments follow three policy recommendations, they should be able to reduce the tension they experience between fiscal responsibility and electoral responsiveness. First, he argues, they should build in larger safety margins during upturns in the business cycle, in order to minimize the risk for a future sovereign debt crisis. This can be achieved by introducing a debt-level target, as a complement to the debt ceiling in the Stability and Growth Pact, and by using backward-looking criteria when compliance with fiscal rules is evaluated. Second, Nyman argues, governments can lower the electoral costs of fiscal discipline by reducing the extent to which public expenditures increase with rising wages or prices. And when countries are caught in a situation where it is either economically or politically unsustainable to consolidate public finances, collective debt restructuring – whereby the creditor countries agree to write off a portion of the debt – may be the best option available. Third, to reduce the tension between responsibility and responsiveness further, measures must be taken to increase public support for fiscal discipline. Fiscal frameworks and fiscal councils should therefore be designed in such a way that they enhance fiscal transparency, increase the salience of the country's fiscal position, and contribute to the public debate on fiscal policy choices.

In Chapter 6, Lars Magnusson and Sofia Murhem review how the Social Dialogue between unions and employers at EU level has evolved over the past twenty years, and ask whether it has a role to play in the 2010s. Their analysis shows that the Social Dialogue, which had its breakthrough with the Amsterdam Treaty in 1999, has diminished in importance over time. The authors identify three factors here. First, the early success of the Social Dialogue was favoured by the involvement of a strong Commission with substantial legitimacy – something the Union lacks today. Second, the Social Dialogue has been weakened by the general decline of the social partners (the trade unions first and foremost). Third, the increase in the number of member states over the past decade has made it difficult to reach agreement; one reason for this is that a tradition of free and independent trade unions is lacking in the former communist states.

Magnusson and Murhem see several reasons to put a stop to this trend and to uphold a strong Social Dialogue in the EU. Over the long run, they contend, the Social Dialogue can strengthen the Union's legitimacy and increase citizens' support for it. Through central agreements between the social partners, the European labour market and European industry can develop in a way that benefits both sides. Furthermore, the authors stress, an active discussion is needed about increasing labour mobility among EU countries at a time of high unemployment in most countries, but of real mass unemployment in only a few. By means of a Social Dialogue, they claim, greater acceptance can be gained for increased labour mobility, and xenophobia can eventually be countered. They also highlight the ageing society, which puts pressure on the welfare and prosperity we have achieved in Europe, and the solution to which will require legitimacy in the form of a dialogue in which as many as possible feel like participants. The authors conclude that policy-makers at national and European level ought to promote the Social Dialogue, as an important tool for reducing the prosperity gap between the member states, enhancing the legitimacy of the EU as a whole, encouraging the mobility of labour, and combatting xenophobia.

In Chapter 7 of the book, Jenny Julén Votinius addresses the differences in prosperity and well-being that follow from the high levels of youth unemployment in the EU. Youth unemployment must be addressed when discussing the prosperity gap between EU countries, for the most deprived member states also have the worst youth unemployment. Equally important, however, is the prosperity gap which is rapidly opening up between different generations within the EU. When young people do not have access to the labour market on the same terms as their elders, clear differences in economic well-being arise. Julén Votinius reviews how youth unemployment has been handled in Europe during the crisis years, and discusses what can be done to reduce the prosperity gap which is being established between the generations. She examines the question with examples taken from labour law reforms that have been introduced recently in order to facilitate the entry of young people into the labour market – particularly such reforms as those that involve weakening protections for young workers specifically.

The idea that hiring young people should be made more attractive by this means – by excluding them from a portion of the labour law protections available to others – is called into question in this chapter. The author rejects such an approach, citing among other things the concept of fundamental social rights – first and foremost the right to protection against age discrimination. She criticizes the compromise-oriented approach taken by the ECJ, which has stated that discrimination on grounds of age may be permissible if its purpose is to promote young people's employability. In the case of young workers too, Julén Votinius avers, respect for fundamental social rights must be seen as a key factor for meeting and reducing the prosperity gap between generations which is becoming established in the European labour market.

In Chapter 8, Jaan Paju analyses the future of national social insurance programmes in the EU. Social insurance is an important part of what makes up a welfare state, and it has been a state responsibility in Europe ever since the first law on workplace accident insurance was adopted in Prussia in the 1870s. In Europe in the year 2017, social insurance remains a national responsibility, but the EU's power to promote the internal market and to develop Union citizenship challenges the autonomy of the member states in such matters. Paju explains and analyses the tensions that arise in this area when different interests contend. The domestic social security systems of the member states are based on a form of solidarity which is nationally and territorially delimited, while the EU's system is based on a concept of economic integration through the free movement of persons and an increasingly significant and freestanding Union citizenship. Legal developments in this field raise the question of how the social security systems of the member states are to be organized in the future, in coordination with an expansive body of EU law.

Paju asks too whether coordination by the Union of national social security systems has a role to play in dealing with increased disparities among the member states, or whether such coordination serves in fact to counteract the EU's social dimension. He finds that the tug-of-war entailed by coordination in this area can only be constructive and sustainable over the long term if the current idea of the nation-state is revised, and migrants start to be seen as an opportunity to jointly promote the development of sustainable welfare systems within the Union. The starting point in this discussion should be what kind of Union the member states wish to see in 25 years, taking into account both current and future regional differences. The models to be developed for the future should aim to bridge the gap in social well-being which currently characterizes the EU, without eroding altogether the differences between the welfare models of the different member states. Paju underlines that, in an increasingly globalized world, the EU's future lies in community – not in national particularity.

In Chapter 9 of the book, Martin Ljunge examines how social trust gets conveyed across generations. Social trust, he points out, enhances health and prosperity. It is the confidence people feel for their fellow citizens in general – that is, for persons with whom they have no direct relation. By studying children of immigrants, Ljunge has managed to trace how social trust is conveyed within the family. He finds that children born to mothers from high-trust countries themselves show greater trust than do children born to mothers from low-trust countries. Children of mothers from high-trust countries also enjoy better health than do those whose mothers hail from low-trust ones. This second correlation shows that greater trust leads to better health. The direction of causality is clear: it is trust that leads to better health, and not vice versa; the child's health, namely, cannot influence the average trust in the mother's home country, inasmuch as the child was born and lives in another country.

Ljunge shows too that high trust has a number of other positive effects. For example, children whose mothers come from high-trust countries have higher incomes than do those whose mothers come from low-trust ones. Those who show high levels of trust also spend more time working than do those who show low levels, and less time unemployed or in retirement. The results indicate that trust is a factor behind persistent differences in health and wealth between individuals – and between countries as well. There are large differences in this regard, namely, between northern, southern, and eastern Europe. Here, the author argues, the EU and its member states have an important role to play. They can work actively to increase trust among citizens, and thus to reduce the long-term prosperity gap within and between EU countries. The most important measure that member states could take, according to Ljunge, would be to institute programmes for inculcating social skills in young people at risk. Experience from a programme focused on boys at risk during their first years of school has been very promising. This is an example of a measure that can dramatically increase young people's chances of educating themselves, to establish themselves in the labour market, and to develop working relationships.

In the final chapter of the book, Chapter 10, Nicholas Charron and Bo Rothstein explore the factors that operate at a societal level to build or destroy social trust. Their analysis in this chapter is based on the unique data available about the quality of public institutions at the regional level within the EU. This data, collected in 2010 and 2013 at the Quality of Government Institute in Gothenburg, enables researchers to compare the quality of public institutions both within and between countries. It includes 206 regions in 25 countries in Europe, and its standardized questionnaire was answered by 85,000 respondents in 2013. Using this extensive material, Charron and Rothstein test the tenability of four common explanations for variations in social trust among groups, countries, and regions: economic inequality, ethnic diversity, the quality of public institutions, and the degree of political participation by citizens.

The authors find sharp variations in social trust within many countries, a phenomenon overlooked in previous studies (based as they were on country-level data). They also find strong evidence to the effect that the quality of public institutions – measured as the degree to which a non-corrupt public sector delivers services in an impartial way – is the strongest factor underlying regional variations in trust within countries. Economic inequality as well proves to be a factor to be reckoned with for explaining variations in social trust. By contrast, the degree of ethnic diversity and the extent to which citizens participate politically have less importance for variations in trust. Charron and Rothstein's results are clearly relevant for the choices the Union and its member states face both in their work of building and reforming their own public institutions and in their encounter with the larger world. The overall conclusion of the chapter is that increasing the quality of public institutions should have first priority if our aim is to reduce the prosperity gap between countries and regions in Europe. Charron and Rothstein also highlight the possibility, as a promising hypothesis for future research, that high-quality public institutions serve to strengthen the capacity of countries to welcome immigrants, since good governance can also be expected to increase trust between those who already live in a country and those who have recently arrived in it.

* * *

The chapters in this book seek to assess the EU's social challenge from the standpoints of economics, law, and political science. An important conclusion from the chapters is that the Union's future role for Europeans depends on its ability to counteract the prosperity gap that has emerged during the crisis. If the Union is to reach the ambitious goals set out in the Europe 2020 strategy, far-reaching measures will be needed. At the same time, the idea of a social Europe faces major opposition from political forces that seek to roll back European integration, to reduce freedom of movement within the Union, and to close the borders to newcomers.

Much will therefore be at stake in the coming months, as the EU formulates its social policy for the years to come. The new initiative to boost growth and jobs recently launched by the Commission includes substantial social investment. In a speech to the EP in Strasbourg, Commission President Jean-Claude Juncker declared: 'Investing in Europe: It means much more than figures and projects, money and rules. We need to send a message to the people of Europe and to the rest of the world: Europe is back in business. This is not the moment to look back. Investment is about the future.'

The question, however, is whether the Commission's growth initiative really stakes out a *new* path for the EU, or whether instead it reflects the past. The social market economy the Union claims to represent is built in all essentials on the member states' own efforts in the social welfare area, while the market on the other hand is common. The EU's contribution is to support economic growth in the weaker regions, thereby promoting social cohesion. Thus it has been since the European Social Fund was created by the Treaty of Rome. But the dream of a social Europe – in the sense of an ambitious social policy pursued at the European level – remains a dream. Some hope that the dream will come true; others prefer that it remains a dream.

REFERENCES

Arnorsson, Agust and Gylfi Zoega (2016), 'On the Causes of Brexit', CESifo Working Paper Series No. 6056, accessed 22 November 2016 at https://ssrn.com/abstract=2851396.

Bakardjieva Engelbrekt, Antonina, Moa Mårtensson, Lars Oxelheim and Thomas Persson (2015), *The EU's Role in Fighting Global Imbalances*, Cheltenham, UK and Northampton, MA: Edward Elgar Publishing.

Beckfield, Jason (2009), 'Remapping Inequality in Europe: The Net Effect of Regional Integration on Total Income Inequality in the European Union', *International Journal of Comparative Sociology*, 50:5–6, 486–509.

Castillo Ortiz, Pablo José (2017), 'The Political De-determination of Legal Rules and the Contested Meaning of the "No Bailout" Clause', *Social and Legal Studies*, 26:2, 249–272.

Committee for the Study of Economic and Monetary Union (1989), *Report on Economic and Monetary Union in the European Community*, Brussels, April 1989, accessed 26 November 2016 at http://ec.europa.eu/economy_finance/publications/publication6161_en.pdf.

Darvas, Zsolt and Guntram B. Wolff (2016), 'An Anatomy of Inclusive Growth in Europe', Bruegel Blueprint 26, accessed 2 November 2017 at http://bruegel.org/2016/10/an-anatomy-of-inclusivegrowth-in-europe/.

EU SPC (2016), *Social Protection Committee Annual Report 2016. Review of the Social Protection Performance Monitor and Developments in Social Protection Policies*, Brussels, October 2016.

European Commission (2010), 'Europe 2020: A Strategy for Smart, Sustainable and Inclusive Growth', COM(2010) 2020 final, Brussels, March 2010.

European Commission (2013a), 'Towards Social Investment for Growth and Cohesion – Including Implementing the European Social Fund 2014–2020', COM(2013) 83 final, Brussels, February 2013.

European Commission (2013b), *Employment and Social Developments in Europe 2013*, Brussels, January 2014.

European Commission (2014a), 'Time for Action – Statement in the European Parliament Plenary Session Ahead of the Vote on the College', European Commission – Speech, Brussels, October 2014.

European Commission (2014b), 'An Investment Plan for Europe', COM(2014) 903 final, Brussels, November 2014.

European Commission (2016a), 'Launching a Consultation on a European Pillar of Social Rights', COM(2016) 0127 final, Brussels, March 2016.

European Commission (2016b), 'The EU Social Acquis', SWD(2016) 50 final, Brussels, March 2016.

European Commission (2017), 'Establishing a European Pillar of Social Rights', COM(2017) 250 final, Brussels, April 2017.

Eurostat (2016), *Europe 2020 Indicators – Poverty and Social Exclusion*, Brussels, October 2016.

Fernandes, Sofia and David Rinaldi (2016), 'Is There Such a Thing as "Social Europe"?', *Tribune*, Jacques Delors Institute, September 2016.

Ferrera, Maurizio (2005), *The Boundaries of Welfare: The New Spatial Politics of Social Protection*, Oxford: Oxford University Press.

Ferrera, Maurizio (2014), 'Social Europe and Its Components in the Midst of the Crisis: A Conclusion', *West European Politics*, 37:4, 825–843.

Greenhill, Kelly M. (2016), 'Open Arms behind Barred Doors: Fear, Hypocrisy and Policy Schizophrenia in the European Migration Crisis', *European Law Journal*, 22:3, 317–332.

Gustavsson, Sverker (1998), 'Double Asymmetry as Normative Challenge', in Andreas Follesdal and Peter Koslowski (eds), *Democracy and the European Union*, Berlin and Heidelberg: Springer, pp. 108–131.

Gustavsson, Sverker (2002), 'What Makes a European Monetary Union without a Parallel Fiscal Union Politically Sustainable?', in Søren Dosenrode (ed.), *Political Aspects of the Economic and Monetary Union: The European Challenge*, Aldershot, UK: Ashgate, pp. 87–118.

Inglehart, Ronald and Pippa Norris (2016), 'Trump, Brexit, and the Rise of Populism: Economic Have-Nots and Cultural Backlash', HKS Working Paper No. RWP16-026, accessed 22 November 2016 at https://ssrn.com/abstract=2818659.

Jabko, Nicolas (2006), *Playing the Market: A Political Strategy for Uniting Europe, 1985–2005*, Ithaca, NY: Cornell University Press.

Keeley, Brian (2015), *Income Inequality: The Gap between Rich and Poor*, OECD Insights, Paris: OECD Publishing.

Kriesi, Hanspeter (2014), 'The Populist Challenge', *West European Politics*, 37:2, 361–378.

Kriesi, Hanspeter, Edgar Grande, Martin Dolezal, Marc Helbling, Swen Hutter, Dominic Höglinger, and Bruno Wüest (2012), *Political Conflict in Western Europe*, Cambridge: Cambridge University Press.

Kriesi, Hanspeter, Edgar Grande, Romain Lachat, Martin Dolezal, Simon Bornschier, and Tim Frey (2006), 'Globalization and the Transformation of the National Political Space: Six European Countries Compared', *European Journal of Political Research*, 45:6, 921–956.

Majone, Giandomeinico (1993), 'The European Community between Social Policy and Social Regulation', *Journal of Common Market Studies*, 31:2, 153–170.

Martinsen, Dorte Sindbjerg, and Hans Vollaard (2014), 'Implementing Social Europe in Times of Crises: Re-established Boundaries of Welfare?', *West European Politics*, 37:4, 677–692.

Portes, Jonathan (2016), 'Immigration, Free Movement and the EU Referendum', *National Institute Economic Review*, 236:1, 14–22.

Raitano, Michele (2016), 'Income Inequality in Europe since the Crisis', *Intereconomics*, 51:2, 67–72.

Scharpf, Fritz W. (2002), 'The European Social Model', *Journal of Common Market Studies*, 40:4, 645–670.

Scharpf, Fritz W. (2010), 'The Asymmetry of European Integration, or Why the EU Cannot Be a "Social Market Economy"', *Socio-Economic Review*, 8, 211–250.

Scharpf, Fritz W. (2012), 'Monetary Union, Fiscal Crisis and the Pre-emption of Democracy', *Zeitschrift für Staats- und Europawissenschaften*, 9:2, 163–198.

Streeck, Wolfgang (2016), 'Exploding Europe: Germany, the Refugees and the British Vote to Leave', SPERI Paper No. 31, Sheffield: Sheffield Political Economy Research Institute.

Thielemann, Eiko and Daniel Schade (2016), 'Buying into Myths: Free Movement of People and Immigration', *Political Quarterly*, 87:2, 139–147.

2. Social rights and EU citizenship

Anna-Sara Lind

INTRODUCTION

The theme for this book is how the European Union (EU) can and should handle the prosperity gap which has grown as a consequence of the global financial crisis. The gap within the Union is evident, both between different national territories and between different groups of EU citizens. The issue as such is neither new nor revolutionary: since the very start of European integration in the 1950s, its organs have had to cope now and then with episodes of economic instability and even crisis. European integration was born of a desire to promote economic cooperation between states, thereby providing the participating countries with better protection against financial problems – with growing prosperity and well-being as a result. After more than a half a century of common history, one might think the Union and its member states would have had many opportunities to consolidate their efforts, and perhaps also to find new ways to handle challenges in this area. Yet Europe is struggling today to survive the aftermath of its biggest economic crisis since the 1930s. This crisis in turn is affecting many different areas in society – our democratic institutions not least – with growing division and mistrust of politicians as a result (see Chapter 3 by Ann-Cathrine Jungar in this book for a discussion of this matter). The recent referendum in the United Kingdom and the Brexit process are further evidence of this trend. Is a more permanent prosperity gap emerging? Can a division be seen between those countries with a rather good financial situation on the one hand, and those which have had a tough time coping with the economic crisis on the other (cf. Kilpatrick and De Witte 2014)? The social challenges the Union faces in this complex scenario stand at centre in this book.

Alongside, then, the serious economic crisis from which Europe is suffering, there is a 'social crisis'. The dimensions of national and European citizenship are being questioned as a consequence of the social crisis, which in turn has led to a new focus on how fundamental social rights within the Union are to be handled. Social rights are numerous and highly various;

they come to expression in many different ways. They may be described briefly as rights which are intimately connected with human dignity and the right to lead a dignified life (Mikkola 2007).

Examples of social rights include the right to work, to health, to housing, to social care, and so on (Lind 2009). The realization of these rights is dependent on many factors: how social programmes are organized; how solidarity is expressed in law; how well individuals are able to support themselves; what people consider the appropriate role of collective measures to be; what they believe economic justice and equal treatment require; and so on. European integration has been a fact for decades, and its organs have had to handle tough economic challenges; but constitutionally guaranteed social rights have never been amongst its primary goals. The EU's competence in these fields has always been extremely limited.

My purpose in this chapter is to examine the role and position of social rights in European law today. The Union is currently facing a major financial crisis, yet social rights have never been so strongly expressed in the EU's fundamental documents. These documents are the Treaty on European Union (TEU), the Treaty on the Functioning of the European Union (TFEU), and the Charter of Fundamental Rights of the European Union (the EU Charter). These fundamental documents represent binding law, both for the member states and for the European institutions. The foremost organ for their interpretation is the Court of Justice of the European Union (CJEU).

But social rights are also expressed in the Community Charter of the Fundamental Social Rights of Workers (hereafter the Community Charter), which the European Economic Community (EEC) enacted in 1989. This charter has influenced the development of social policy in the EU, and the Court of Justice uses it as an interpretative tool. The EU is not yet a member of the Council of Europe (cf. Opinion of the Court, 2/13), but two of the latter body's conventions have had a special importance within EU law. These are the European Convention on Human Rights and Fundamental Freedoms (ECHR) and the Council of Europe's Social Charter. Both of these conventions are cited in the EU's treaties, and they have served as a point of departure for the creation of a bill of rights for the Union: the EU Charter of Fundamental Rights (see the Explanations relating to the Charter, 14.12.2007, C/303/17). The European Court of Human Rights is the final interpreter of the ECHR. Where the Social Charter is concerned, the European Committee of Social Rights has responsibility for interpreting it. These two conventions are binding for the states that have ratified them (such as the member states of the EU), but they also have an indirect impact – through EU law.

In this chapter, my focus is on the chapter on social rights that forms part of the EU Charter, and on the new introductory articles in the treaties that were added in 2009, when the Treaty of Lisbon entered into force. What has happened in this area since the enactment of the Lisbon Treaty? Has the altered 'constitutional tone' in the treaties made any practical difference in how social rights are approached? Questions arise here about the impact of the social-market economy, the treatment of social issues in the CJEU, the ability of individuals to demand social rights (such as the right to health care or to social security), and so on.

The wording in the basic articles of the treaties changed considerably with the entry into force of the Lisbon Treaty. Issues of welfare and social rights are described or at least expressed differently. The question is thus whether social rights have been given or could be given a new, general, and overarching meaning. This question is particularly apposite in view of the legacy from recent decades of 'social policy' at the European level (where the Union has, amongst other things, embraced goals of full employment and social protection), and in view of the enactment of the Community Charter and the Council of Europe's Social Charter. All of these developments in the field of social policy have come about due to the challenges posed by economic hard times. Perhaps a new pattern is visible in the case law of the CJEU. There has also been a clear movement towards the individualization of rights – a movement that was already evident before the Lisbon Treaty entered into force.

In legal doctrine, a distinction is often made between collective rights, which devolve upon groups, and individual rights, which only individual persons can invoke (vis-à-vis public authorities or the state) (Lind 2011). The 'individualization' of rights means that a greater number of individuals can appeal their case in a court of law (or in an instance resembling a court) and have the protection of their rights tested. This may seem helpful from the standpoint of collective rights too, inasmuch as rights thereby become stronger, clearer, and more concrete both to the individual and to society. But it poses a danger as well, since too strong a focus on the individual dimension of social rights can be seen as a threat from a welfare perspective. In a strong welfare state, the stress on the collective dimension of rights is an expression of solidarity. Such a stress furthermore leads – hopefully – to a high minimum level for the rights in question.

The fundamental idea behind social rights is that they should be accessible to all, regardless of ability to pay. Is it now the case that the collective dimension has been dismantled, and that only the individual aspects of such rights are underlined (especially in connection with the European motto of free movement)? The way social rights are described in European law can have an impact on the national welfare state in various ways.

Stronger social rights can be an asset for the national welfare state, but also a challenge or even a threat to it (cf. Newdick 2006).

In this chapter, I first comment on the new points of departure regarding welfare that were introduced into the treaties in 2009. After that, I turn my attention to the social rights codified in the EU Charter of Fundamental Rights. In order to ascertain the meaning of these rights up to now, I start by discussing the CJEU's interpretation of the articles in question, as well as the sources selected by the Court when establishing the area over which these rights apply. In the subsequent section, solidarity within the Union stands at centre, in two ways. First, it figures centrally in a discussion of how the member states and the Union have divided decision-making competence in the social field amongst themselves. But solidarity is also expressed in the realization of fundamental rights, which in itself demands that the member states and the Union accept certain duties. This matter is the second aspect studied in this section. The realization of a right and the measures required for its realization are in turn dependent upon whether the right is considered to be individual in nature or – as is often the case for social rights – both individual and collective in character. Even when an individual social right is at stake, a strong collective dimension is typically involved as well, inasmuch as welfare programmes are often organized as something for both the individual and the collective to enjoy. One could also argue that a collective dimension is always present, since the realization of social rights entails the redistribution of large-scale resources from society as a whole. A substantial effort is sometimes required, therefore, to apply an individually oriented perspective to the collective provisions of the welfare state. For example, realizing social rights at a European level would automatically lead to major costs for the member states. We must therefore ask: does a European structure for the realization of social rights exist? And, if not, how can such a structure be built in order to meet the constitutional demands set forth in the treaties? I close the chapter with a policy recommendation along these lines.

THE STARTING POINT: A SOCIAL DEFICIT IN EUROPEAN INTEGRATION

Prior to 2009, the Union had no exclusive competence in social policy. Ambitions for a 'social Europe', therefore, were founded on the welfare systems of the member states themselves. Due to several situations which have arisen, however, it has become clear that national welfare is not always easily reconciled with the Union's internal market. National welfare systems are constructed in such a way as to be limited to the territory of a given member state. It is only within its own territory that a member state has enough control over a complex welfare system – including over how it is financed – to ensure its proper operation.

Such territorial limitations conflict with the goals laid down in the fundamental documents of the Union. One major challenge for the national systems is how to handle the many EU citizens who have the right to access said systems despite not being citizens of the state in question. For more than 15 years, EU citizens have been guaranteed certain rights – as long as they meet certain criteria – even if they are not nationals of their host state. For countries where the basic idea behind the welfare system is that social security is something one obtains as a right of citizenship, or that one receives after having contributed through taxes and the like, this poses a challenge (Erhag 2016, pp. 211–212).

The EU strives to realize the internal market through freedom of movement. For this to happen, the obstacles to freedom of movement – including those arising from the organization of welfare systems – need to be removed. This may necessitate a number of changes in national welfare systems. For example, a greater number of persons may have to be covered by a given national social-security system. Or it may be necessary to make mixed arrangements, as when health-care services are financed by a patient's home country, even while being provided in another.

For decades, EU regulations and directives have governed the coordination of member states' welfare systems, as well as the procedures by which migrant Union citizens can gain access to the social-security system of their host state (Jaan Paju describes this further in Chapter 8 of this book). The principle of free movement for Union citizens has always formed the foundation for these regulations and directives (see also Chapter 4 by Joakim Ruist in this book).

While the EU's competence and budget are both too limited for the Union to be able to conduct its own policy of redistribution, we should remember that the rules relating to the internal market also have a type of redistributive function, inasmuch as they affect the market's operations in various ways. The fundamental principle of non-discrimination, taken together with freedom of movement, redistributes assets through its recognition of certain persons or groups of persons as having rights. But since the Union has no competence to intervene in national welfare matters, this recognition is not accomplished through EU law. Furthermore, a clear social dimension is associated with the internal market, and it serves to shape policy in the social field, as in the case of measures (e.g., labour policies) that bear directly on the market.

Economic integration and the internal market are thus seen as preconditions for achieving the social goals of the Union, which prior to 2009 had to be accomplished through measures that fell within the EU's competence at the time. Article 3 of the former Treaty on European Union, which was in force until 2009 when the Lisbon Treaty brought in the current treaty, invested the Union with the competence to promote economic and social cohesion, to contribute to a high level of public health, and to coordinate the employment policies of the member states. The section outlining these objectives, however, only came after the paragraphs detailing the internal market and the four freedoms. The legislation of the different member states would be coordinated to the extent that the functioning of the internal market required it. The tensions to which EU law gives rise in the social realm are already evident in these provisions. The articles relating to freedom of movement and the internal market, namely, have stronger legal effect than those which provide for exceptions from said articles. In the social field the expressions are vaguer: the EU shall *contribute*, *promote*, *coordinate*, and so on.

But an EU basing its social commitment solely on a quest for welfare linked to economic integration seemed to be insufficient. The idea of a socially stronger Europe committed to the defence of fundamental human rights gathered momentum at the beginning of the twenty-first century, when proponents of integration were seeking a constitution for Europe in the hope of imparting greater legitimacy to the European project. The common quest upon which the EU had been built – to achieve certain economic goals – was considered insufficient, in view of the legal changes that had been made during the preceding couple of decades. Questions of social welfare, however, were intimately linked to matters of national identity, and to the expectations citizens had of what their own state would provide. This is the inherent dynamic and tension which lies behind the changes outlined in the next section.

SOCIAL QUESTIONS GAIN A PLACE IN EU LAW

The tension between the economic goals of the Union and the desire of the member states to decide on their own over social matters – a tension which has long been present – is conditioned by the structure of the treaties and by the division of competence on social questions laid out therein. EU law needs to be able to address social questions if the free movement of persons and services is to be guaranteed, and if the tension in relation to the economic goals of European integration is to be mitigated. In its 'Preliminary Guidelines for an EC Programme of Social Policy', adopted in 1971, the European Commission stressed that the treaties did not call for any harmonization of social benefits. Two years later, it underlined in a report that it did not seek to reduce differences in social policy between the member states.

In the second half of the 1980s, after the release of the Commission's white paper on the implementation of the internal market, there was concern that, due to the operation of said market, job opportunities would be lost to low-wage countries, and national attempts to regulate wages and working conditions would be undermined. In connection with this, the Commission presented a common social charter in 1989: the so-called Community Charter of the Fundamental Social Rights of Workers. This charter was created due to the inability of the member states to agree upon common rules in the area of social policy. The idea was to confirm and to strengthen the European social model, by creating and securing rights in relation to work. While not legally binding, it has had legal consequences, especially in connection with the working environment.

In 1993, the Commission presented the 'Green Paper – European Social Policy – Options for the Union', wherein it stressed that social matters must not take a back seat to economic growth. In the subsequent white paper, from 1994, the Commission made some suggestions of a more concrete nature, and underlined that the EU did not seek total harmonization in the area of social policy. A new chapter on social policy was then included in the Treaty of Amsterdam. Article 2 in the treaty establishing the European Community (the EC Treaty, in force until 2009) also set out goals of a different kind. One illustration of this is the formulation that the Community shall promote not just 'a high level of employment and social protection, [as well as] equality between men and women', *but also* 'sustainable and non-inflationary growth, a high degree of competitiveness and convergence of economic performance'. Before 2009, Community activities in the social field were regulated by Article 136 (harmonization of social systems) and Article 152 (means and ends of public-health policy). With these articles as a basis, so-called minimum directives were issued. The targets were 'soft'; that is, the mentioned articles made no explicit reference to social rights, or to any human rights.

The goal of economic integration after the War was to secure peace and prosperity; human rights and fundamental rights were not thought relevant in connection with this. Towards the end of the 1950s, for example, the CJEU found that it lacked the competence to address whether or not a certain decision taken within the framework of the Coal and Steel Community constituted a violation of a fundamental right recognized in the constitution of a member state (Case 1/58 *Stork v. High Authority*).

NEW POINTS OF DEPARTURE FOLLOWING THE LISBON TREATY?

As the brief account above has shown, rules on social matters are nothing new in the EU. Social progress and solidarity were already set out as goals in the preamble to the EC Treaty. The preamble to the present Treaty on European Union stresses the centrality of human rights, fundamental freedoms, and the rule of law. Also included are the social rights set out in the Social Charter of the Council of Europe and in the Community Charter. Today, in Article 2 TEU, the fundamental values are expressed as follows:

> The Union is founded on the values of respect for human dignity, freedom, democracy, equality, the rule of law and respect for human rights, including the rights of persons belonging to minorities. These values are common to the Member States in a society in which pluralism, non-discrimination, tolerance, justice, solidarity and equality between women and men prevail.

The Union furthermore strives to 'promote peace, its values and the well-being of its peoples', as set out in Article 3 TEU.

The Treaty of Amsterdam included a chapter on social policy. Today, this chapter forms part of the section on social policy in the TFEU (Articles 151 to 161). These articles mention measures aimed at cooperation in the social field, dialogue between the social partners, the harmonization of social-security systems, and the like. Article 151 describes the objectives of EU social policy as follows:

> The Union and the Member States, having in mind fundamental social rights such as those set out in the European Social Charter . . . and in the . . . Community Charter of the Fundamental Social Rights of Workers, shall have as their objectives the promotion of employment, improved living and working conditions, so as to make possible their harmonisation while the improvement is being maintained, proper social protection, dialogue between management and labour, the development of human resources with a view to lasting high employment and the combating of exclusion.

Article 160 calls for the establishment of a 'Social Protection Committee'. The primary aim of the competence mentioned in the chapter is to prevent member states from acting in such a way as to distort competition in the Union. In line with this, Article 154 enjoins the Commission to promote dialogue between the Union and the social partners (management and labour). Article 155 stipulates that the social partners, acting together, may request of the Council that it take a decision on certain matters, on the basis of a proposal from the Commission (on the social dialogue, see Chapter 6 by Lars Magnusson and Sofia Murhem in this book).

Furthermore, the provisions of EU law on work-related rights have been broadened to encompass how jobs are *created* (Title IX, Articles 145 to 150, which treat strategies for creating employment).

The entry into force of the Lisbon Treaty did not lead to any major changes in the EU's provisions for social policy. One novelty is the inclusion, in Article 2 TEU, of solidarity amongst the fundamental values of the Union. Another new feature, contained in Article 3 TEU, is that the Union proclaims the promotion of peace, its values, and the well-being of its peoples to be amongst its fundamental goals; and it declares that the internal market shall be built on a highly competitive social-market economy aiming at full employment and social progress. The same article commits the Union to combating social exclusion and discrimination; to promoting social justice and protection, equality between women and men, and solidarity between generations; and to furthering economic, social, and territorial solidarity amongst the member states.

Article 2 (3) TFEU enjoins the member states to 'coordinate their economic and employment policies within arrangements as determined by this Treaty, which the Union shall have competence to provide'. This is further explained in Article 5. Article 5 (2) regulates the coordination of the member states' employment policies, for which the Council is to furnish guidelines. Paragraph 3 adds that the Union may take initiatives to ensure coordination of the social policies of the member states. According to Article 2 (5), however, this shall not include harmonization of national laws or regulations.

Article 9 states that social requirements are to be taken into account when the Union defines and implements its policies and activities. The EU shall promote a high level of employment, guarantee adequate social protection, fight against social exclusion, and ensure a high level of education, training, and protection of human health. The TFEU underlines the member states' competence in the areas of employment (Title IX, Articles 145 to 150) and social policy (Title X, Articles 151 to 161). The close connection between the employment policies of the member states and the economic policies of the Union is evident in Article 146. The fundamental social rights listed in the Social Charter and in the Community Charter from 1989 are to continue to form the basis for EU social policy. The novelty of Title X lies in its emphasis – in a chapter on social policy – on the importance of the social dialogue and the role of management and labour. In addition, the Union must support and complement the activities of the member states in regard to social security and the social protection of workers, as stated in Article 153 (1) (c), as well as in regard to the combating of social exclusion (j). As before, the aims of social policy are to be realized progressively through the enactment of minimum directives in the ordinary legislative process (Articles 151 to 153).

The express goal of the EC was to promote economic cooperation, and to create peace and stability thereby. Yet human rights have long been part of EU law, albeit indirectly. The case law of the CJEU has contributed to the inclusion of human rights, leading to a change in what the Court considers to be a fundamental right. According to Article 6 TFEU, the Union shall be built upon the principle of respect for human rights and fundamental freedoms. This gives the Court strong support in developing its case law. In view of this, creating the Union's own bill of rights – the Charter – was a logical step to take.

THE EU CHARTER: NEW OR REVISED FUNDAMENTAL RIGHTS?

As early as the year 2000, the EU Charter of Fundamental Rights had been proclaimed by the European Parliament, the Council, and the Commission. It became legally binding on the member states and the EU's institutions in 2009, when the Lisbon Treaty entered into force. The EU Charter is to a great extent inspired by the work on human rights that has been done in the Council of Europe, as can be seen in the Social Charter and the European Convention on Human Rights (ECHR). Several of the rights in the EU Charter are supposed to be the equivalent of rights in the ECHR. Interestingly, social rights were also included in the EU Charter. In the Presidency's conclusions (Annex IV) from the 1999 summit in Cologne, the member states underlined that: 'In drawing up such a Charter account should furthermore be taken of economic and social rights as contained in the European Social Charter and the Community Charter (Article 136 TEC), insofar as they do not merely establish objectives for action by the Union.'

The preamble to the EU Charter states that: '[T]he Union is founded on the indivisible, universal values of human dignity, freedom, equality and solidarity; it is based on the principles of democracy and the rule of law.' Through EU citizenship, the human person is put front and centre. The EU Charter, like the international conventions for protecting human rights, is based on the principle of human dignity. The focus is on the human being, not just the market.

The Charter is a product of its time. Human rights in the twenty-first century include all generations of rights, and this is mirrored in the Charter. The document enumerates rights that are common to the member states' constitutional traditions, and includes international human rights as well. As a result, rights of three different types are gathered in one document: civil and political rights (e.g., the right to freedom from torture and the right to freedom of expression, set out in Articles 4 and 11 respectively); economic and social rights (e.g., the right to choose an occupation and the right to engage in work, set out in Article 15); and rights specific to the EU and to Union citizens (such as the right to vote in EU elections, set out in Article 39). A large part of the Charter is devoted to codifying already existing rules and principles of EU law. Many of the most important rights set out in the Charter have their roots in the principle of free movement.

By choosing to create the Charter, the EU has clearly signalled that the purpose of its existence goes beyond the initial economic goals. This is evident both from the process behind the Charter's creation and from the content of the document itself. The Charter points out, moreover, that there are tensions between the member states and the EU's institutions, as well as between traditional and newer perspectives on what human and fundamental rights really consist of.

The Charter addresses the EU's institutions, as well as the member states when they are implementing Union law. It enjoins them to respect the rights and to observe the principles which it sets out, and to further their realization within their respective areas of competence. This is stated in Article 51 (1). Paragraph 2 thereof explains that the 'Charter does not extend the field of application of Union law beyond the powers of the Union or establish any new power or task for the Union, or modify powers and tasks as defined in the Treaties'. At the same time, the EU shall be based on respect for human rights, and one of the fundamental goals of the Union is to promote them. The Charter does not demarcate exactly which rights are to be regarded as social. It does include rights relating to work in this group, such as the right of workers to information and consultation within the undertaking (Article 27), the right of collective bargaining and action (Article 28), the right of access to placement services (Article 29), and the right to protection against unjustified dismissal (Article 30). Workers further have the right to fair working conditions (Article 31), and to legal, economic, and social protection for themselves and their family (Article 33) (see, for example, Case C-176/12 *Association de médiation sociale v. Union locale des syndicats CGT and Others*; see also Chapter 7 in this book by Jenny Julén Votinius, the focus of which is on youth and labour law within the Union). Article 34 sets out the right to social security. In addition, the Charter contains articles that pertain not to workers in particular but to individuals in general. The right to education (Article 14), the right of persons with disabilities to integration (Article 26), and the right to health (Article 35) are some examples. By including civil, political, and social rights in a single document, the Charter underlines the indivisibility of rights. Thus, the EU does not automatically divide rights into different categories (a separation that had been common in international law up to the 1990s). The relatively modern character of the Charter is underlined by the fact that it also enumerates rights of other kinds, such as collective rights and bio-ethical rights. Social rights figure centrally, as seen in the fact that a entire chapter (entitled *Solidarity*) is devoted to them. The right to strike and the right to freedom of assembly – neither of which had formed any part of EU law before – are guaranteed as well.

The tension between what can be considered new knowledge of law on the one hand and already confirmed knowledge of law on the other – between classical and modern versions thereof – is evident in Articles 51 to 54 in the Charter. From these we can conclude that the EU's institutions are only bound by the Charter within their field of competence, and that the member states are only bound by it when they are implementing Union law. The purpose of the Charter is not to give the Union any more tasks or competences, or to affect already existing tasks or competences. Rights enunciated in the treaties are to be exercised under the conditions defined by those treaties (Article 52 (2)), and full account shall be taken of national laws and practices as specified in the Charter (Article 52 (6)). Article 52 (4) states that rights resulting from constitutional traditions common to the member states shall be interpreted in line with said traditions. (Cf. Article 6 TEU.)

In Article 52 (5) of the Charter, we can see the tension between two types of rights: 'principles' and 'rights'. However, the difference between principles and rights is not explained in the Charter itself. Instead it may be up to the courts to elucidate this difference when they interpret the Charter in future. It is hard to know, therefore, whether a line can be drawn between binding 'rights' which are justiciable in court and non-binding 'principles' which are not. Up until now, the Court of Justice has refrained from direct comment on this question. Article 51 (1) states that rights shall be respected and principles observed. It is not clear, however, what is to be considered a right and what a principle. To some extent, this is clarified in the explanatory report which accompanied the Charter. Principles, according to this document, can be regarded more as goals; thus they are something to be *observed*, rather than respected. Moreover, according to Article 52 (5):

> The provisions of this Charter which contain principles may be implemented by legislative and executive acts taken by institutions, bodies, offices and agencies of the Union, and by acts of Member States when they are implementing Union law, in the exercise of their respective powers. They shall be judicially cognisable only in the interpretation of such acts and in the ruling on their legality.

This might be taken to mean that only some of the rights in the Charter are potentially justiciable for citizens, and that these are the rights mentioned in the treaties or confirmed by the Court of Justice. If a right is not respected when the Union or its member states decide to take a certain measure, then said measure (a legislative act, for example) can be tested in court. It is not clear, however, how the CJEU is to apply these distinctions in concrete rulings. To some extent, the division between rights and principles seems to represent a powerful political aspiration – an aspiration which is not, however, easily converted into legal practice.

The provisions of the Charter contain a tension between social rights on the one hand and civil and political rights on the other. The former rights, namely, are expressed in a different manner to the latter ones. The Court of Justice has not yet provided any clear interpretation on how this is to be handled. In some cases social rights are expressed as positive rights, in accordance with national law and practice – that is, rights which require that the state act in order to realize the right in question. In other cases social rights are not even expressed as rights: see, for example, Article 33, which states that the family should enjoy legal, economic, and social protection. At times the Charter also mentions the Union's 'duty to respect' certain rights (such as the rights of disabled persons); at other times, however, it does not even link a given duty to a right (as in the case of Article 22, which enjoins the EU to respect cultural, religious, and linguistic diversity).

The range of ways in which rights are expressed in the Charter is explained by the variety of purposes behind the creation of the document. Besides endowing the EU project with legitimacy and creating a Europe for the people, the aim of the Charter is to prevent the economic competences wielded by the Union from limiting economic and social rights at member-state level. The Charter can thus function as a means for the member states to protect themselves against an excessive accumulation of competences by the EU. A legally binding Charter also binds the Court of Justice; and the latter's possibilities of elaborating still more general principles is limited by the requirement that it respect the Charter and follow its provisions. But the Charter also seeks to protect the individual, as one of its central purposes is to serve as a tool for preventing the Union from limiting fundamental rights. The Charter can also have repercussions in the national context, since it can be used against the legislation of the member states themselves. If a national rule falls within EU law, then the Charter is applicable (see cases C-399/11 *Melloni* and C-617/10 *Åkerberg Fransson*).

In the area of health care, competence still lies first and foremost with the member states, as Article 35 of the Charter confirms:

> Everyone has the right of access to preventive health care and the right to benefit from medical treatment under the conditions established by national

laws and practices. A high level of human health protection shall be ensured in the definition and implementation of all the Union's policies and activities.

The first sentence in this article, giving everyone a right in accordance with national law, is taken from Article 11 in the Council of Europe's Social Charter. Access to preventive health care is important here, since it is a prerequisite for good health in some measure. The exact meaning that 'right of access' will take on remains to be seen. The second sentence repeats the content of Article 168 TFEU, and broadens the application to include the whole of the Union.

The economic and social rights enumerated in the Charter can be divided into three categories. Rights which are clearly and obviously individual in nature fall into the first category; rights that the Union recognizes and respects fall into the second; and rights which amount simply to social objectives comprise the third. In that case Article 35, according to its literal meaning, would fall into the third group; and there would be scant possibility of claiming it as a justiciable right in court, even though the Charter is legally binding.

The preamble to the EU Charter cites the Social Charter of the Council of Europe, and contains several articles directly inspired by the latter convention. The Social Charter is also explicitly mentioned in Article 151 TFEU, making it a relevant source of EU law. One question here is whether the interpretations provided by the Council of Europe's Committee on Social Rights (in decisions, conclusions, and collective complaints) have import for the meaning of the articles in the EU Charter that (like Article 35) are directly inspired by the Social Charter. It would be logical to conclude that they do have such import, inasmuch as the Committee is the institution responsible for interpreting the Social Charter. The member states must respect the EU Charter when implementing Union law; however, this provision was given a broader meaning in the explanatory report which accompanied said Charter (cf. Article 52 (7)). If the CJEU were then to interpret references to the Social Charter and its Committee as forming part of the law (as 'fall[ing] within the scope of Community law'), then the effects of the EU Charter would be greater. If the Court of Justice were to conclude that preventive health care and access to medical care *is* a human right, then the member states' margin of appreciation would diminish in the field of health care.

The articles in the Charter would take on a broader meaning if, together with the general principles of EU law, they could issue in justiciable rights for the individual. If human rights were furthermore regarded – as increasingly they tend to be – as interdependent and indivisible, then the courts could give Article 35 a greater importance than may have been intended for it when the Charter was written. Article 35 could then be combined with other articles in the Charter – for example, the prohibition of discrimination (Article 21), the right to dignity (Article 1), and the right to good administration (Article 41). Article 35 could also be used by the courts as a tool of non-binding soft law – for interpreting EU law and for developing measures in accordance with EU law.

As we have seen, some social rights can be compared to principles, and such rights do not have the same status as the ones which are formulated more distinctly. The member states accordingly argue that social rights belong to the political sphere, and that it is therefore the responsibility of politicians to ensure their realization. At no point, however, has the Court of Justice explicitly stated this in its rulings. National welfare policies could be undermined if the Union were to gain too much influence in the social field – which it could if the social rights in the Charter were made justiciable for individuals.

Even if the member states wish to limit the application of EU law in the shaping of the EU Charter, national courts need to ask the Court of Justice for guidance in preliminary rulings, leaving the latter with an option to test questions in areas where its competence is limited. When the Court is itself asked to issue a preliminary ruling, its guidance is authoritative for national courts (cf. Article 4 (3)). And since the principles in the Charter can also be implemented through legislative acts enacted by the Union and through legislation passed by the member states, there is a potential for the application of EU law to be broadened. Several of the rights and principles enunciated in the Charter are also found in the ECHR, which in turn has a special constitutional status in each and every member state.

Article 53 in the Charter states that no article may be interpreted in such a way as to restrict human rights or fundamental freedoms that are recognized in EU law, in international law, and in the conventions to which the Union or all the member states are party. This reinforces the importance of the two main sources of the Charter: the ECHR and the Council of Europe's Social Charter. Consulting these documents is necessary for interpreting the EU Charter's content, although the Court has stated that it will cite the Social Charter and Article 6 TEU as long as the Union has not ratified the Convention (Case C-218/15 *Gianpaolo Paoletti and Others v. Procura della Repubblica*, paras 21 and 22). This has also given the Social Charter a higher status. However, the duty to *respect* and *recognize* a right is only a duty to abstain from acting. In this case, it means a duty on the part of the Union not to meddle in the social policies of the member states. I am of the opinion that the Union must, if it is to respect and recognize rights, devote greater attention to how its policies and legislative acts can *influence* the rules enacted by the member states in the area in question.

If the member states have not recognized any rights in the field, then the EU has nothing it needs to respect. This means it can take another step towards creating rights.

OPPORTUNITIES FOR THE EU ON THE BASIS OF ARTICLE 34: THE RIGHT TO SOCIAL SECURITY

Taking such a step towards creating rights could have a great impact in connection with social and housing assistance. Article 34 in the Charter proclaims the right of all Union residents to social security and social assistance. The Charter could contribute here to ensuring a minimum level of protection (or, in the lingo of international human-rights law, to guaranteeing a core of the right in question). Article 34 reads as follows:

> 1. The Union recognises and respects the entitlement to social security benefits and social services providing protection in cases such as maternity, illness, industrial accidents, dependency or old age, and in the case of loss of employment, in accordance with the rules laid down by Union law and national laws and practices.
> 2. Everyone residing and moving legally within the European Union is entitled to social security benefits and social advantages in accordance with Union law and national laws and practices.
> 3. In order to combat social exclusion and poverty, the Union recognises and respects the right to social and housing assistance so as to ensure a decent existence for all those who lack sufficient resources, in accordance with the rules laid down by Union law and national laws and practices.

The Council of Europe's Committee on Social Rights, which oversees compliance with the Social Charter, has established a minimum level for social security, and it is included in Article 12 of the EU Charter. Through Article 34 in said Charter, this minimum level would then have effect in EU law in areas where the Union legislates and takes measures on social security. Article 34 (1) of the EU Charter states that the Union recognizes and respects the right of access to social security and social benefits providing protection in the event of illness, motherhood, old age, unemployment, and the like, in accordance with the rules of EU law and national legislation and case law.

Article 34 (1) could also be relevant for the work carried out in connection with the Social Agenda, the Commission's action programme on social matters. The Social Agenda has been implemented through the open method of coordination and legislation. Article 34 could provide indicators and criteria when member states, cooperating on the basis of the open method, seek to prevent social security from being reduced to social assistance. While Article 34 (1) cannot serve as a legal basis for legislation in the EU, since the Union has no competence in the field, it could prove influential in connection with the open method of coordination or other fields of cooperation in the EU. For example, the level of benefits and the number of insurance schemes and beneficiaries could serve as useful indicators and benchmarks under the Social Agenda. The criteria and time limits set out in Article 12 (2) of the Social Charter could serve as minimum norms for the member states.

If Article 34 (1) in the EU Charter were interpreted as a right or a freedom, then Article 52 (1) of said Charter would be applicable. According to this article, limitations on the rights and freedoms recognized by the Charter may only be made if they are prescribed by law, and if they are necessary and respond to an important societal interest or if their aim is to protect the rights and freedoms of others. Furthermore, the principle of proportionality must always be observed when a right in the Charter is restricted.

Article 34 (2) of the Charter mentions both social security and social assistance. It gives everyone who resides and moves legally within the EU a right to social security and social benefits in accordance with EU law and national legislation and case law. It is based on Article 13 (4) of the Social Charter, and it also reflects the rules laid down by EU Regulation 883/2004 and EU Directive 2004/38. These acts contain rules on how citizens from other member states are to be treated in regard to social security. Article 13 (4) of the Social Charter becomes important for interpreting the right to social assistance. Article 12 (4) of the Social Charter becomes applicable too, since it deals with social security and so can provide information relevant for interpreting Article 34 (2) of the EU Charter.

In Article 34 (3) of the EU Charter, a right to social and housing assistance is now recognized. This is the first time that housing assistance forms part of EU law. This article is inspired by Articles 30 and 31 in the Social Charter. Article 30 of the Social Charter proclaims the responsibility of the signatory states to fight poverty and social exclusion, by amongst other things extending social and housing assistance. Article 31 of the Social Charter sets out the obligation of the signatory states to strive for access to affordable housing, to combat and gradually eliminate homelessness, and to regulate housing costs so as to assure that those without adequate resources can afford housing. Declarations of the same kind are found in the Commission's action plan against social exclusion, based upon former Article 137 of the EC Treaty, and in the programme for combating poverty and social exclusion in Europe 2020, the EU's strategy for achieving growth.

Article 30 of the Social Charter proclaims the right to protection against poverty and exclusion. Moreover, the explanatory report accompanying the EU Charter explicitly cites Article 30 of the Social Charter in relation to Article 34 (3) of the EU Charter, which means that Article 13 (1) of the Social Charter also becomes relevant. The latter article namely obliges the signatory states, as far as possible, to eliminate all causes of ill health. Articles 30 and 13 (1) of the Social Charter overlap. Exactly how social assistance is to be organized is not specified, but the articles make clear that everyone has the right to social assistance and that the state must guarantee this right. The same goes for the right to medical care and assistance, as declared in Article 13 (1), which is also relevant through Article 34 (3) in the EU Charter. The different benchmarks applied by the Social Committee when interpreting Article 13 (1) could also be useful for the EU, for example by supplying a basis for cooperation amongst the member states on social matters through the open method of coordination. The right to social assistance shall also, according to the Social Charter, include the right of appeal. This in turn strengthens the individual right to social and housing assistance set out in Article 34 (3) of the EU Charter.

THE CJEU AND THE MEMBER STATES: SLOWING DOWN PROGRESS

After more than half a decade with the EU Charter in force, we can start drawing some conclusions. To begin with, only a small number of legal cases have arisen where the social rights in the Charter are taken up. In these few cases, moreover, the CJEU's interpretation has not been explicit enough to make it possible to ascertain the scope or applicable area of the right in question. For example, in Case C-571/10 *Servet Kamberaj mot Istituto per l'Edilizia sociale della Provincia autonoma di Bolzano (IPES) and Others*, the wording of Article 34 on the right to housing assistance was mentioned. The Court chose, however, not to cite the Charter, contenting itself instead with discussing the directive that was at stake. The Court put Article 34 aside, on the grounds that it refers to national law.

But at the same time, the case-law and legal usage established in relation to other rights in the Charter may help to clarify what the social rights in the Charter really mean. The explanatory report should serve as our point of departure in seeking to ascertain this. This report is not *travaux préparatoires*, but it does provide a way for the Court to find support for its reasoning regarding the articles in the Charter. Since the report was drafted by the legislator, moreover, the Court echoes the will of the legislator when it accepts, interprets, and applies the explanations provided therein. But the references to the Charter may also open up for some exciting new developments regarding the rights enumerated in the EU Charter, for the report cites international conventions that have inspired the authors of the Charter (see Case C-279/09 *DEB v. Bundesrepublik Deutschland* and Case C-617/10 *Åklagaren v. Åkerberg Fransson*).

As to the *welfare systems in the different member states* today, it can be said that the latter have lost influence over the determination of *who* shall be entitled to demand welfare rights and services. The ban on discrimination and the demand for equal treatment in EU law have reduced the member states' room for manoeuvre, since their ability to differentiate between different groups of people has diminished. Citizens from other EU member states can no longer be treated differently from a country's own citizens, unless certain criteria in EU law are met. The effect hereof is to reduce the ability of the member states to parry financial blows. On top of this, the budget restrictions that follow with the Economic and Monetary Union (EMU) and the euro leave less room for choice in the design of welfare systems.

How, then, can a member state respond to financial difficulty within these narrower new confines? A more market-oriented way of approaching the matter would be to insist that the member states create a business climate conducive to economic growth, by which means they will then be able to secure their national welfare arrangements. The Union must also be capable of balancing considerations of overall European welfare with the strong market perspective that forms the ideological basis of the EU. One way to do that would be to try to find a common path to social security in Europe. This, however, is not a path easily taken, given the distribution of competences that we see today between the Union and the member states. On the other hand, an excessive social deficit will lead to a lack of legitimacy for EU law, which in turn may undermine the process of democratic decision making within the Union.

The Court still has difficulty, then, on matters having to do with how the member states organize their national welfare systems. More than ten years ago, for example, it already became clear in certain cases relating to freedom of movement in connection with health care – such as Case C-158/96 *Kohll v. Union des caisses de maladie* – that the principle of free movement does not supply a sufficient basis for handling the welfare-state dimension of European integration. Strong concern was expressed in these cases for the ability of the member states to organize national welfare in such a way as to secure its financing, to ensure its accessibility throughout the national territory, and to make it possible to plan effectively enough to retain expertise and to confront new challenges. The Court was very explicit that exceptions to the rules on freedom of movement could not be justified solely by reference to financial problems or the need for economic stability. The member states' answer to this, after some years, was to enact new legislation in the field. Today the Court's interpretative margin has been limited, through a directive on the free movement of patients.

It is in the interest of both the Union and the member states to ensure that nationally guaranteed welfare is in line with EU law. The trend towards viewing social rights as individual and justiciable rights with a certain economic value is here to stay, but the CJEU has not entirely followed this trend, and it is a bit reluctant to fall into line altogether with the relatively clear indications on the subject given by the Union legislator.

Upon reading the most recent rulings of the Court bearing on social security and/or social assistance, we see that not so much has actually happened, notwithstanding the recognition of social rights in the EU Charter and new wording in the treaties regarding a social-market economy. The social rights set out in the EU Charter can certainly be made the object of deliberation by the Court, but in fact that does not happen. Following a comfortable old pattern, the Court avoids the subject of social rights. Instead it cites Union citizenship and the principle of non-discrimination, seeking thereby to guarantee the rights of free movement which are set out in the directives and regulations applicable in a given case (see, for example, Case C-140/12 *Brey*, as well as cases C-22/08 and C-23/08 *Vatsouras* and *Koupatantze*).

In one case not long ago, this old pattern was confirmed. The opinion submitted by Advocate General Wathelet in the case made this clear, as did the verdict of the Court of Justice itself. The case in question, C-333/13 *Elisabeta Dano, Florin Dano v. Jobcenter Leipzig*, brought several important questions concerning social rights to a head. The case concerned access to social assistance for migrating EU citizens without income. The Court had a golden opportunity here to refer to its old case law, as well as to consider the EU Charter and possibly to interpret the social rights set out therein. The opinion submitted by the advocate general concentrated on EU citizenship, and on the classification of persons into different groups according to level of economic activity. The persons in question were extremely vulnerable, yet the fundamental rights enumerated in the EU Charter were not discussed. The advocate general consulted the directive on freedom of movement for EU citizens, the treaty provisions on citizenship and equal treatment, and the regulations relating to the coordination of social-security programmes.

The advocate general did a thorough analysis of the case law, and found that the economic ties of an EU citizen to his/her host state – including his/her degree of integration – should continue to be decisive for ascertaining how many social rights the person in question is entitled to claim. The Court reasoned in the same way, emphasizing the importance of a person's legal presence and economic activity in the host state for establishing his/her right of residence. The EU Charter was not mentioned in the ruling, leaving it without any immediate implications for the interpretation of EU law.

For the member states, this ruling serves as a guarantee against having to assume greater social responsibility for economically inactive EU citizens, inasmuch as it allows national rules that make social assistance conditional upon fulfilling residential criteria. Solidarity, then, is not about the bond between the individual and the EU, or about the needs that individuals might have. It consists rather in observing the principle of free movement and in carrying out the commitments that the Union and its member states have long had towards each other. The changes made in the treaties in 2009 have not yet had any major breakthrough in the case law of the CJEU. The previous pattern in this regard has continued. Fundamental social rights for EU citizens are interpreted first and foremost through secondary law, and the Charter is seldom cited. Thus, the directive on the right of citizens of the Union and their family members to reside and move freely within the territory of the member states (Directive 2004/38) ultimately decides the content of the social rights in question, without regard to the Charter or the fundamental goals of the Union (see Case C-67/14 *Jobcenter Berlin Neukölln v. Nazifa Alimanovic and Others*; Case C-308/14 *European Commission v. the United Kingdom*; and Case C-299/14 *Vestische Arbeit Jobcenter Kreis Recklinghausen v. Jovanna García and Others*). This is underlined in a recent proposal from the Commission. It is suggested that Directive 2004/38 should be referred to expressly in Regulation 883/2004 on the coordination social security systems. Through this proposal, COM(2016) 815, the Commission suggests strengthening the rules for EU citizens that are economically active and preventing abuse of the social security coordination framework. EU citizens lacking the legal right to reside in a host state will, if the proposal is accepted by the Council and the Parliament, have even less possibility to refer to rights based on citizenship.

CREATE A EUROPEAN STRUCTURE FOR REALIZING SOCIAL RIGHTS!

The dignity of the human person has been granted a more central and prominent place in European law since the EU Charter and the new treaties entered into force in 2009. The EU's institutions and the member states have underlined that fundamental rights must furnish critical guidance, and that they must mean something in EU law. One question to consider, therefore, is whether this now requires the Union to introduce an even stronger social dimension in relation to its citizens. And what role, in that case, might social rights play?

The CJEU plays a crucial role in the development of EU law, because it has the last word on how potential conflicts between EU and national law are to be interpreted and handled. To a large extent this also means resolving direct conflicts between norms, as national rules often collide with EU law. It is in such a situation, furthermore, that the question of competence is put to the test. The member states seem a bit hesitant in regard to social rights, and for its part the Court tries to avoid entering legally complicated territory where it must make decisions which are in fact political. It is in relation to the welfare state that it becomes evident that the economic advantages of European integration have to some extent been erased. This is above all true in the case of the older member states. But if the member states themselves do not start actively interpreting and observing the fundamental rules bearing on social rights, then the Court may feel called upon to impose these rules itself. That would mean taking another step towards a paradigm shift in the EU's legal narrative.

The Commission has taken the initiative to create a European Pillar for Social Rights, starting with the State of the Union speech by President Juncker (see COM(2016) 127 final). The Pillar is intended to serve as a framework for promoting reforms at the national level, for monitoring the employment and social performance of participating member states, and more specifically for encouraging renewed convergence within the eurozone. The idea is that the euro countries will work actively within the Pillar, and that member states outside the eurozone will be welcome to join in. With a view to finalizing the Pillar in 2017 (Annex 1, COM(2016) 127 final, p. 3), the EU's institutions and all of the member states carried out consultations throughout 2016. The entire social acquis is assembled in the Pillar, but it is arranged under three different themes: fair working conditions; equal opportunity and access to the labour market; and adequate and sustainable social protection. The Commission has stressed on several occasions that the Pillar will not change anything in regard to competence; nor will any new rights be created (see Garben et al. 2017).

The fact that fundamental social rights have not been highlighted during the present economic crisis is a matter of great concern. It is particularly important during difficult times that citizens feel trust towards the legal framework of society, and that they are able to foresee its impact upon their own lives. This is fundamental for the rule of law. Perhaps, if social rights had been more prominent in the political discourse during this difficult period, citizens would have had greater understanding for the measures that were taken. With law serving as a real tool for building society, moreover, these measures might have been taken in a better way.

Assuming the member states did not wish solely to achieve short-run political gains when they enacted the EU Charter and introduced the new treaty provisions, they acted unwisely in enacting binding rules at first, and then pretending that fundamental rights are a matter of fickle opinion and shifting political winds.

The crisis agreements adopted in the Union during recent years would have been justified and explicated in a different fashion if fundamental rights had been taken into account. They could also have been given a different content. If difficult decisions are elaborated and legitimized with a clear connection to both politics and law (in the form of human and fundamental rights), then a united EU might finally make a strong contribution to finding new ways of dealing with imbalances of prosperity and welfare within and between the member states. We could have a structure of European integration that respects – and in some measure ultimately defines – the full extent of what can be considered human dignity today.

REFERENCES

Court of Justice (www.curia.eu)

Opinion of the Court, 2/13, Avis rendu en vertu de l'article 218, paragraphe 11, TFUE.

Case 1/58 *Stork v. High Authority* (ECR 1959 p. 17) (EU:C:1959:4).

Case C-158/96 *Kohll v. Union des caisses de maladie* (ECR 1998 p. I-1931) (ECLI:EU:C:1998:171).

Cases C-22/08 and C-23/08 *Vatsouras and Koupatantze* (EU:C:2009:344).

Case C-279/09 *DEB v. Bundesrepublik Deutschland* (EU:C:2010:811).

Case C-571/10 *Servet Kamberaj mot Istituto per l'Edilizia sociale della Provincia autonoma di Bolzano (IPES) and Others* (EU:C:2012:233).

Case C-617/10 *Åklagaren v. Åkerberg Fransson* (EU:C:2013:105).

Case C-399/11 *Melloni* (EU:C:2013:107).

Case C-140/12 *Brey* (EU:C:2013:565).

Case C-176/12 *Association de médiation sociale v. Union locale des syndicats CGT and Others* (EU:C:2014:2).

Case C-333/13 *Elisabeta Dano, Florin Dano v. Jobcenter Leipzig* (EU:C:2014:2358).

Case C-67/14 *Jobcenter Berlin Neukölln v. Nazifa Alimanovic and Others* (EU:C:2015:597).

Case C-299/14 *Vestische Arbeit Jobcenter Kreis Recklinghausen v. Jovanna Garcia and Others* (EU:C:2016:114).

Case C-308/14 *European Commission v. the United Kingdom* (EU:C:2016:436).

Case C-218/15 *Gianpaolo Paoletti and Others v. Procura della Repubblica* (EU:C:2016:748).

Literature

Erhag, Thomas (2016), 'Under Pressure? – Swedish Residence-Based Social Security and EU Citizenship', *European Journal of Social Security*, Vol. 18, No. 2, pp. 207–231.

Garben, Sacha, Claire Kilpatrick, and Elise Muir (2017), 'Towards a European Pillar of Social Rights: Upgrading the EU Social Acquis?', College of Europe Policy Brief, No. 1/2017.

Kilpatrick, Claire and Bruno De Witte (2014), 'A Comparative Framing of Fundamental Rights – Challenges to Social Crisis Measures in the Eurozone', Sieps European Policy Analysis, November 2014.

Lind, Anna-Sara (2009), *Sociala rättigheter i förändring. En konstitutionellrättslig studie*. Academic Thesis, Uppsala University, 2009, 497 pp.

Lind, Anna-Sara (2011), 'The Right to Health from a Constitutional Perspective – The Example of the Nordic Countries', in Elisabeth Rynning and Mette Hartlev (eds), *Nordic Health Law in a European Context – Welfare State Perspectives on Patients' Rights and Biomedicine*, Leiden: Martinus Nijhoff Publishers, pp. 67–76.

Mikkola, Matti (2007), 'Social Human Rights of Migrants under the European Social Charter', *European Journal of Social Security*, Vol. 10, No. 1, pp. 25–59.

Newdick, Christopher (2006), 'Citizenship, Free Movement and Health Care: Cementing Individual Rights by Corroding Social Solidarity', *Common Market Law Review*, Vol. 43, No. 6, pp. 1645–1668.

Other Sources

Explanations relating to the Charter of Fundamental Rights, 14.12.2007, C/303/17.

COM(2016) 127 final, Launching a Consultation on a European Pillar of Social Rights, 8.3.2016.

COM(2016) 815 final, Proposal for a REGULATION OF THE EUROPEAN PARLIAMENT AND OF THE COUNCIL amending Regulation (EC) No 883/2004 on the coordination of social security systems and regulation (EC) No 987/2009 laying down the procedure for implementing Regulation (EC) No 883/2004.

First preliminary outline of a European Pillar of Social Rights, Annex 1 COM(2016) 127 final, Launching a Consultation on a European Pillar of Social Rights, 8.3.2016.

3. Repercussions of right-wing populism for European integration

Ann-Cathrine Jungar

INTRODUCTION

In 2014, as elections to the European Parliament (EP) approached, populist parties with nationalist, fascist, and Eurosceptic agendas were expected to meet with great electoral success. In this chapter, I analyse right-wing populist parties in Europe: their policies, their relationship to their voters, and their possible impact on the orientation of the European project. The title of this book highlights the economic and social disparities within and between EU member states. An important question for this chapter is whether prosperity gaps of this kind contribute to the success of right-wing populist parties. Are supporters of the latter mainly motivated by dissatisfaction with the established parties, or by agreement with the policies proposed by the right-wing populist parties? In this chapter, I show that the presence of these parties in the parliament of many member states reflects a demand within the electorate for Eurosceptic and anti-immigration policies. For such voters, the policies for which these parties stand in these areas is crucial for how they vote: their choice of party is not first and foremost a general expression of dissatisfaction with the political system. The right-wing populist parties that exist today have long been present in the political systems of Europe; they are not, as was often assumed earlier, ephemeral or 'flash-in-the-pan' phenomena. Their persistence and increased voting share reflect the fact that, due to their greater parliamentary representation, they have acquired the resources to establish professional channels of communication and to build up effective party organizations with national coverage (Heinisch and Mazzoleni 2016). Despite the varying origins of these parties – in anti-tax protest, in agrarian populism, or in nationalist and regionalist movements – they have increasingly converged ideologically, and transnational cooperation among them has grown (Jungar and Jupskås 2014).

In the wake of the far-reaching economic crisis, a larger number of anti-establishment parties of various ideological hues – some newly formed, others long established – have found themselves in parliament in a number of EU member states (Kriesi and Pappas 2015). In the election year of 2014, many believed it was the turn of the EP to be invaded by political parties opposed to freedom of movement, the common currency, and the EU's supranational character. Warnings were issued by leading representatives of the Union's institutions (the Council of Ministers, the Commission, and the EP), as well as by many heads of government of the member states, that the project of European integration would suffer a grievous setback, and the ability of the Union to solve problems in Europe's societies would be lost. If nationalist and anti-immigration parties gained greater representation in the EP, freedom of movement would be restricted, the formulation of common policies would be hampered, and the fundamental values of the Union would be threatened. The mass media too stressed the threat to European integration posed by right-wing populism. *The Economist* started off the year 2014 with an article entitled 'Political Insurgency: Europe's Tea Parties', together with a front page adorned by a right-wing populist trio – *Marine Le Pen* of the Front National in France, *Nigel Farage* of the United Kingdom Independence Party (UKIP), and *Geert Wilders* of the Freedom Party in the Netherlands – sailing a stormy (European) sea at full speed in a teapot (*The Economist* 2014).

This dark picture, which dominated debate in politics and the mass media, served partly to conceal a political discussion about how the project of European integration has developed, particularly during and after the economic crisis. Eurosceptic parties contended, as Farage did in UKIP's election manifesto, that a 'lot of lies have been told about the EU', and that the time had now come to lift the smokescreens which had kept European citizens from realizing how the policy packages for rescuing the euro had both worsened the EU's democratic deficit and deepened its supranational character (UKIP 2014). Alternative for Deutschland (AfD), the Eurosceptic party in Germany, claimed in its election manifesto that 'Never since World War II have so many politicians broken so many promises and disregarded so many laws as has been the case since May 2010 in the attempt to preserve the common currency' (Alternative for Deutschland 2014). The power of EU institutions with a weak democratic mandate or none at all – more precisely, the European Commission and the European Central Bank (ECB) – had grown. Together with the International Monetary Fund, these constituted the widely despised troika, which according to Alternative for Deutschland 'establish[ed] institutions [read: the European Stability Mechanism (ESM) and the banking union] that lack any kind of parliamentary control'. As a result, '[e]specially citizens in the highly indebted countries of the eurozone suffer from the [democratic] deficit' when demands for spending cuts and financial savings are imposed on them without any mandate from democratically accountable bodies (Alternative for Deutschland 2014).

At the same time, the threatening portrayal of right-wing populist parties in political debate and the mass media diverted attention from the issues by means of which these parties mobilize their voters. In fact, these parties pose important and basic questions about the EU's development in an ever more supranational direction, about the deepening of the Union's democratic shortcomings, and about the implications of freedom of movement for national identity and social welfare. These parties tend, however, to offer simplistic and unrealistic solutions to these challenges. From this perspective, the success of Eurosceptic parties may constitute a possible corrective, forcing the emergence of political leaders in the EU who are more responsive to citizens and more sensitive to their concerns (Mudde and Kaltwasser 2012). Populism can be a threat, if the established parties respond to it by embracing elements of xenophobia and nationalism in order to make short-term gains among voters; but it may also serve as a wake-up call to the established parties, reminding them of the need to explain their policies, to try to influence public opinion, to consider their democratic mission – and to act accordingly. In the wake of the economic crisis, in the eurozone especially, criticism of the growing power of the Union and dismay at its democratic deficit have gathered steam in the member states. The success in Greece of Golden Dawn, a party of the extreme right, came in reaction to the deep economic crisis in that country and the far-reaching cutbacks in public spending which the EU has exacted from Greece in exchange for financial assistance. In other countries, radical-right parties have mobilized resistance to the provision of economic assistance on a solidaristic basis to financially troubled members of the eurozone. The electoral success of right-wing populist parties can be seen as a sign that the mainstream parties and the EU establishment have not been able to explain their policies adequately. They have garnered popular support neither for the way in which they have handled the economic crisis in particular, nor for the direction in which they have taken European integration in general. A good many citizens of the Union do not perceive benefits from the European project; instead they see it as a threat to their jobs, to their prosperity and welfare, and to national self-determination.

The influx of refugees into Europe from war-torn areas, Syria in particular, has further contributed to a situation where the questions raised by parties of the radical right have dominated the political agendas of the member states. New parties of the radical right have been formed. Alternative for Deutschland, which started out mainly as a Eurosceptic party, has won seats in several German state legislatures by adopting more radical positions against immigration and against Islam. In Estonia, the newly formed radical-right populist party EKRE (Eesti Konservativne Rahvaerakond) secured seats in the parliamentary election of 2013 by strongly opposing the EU's proposal for a solidaristic sharing-out of refugees (Jungar et al. 2016). Radical-right parties that already held parliamentary seats have continued to enjoy electoral wind in their sails, even when the established parties – in the wake of the refugee crisis – have adjusted their posture more and more to the anti-immigration rhetoric of the radical-right parties, and to the picture the latter have painted of a failed EU project of multicultural integration. Europe's radical-right parties have also seen their chance after the referendum in the UK on EU membership, which the Leave side won. Indeed, that referendum was held in reaction to the rising popular support garnered by UKIP since 2010.

This chapter is organized in the following manner. To start with, I describe the policies of the right-wing populist parties, as well as their ideological position in European party systems. Do they form a cohesive party family, or are there significant differences between them? I then review the electoral successes of these parties, as well as the formation of party groups following the EP elections of 2014. Finally, I ask what policies these parties can be expected to pursue in the EP, and what prospects they may have for influencing political decision making.

WHICH PARTIES? CONCEPTS AND DEFINITIONS

The parties analysed in this chapter make up a motley crew, and various labels have been used for them in public discourse and in academic literature. Right-wing populism, right-wing extremism, and rightist radicalism are some of the terms commonly used to describe parties that combine an anti-establishment posture with xenophobia, nationalism, Euroscepticism, and opposition to immigration (Mudde 2007). 'Far right' is an overarching term for these parties; however, 'right' does not relate here to their position on the socioeconomic left–right spectrum, but rather to their position on the values-based left–right spectrum – what political scientists call the liberal–authoritarian (or sometimes the nationalist–cosmopolitan, should be nationalist-cosmopolitan) spectrum.

The political space in European party systems is usually envisioned in terms of (at least) two lines of conflict, along which parties place themselves when formulating policies and competing for voter support (Kitschelt and McGann 1997). The first line of conflict is the socioeconomic left–right axis, which reflects the range of views on issues like taxes, welfare, and the relationship between market and state. The Left wants more in the way of government regulation, tax-financed redistribution, and publicly funded social welfare; the Right seeks lower taxes, market-based solutions, and stronger incentives for entrepreneurship. The other line of conflict, often termed the liberal–authoritarian axis in political science, reflects the range of views on sociocultural issues, such as defence, law and order, animal rights and the environment, nationalism (immigration and multiculturalism), and family issues (equality for sexual minorities and between men and women). Opposition to immigration, calls for longer prison sentences, and a traditional view of the family are found on the authoritarian side; while favourable attitudes towards multiculturalism, gender equality, the rights of (sexual) minorities, and the need to protect the environment reflect a liberal position. Views on the EU constitute an axis of their own, disconnected from the socioeconomic and sociocultural lines of conflict. Euroscepticism can be found on both the left and right sides on the socioeconomic axis, and at both liberal and authoritarian points along the sociocultural axis.

In western Europe, and in the Nordic countries especially, the socioeconomic left–right axis has been the dominant one in structuring party-political conflict; however, the liberal–authoritarian dimension has become more important. The prominence of the latter dimension has grown in connection with the success of green parties and (especially) with the emergence of right-wing populist parties. The core issues of the two types of parties – cosmopolitanism and the environment on the one hand, opposition to immigration and defence of the national culture on the other – place prominently on the liberal–authoritarian dimension. The parties analysed in this chapter typically take a polar position on both the liberal–authoritarian and EU axes within their respective party systems. Their positions vary, however, when it comes to socioeconomic questions, although they have recently tended to converge on these matters too. Economic liberalism in combination with authoritarianism was previously thought to be the key to success – the 'winning combination' – for parties of the radical right; however, more and more of these parties are now staking out a position within the middle portion of the socioeconomic spectrum (Kitschelt and McGann 1997; De Lange 2007). The winning formula today is a socioeconomic centrist position combined with an authoritarian stance. Where these parties have shifted their position on the socioeconomic spectrum, their motivation has often been strategic in nature: increasingly, they have been mobilizing working-class voters with culturally conservative views.

In the two figures below, we see how a number of Europe's so-called right-wing populist parties position themselves on the socioeconomic and sociocultural dimensions of conflict. The data employed are from an expert survey (Chapel Hill Expert Survey, CHS: Bakker et al. 2014), in which national experts on political parties have evaluated the positions taken by different parties in their respective countries on a variety of issues, and ranked them along different dimensions. Unlike data based on electoral manifestoes, which are based solely on the electoral platforms of the parties, expert data include the parties' actions and political moves in parliament. Not all of the parties examined in this chapter are included in the CHS, because several of the populist parties with seats in the EP are relatively new, and they are not represented in any of the parliaments of the member states.

As can be seen in Figure 3.1, right-wing populist parties take a polar position on the liberal–authoritarian spectrum and (in most cases) a

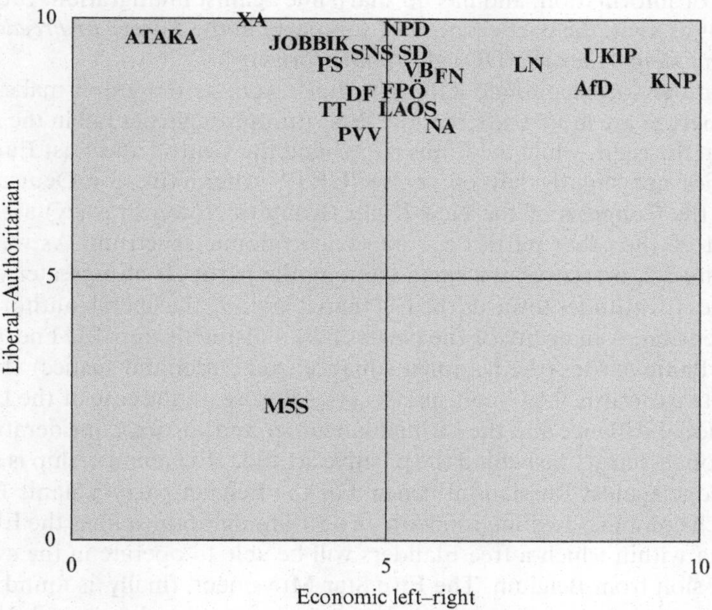

Note: The position of each party along the socioeconomic dimension is measured on a scale of 0 to 10, where 0 means left and 10 means right. The position of each party along the sociocultural dimension is measured on a scale of 0 to 10, where 0 corresponds to a liberal position and 10 to an authoritarian one.

Source: Chapel Hill Expert Survey 2014.

Figure 3.1 The positions of the parties along socioeconomic and sociocultural lines of conflict

middle position on the socioeconomic spectrum. The figure shows too that these parties cluster together at the authoritarian end on the values dimension, and that they are scattered more widely on the socioeconomic dimension. The more radical and extreme of these parties take, relative to the other right-wing populist parties, a marginally more radical position on the sociocultural dimension – that is, Jobbik from Hungary, the Slovak Nationalist party, Golden Dawn from Greece, and Ataka from Bulgaria. The parties are thus concentrated at the authoritarian end on the values dimension; moreover, the differences in this regard between the various radical-right parties are marginal, in the judgement of the country experts. However, the Five Star Movement in Italy stands out from the other parties with its clearly liberal position on the values dimension. This party champions environmentalism, takes a libertarian stance on the dissemination of information, and has no sharp line against immigration. From this point of view, the participation of this party in the *Europe of Freedom and Direct Democracy* (EFDD) group is surprising.

On the socioeconomic left–right dimension, as the graph makes clear, the parties are more scattered: the West European parties fall in the middle or on the right, while the Finns party[1] and the Central and East European parties are slightly left of centre. UKIP, Alternative for Deutschland, and the Congress of the New Right (Kongres Nowej Prawicy) are to the right of the other parties on the socioeconomic spectrum. As we see in Figure 3.2, moreover, the spread among the parties is also greater when it comes to attitudes towards the EU than it is along the liberal–authoritarian dimension. A majority of the parties take a distinctly anti-EU line, but the two Baltic parties (the National Alliance, and Order and Justice) are more positive towards the Union, as is Vlaams Belang. In the case of the Latvian National Alliance and the Lithuanian Order and Justice, considerations of national security lie behind the positive attitude: EU membership is seen as a hedge against Russian influence. For the Belgian party Vlaams Belang, which combines regionalism with an anti-immigration stance, the EU is an arena within which a free Flanders will be able to operate in the event of secession from Belgium. The Five Star Movement, finally, is found within the main cluster of the parties when it comes to attitudes towards the EU; it is this which explains the participation of this anti-establishment Italian party in EFDD.

The other parties are in varying degrees Eurosceptic – that is, they are opposed to European integration in a variety of ‘harder’ or ‘softer’ ways. I shall return to this in greater detail later in this chapter.

These parties are sometimes depicted as one-issue parties, their sole concern being to oppose immigration or European integration. Indeed, the historical origins of many of these parties do lie in a specific political

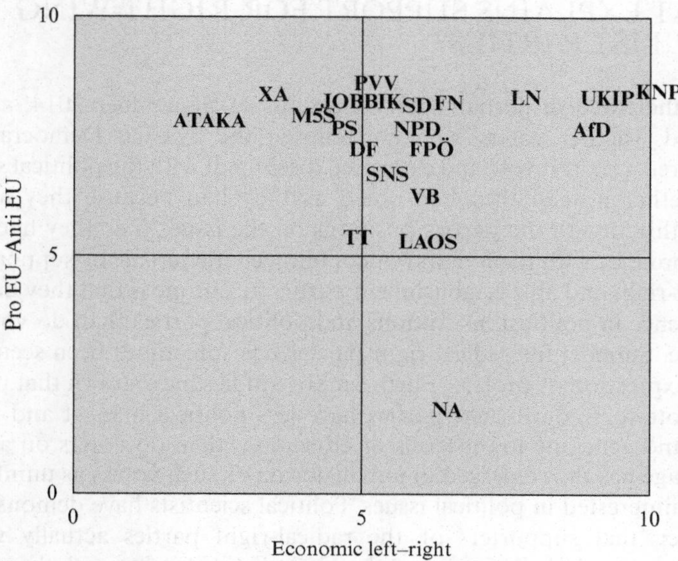

Note: The position of each party along the socioeconomic dimension is measured on a scale of 0 to 10, where 0 means left and 10 means right. The position of each party along the EU dimension is measured on a scale of 0 to 10, where 0 means pro EU and 10 means anti EU. See Table 3.A3 in the appendix for a key to the party abbreviations used in this figure.

Source: Chapel Hill Expert Survey 2014.

Figure 3.2 Party positions along economic left–right and EU dimensions

question; however, as they have gained a firmer foothold in parliament and in some cases also taken part in government, these parties have necessarily developed a broader political agenda. Yet immigration and the EU remain the most important issues for these parties, as can be seen from their programmes, their rhetoric, and their voters. They continue to see such questions as central, and to connect other issues to these core concerns. For example, many of these parties resort to welfare-chauvinist arguments in which cuts in pensions or other social programmes get blamed on costs arising from immigration, or are linked to membership fees and financial transfers to the EU.

WHAT EXPLAINS SUPPORT FOR RIGHT-WING POPULIST PARTIES?

After the Swedish parliamentary elections of September 2014, analysts debated whether voters who had chosen the Sweden Democrats had registered a protest vote and expressed discontent with the political system, or whether instead they had voted as they had because they actually sympathized with the party's positions on the issues (i.e., they had voted in accordance with their views). A common characteristic of supporters of radical-right and anti-establishment parties in Europe is that they have less confidence in political institutions and political parties than do voters on average. Support for radical-right parties has sometimes been seen, then, as an expression of protest. Furthermore, studies have shown that persons who vote for radical-right parties have less political interest and knowledge, and generally lower levels of education, than do voters on average. An image has thus emerged in public debate of such voters as uninformed and uninterested in political issues. Political scientists have demonstrated, however, that supporters of the radical-right parties actually vote in accordance with their views, and that their dissatisfaction with the political system *derives* from their opposition to prevailing policies on immigration and the EU (Ivarsflaten 2008; Werts et al. 2013).

How we ascertain the answer here – as to whether such voters are lodging a protest vote or voting in accordance with their views – depends ultimately on how protest voting is defined, and on how the relationship between political views and low levels of trust in institutions is understood. In other words, do supporters of the radical-right parties vote as they do in order to protest against the establishment or do they vote as they do because they sympathize with the policies espoused by these parties? In a far-reaching study entitled 'Anti-immigration Parties in Europe: Ideological or Protest Vote?', Wouter van der Brug, Meindert Fennema, and Jean Tillie (2000) show that support for radical-right parties reflects sympathy with their policies, above all in connection with immigration. In a subsequent article, 'Protest or Mainstream?: How the European Anti-immigrant Parties Developed into Two Separate Groups by 1999', Brug and Fennema (2003) contend that the radical-right parties are in fact more modern than their established counterparts. Their voters support them to a higher degree on the basis of a concordance of views. To a greater extent than supporters of the established parties, persons who support radical-right parties place their vote not on the basis of the social group to which they belong, but instead on the basis of ideology – that is, they are more focused on the issues than other voters are. These authors have drawn criticism for defining protest voting too narrowly – for equating protest voting with choosing a party not on the basis of its policies, but instead on the basis of a perceived need to lodge a protest against the political establishment. However, research on the relationship between political preferences and political trust gives further support to the congruence-of-views hypothesis. Studies on the causal connection between opposition to multiculturalism and immigration on the one hand, and trust in political institutions on the other, have shown that persons who perceive multiculturalism and immigration as a threat to the national community are more likely to lose trust in the state, inasmuch as they feel that its leaders are no longer showing due regard for the concerns of their own people. In an article entitled 'The Cultural Divide in Europe: Migration, Multiculturalism, and Political Trust', Lauren McLaren (2012b) shows that discontent in the form of lower levels of political trust is associated with dissatisfaction with immigration policy. In 'Multicultural Policy and Political Support in European Democracies', Jack Citrin, Morris Leavy, and Matthew Right (2014) reach a similar conclusion: low levels of political trust correlate – even after control for other factors that affect political trust – with anxiety over the impact of immigration on the national community. The causal link, they hypothesize, works as follows: 'Those most concerned about the problem may believe that the political system (the elites and institutions) have sold out the public by failing to protect the national community from the potentially disruptive and divisive force of immigration.'

The parties of the radical right gain as many votes as they do because there is a demand in the electorate for the policies they espouse. Moreover, the congruence in views between these parties and their voters is particularly pronounced on their core issues, namely immigration and the EU. In order to assess the degree to which these parties and their voters hold the same views, I have relied on data from the CHS about the positions of the parties, and from the European Election Survey 2014 (Schmitt et al. 2016) about the views of the voters. The right-wing populist parties have a unique take on these issues: they alone propose such policies within their respective political systems. Figures 3.3 and 3.4 depict the degree of opinion congruence between political parties and their voters in eight EU member states. They make clear, first of all, that the right-wing populist parties take the most extreme positions on immigration and the EU – that is, they are most opposed to immigration and to a deepening of European integration. They offer a unique political choice on these two issues; they face no political competitors in this area. Second, the congruence in views between these parties and their voters is particularly pronounced on these core issues. On matters of this kind, these parties are faithful representatives of their constituents. It is also clear from the graphs that, according to data from 2014, European political parties are

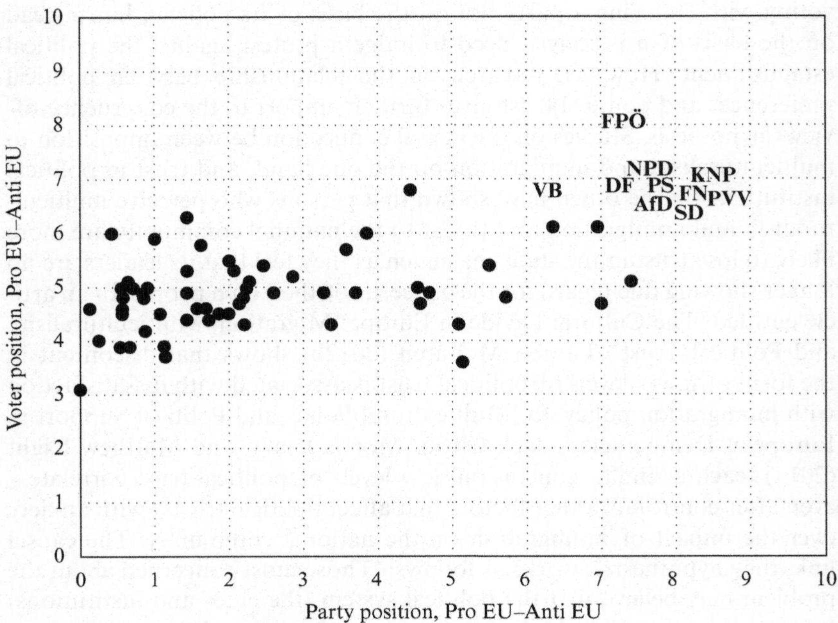

Note: The positions of the parties and the voters are measured on a scale from 0 to 10 where 0 means pro EU and 10 means anti EU. See Table 3.A3 in the appendix for a key to the party abbreviations used in this figure.

Sources: Chapel Hill Expert Survey 2014; European Social Survey 2014.

Figure 3.3 Party–voter congruence on the European Union

more favourably disposed to both immigration and European integration than their voters are. A change in voter opinion has taken place since 2010: the average voter has become more critical of immigration, and the degree of opinion congruence between the parties and their voters on this issue has diminshed (see Appendix). European political parties in general are more well-disposed to immigration than their voters are. The parties of the populist right, on the other hand, take positions on these matters – both immigration and the EU – which coincide closely with the views of their voters. These parties contribute, then, to an improved representativity in European party systems where public opinion is concerned, because they respond to the pool of Eurosceptic and anti-immigration voters by offering a unique policy approach – that is, they are often the only parties to offer a strictly Eurosceptic or anti-immigration option. In this way,

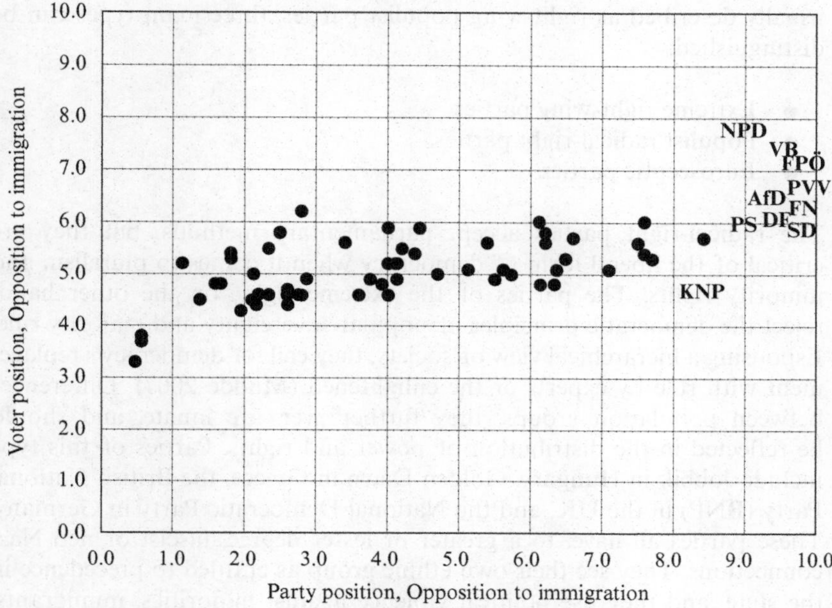

Note: The positions of the parties and the voters are measured on a scale from 0 to 10 where 0 means pro-immigration and 10 means anti-immigration. See Table 3.A3 in the appendix for a key to the party abbreviations used in this figure.

Sources: Chapel Hill Expert Survey 2014; European Social Survey 2014.

Figure 3.4 Party–voter congruence on opposition to immigration

these parties may serve to mobilize voters and to strengthen the system, by offering a parliamentary alternative for voters who might otherwise stay at home, or turn their back on politics, or come to sympathize with truly extreme movements. In articulating the concerns of these voters within the conventional political system, the activities of these parties may in fact strengthen the latter.

ONE FAMILY PARTY OR SEVERAL?

Notwithstanding ideological similarities between these parties, they do not form a cohesive party family. One important dividing line here – between extreme and merely radical parties – reflects differing attitudes towards democratic values and principles. Within the broad group of parties usually described as right-wing populist parties, three main types can be distinguished:

- Extreme right-wing parties
- Populist radical-right parties
- Eurosceptic parties.

The radical-right parties accept parliamentary methods, but they are critical of the liberal form of democracy when it comes to pluralism and minority rights. The parties of the extreme right, on the other hand, reject the democratic principles of popular sovereignty and majority rule. Espousing a hierarchical view of society, they call for democracy's replacement with rule by experts or the enlightened (Mudde 2007). Differences between population groups, they further aver, are innate, and should be reflected in the distribution of power and rights. Parties of this type include Jobbik in Hungary, Golden Dawn in Greece, the British National Party (BNP) in the UK, and the National Democratic Party in Germany. These parties all have, to a greater or lesser degree, fascist or neo-Nazi connections. They see their own ethnic group as entitled to precedence in the state, and they use political violence against minorities, immigrants, and political opponents.

Most of the parties analysed in this chapter can be defined as populist radical-right parties. These parties accept the rules of democracy, they disavow extraparliamentary methods, and they operate within the framework of parliamentary institutions. They do not seek to replace democracy with another form of government. They have a (somewhat limited) ideological core in common, consisting of *populism*, *nationalism*, and *authoritarianism* – where different populist radical-right parties put differing emphases on the one or the other component (Mudde 2004). 'Populism' refers to an anti-establishment position, according to which the fundamental conflict in society is between a unified and homogeneous people on the one hand, and a cohesive, corrupt, and non-responsive elite on the other. Populism takes an antagonistic stance not just towards the political establishment, but also towards the ideas and values that predominate in society (Canovan 1999).

The idea that the political community should be based on a homogeneous and cohesive people is central to populism. In this populism differs from ideologies based on class or other interests, which fasten on the situation of more specific groups in society. However, the people championed by populism can be visualized in a variety of ways (Canovan 1999). For example, they can be conceived as the democratic people – the *demos* – who have been betrayed by their elected representatives. They can also be seen as the 'man in the street' (less often the woman), or as the 'silent majority'. The people here consists of a certain segment of the population: the 'authentic', 'typical', or 'normal' people, who are neglected by the establishment or threatened by changes in society. The people can also be understood as 'our own people' – that is, those who share our ethnicity, language, history, or culture.

The nationalism of the populist radical-right parties is expressed in ideas of the people as an 'ethnos': a people united by common characteristics and bound by shared origins, language, or culture. Where policy is concerned, nationalists tend to oppose immigration and to reject multiculturalism, which they contend leads to social tensions and conflicts. They defend Western culture, tradition, and religion; and they perceive Islam as incompatible with Western values, such as freedom of expression and equality between men and women. In the member states of central and eastern Europe, which do not have large groups of immigrants, nationalist parties aim their ire mainly at minorities resident within the country, such as Roma in Hungary or Russians in the Baltic states. The authoritarianism of these parties finds expression in cultural conservatism, in respect for authority and tradition, and in a high estimation of the value of orderliness. In political terms, these parties support stricter punishment, a strong defence, conventional family values, and traditional methods for bringing up children.

The third group of so-called anti-establishment parties has shrunk. UKIP was strictly a Eurosceptic party to begin with, but the question of immigration – both from within the Union and from outside it – gained ever greater prominence within it after 2008 (Ford and Goodwin 2014). The party's opposition to the EU, rooted in its insistence on national self-determination, was increasingly combined with opposition to free movement within the Union (which was also a dominant theme for the Leave side in the Brexit referendum of 2016). Alternative for Deutschland too started out as a mainly Eurosceptic party, in the EP elections of 2014. But it was rent by tensions between supporters of party leader Bernhard Lucke, for whom economic liberalism was central, and adherents of national conservatism, who espoused a tougher line on immigration and Islam. At the party congress in June 2015, the struggle for the leadership was won by Frauke Petry, who hailed from the anti-immigration wing. The image of the party then underwent a drastic change. The former leader left the party, as did many others, including five of the party's MEPs. In 2016, Alternative for Deutschland began cooperating with the Freedom Party of Austria, a party of the radical right, further underlining the change in the party's direction. This also had implications for Alternative for Deutschland's party-group affiliation, as I describe below. In sum, UKIP and Alternative for Deutschland can be seen as populist radical-right parties, but with an economic policy to the right of that favoured by most parties of this type.

The Five Star Movement, for its part, is clearly an anti-establishment party with a soft Eurosceptic profile. It calls for a referendum on Italy's participation in the common currency, and it combines Euroscepticism with environmentalism. It also champions direct democracy and a guaranteed minimum income. Opposition to immigration has not figured prominently in this party, although its former leader, Beppe Grillo, has criticized Italian immigration policy.

THE EARTHQUAKE THAT PETERED OUT?

'Create an earthquake', read the call to voters on the title page of UKIP's manifesto for the European elections of 2014 (UKIP 2014). Eurosceptic parties did indeed advance in those elections, but the results were not unequivocal. New parties won seats in the EP; some of the established parties were strengthened; other parties lost their seats. This variation in electoral outcomes would have great importance for the process of forming party groups, which got underway as soon as the polling stations closed their doors. In the previous parliament, radical-right and Eurosceptic parties had been represented in two party groups – *Europe of Freedom and Democracy* (EFD) and *European Conservatives and Reformists* (ECR) – as well as among those without any party-group affiliation. Electoral results of three different kinds can be identified for the Eurosceptic, nationalist, and anti-immigration parties in the EP elections of 2014. We can start with the parties – both newcomers and established ones – that significantly increased their presence in the EP. The most successful among these were the Five Star Movement, the Eurosceptic anti-establishment party from Italy (21.2 per cent of the vote; 17 seats); Alternative for Deutschland in Germany (7.1 per cent; 7 seats); the populist radical-right Sweden Democrats (9.7 per cent; 2 seats); and the far-right Greek party Golden Dawn (9.4 per cent; 3 seats). The Congress of the New Right, a Eurosceptic and economically liberal party from Poland, made its debut in the EP with 7.2 per cent of the vote and 4 seats (grabbing headlines, moreover, with its proposal to deprive women of the right to vote). Three of the parties already represented in the EP made heavy gains; indeed, they became the largest parties from their respective countries. These were UKIP, the Front National, and the Danish People's Party. A quarter of the voters in France, Denmark, and the UK opted for a populist radical-right party. With nearly 25 per cent of the vote, the Front National increased its number of seats from 3 to 23; UKIP and the Danish People's Party each took 27 per cent of the vote. The Freedom Party of Austria (19.7 per cent; 4 seats) and the Finns party (12.9 per cent; 2 seats) also gained ground; for the latter party, however, the results were a disappointment, as compared with the nearly 20 per cent of the vote it received in Finland's parliamentary elections in 2011.

Other parties lost seats or even fell out of the EP altogether. Among the right-wing populist parties of central and eastern Europe, several Eurosceptic and nationalist parties – Slovak Nationalist party from Slovakia, the Greater Romanian Party, and Ataka from Bulgaria – failed to gain any representation in the new parliament. The far-right BNP from the UK lost both of its seats, probably because UKIP succeeded in mobilizing British voters of a Eurosceptic and anti-immigration disposition. While far-right Golden Dawn made its debut in the EP, its fellow Greek party, the Popular Orthodox Rally, a religious right-wing populist party, lost its two seats. Vlaams Belang in Belgium and Lega Nord in Italy lost half their seats. The isolation imposed on the former party by Belgium's established parties – the 'cordon sanitaire' – appears to have borne fruit, inasmuch as Vlaams Belang's electoral support had successively fallen in both national and local elections, and now fell in the EP elections as well. One can assume that some of Vlaams Belang's voters switched to NVV (Nieuw-Vlaamse Alliantie), which has a more moderate profile on immigration and on regional issues, and which unlike Vlaams Belang is well disposed to the EU (Pauwels 2011). Lega Nord's decline mostly reflected internal party scandals in connection with corruption and abuse of power (Albertazzi and McDonnell 2015).

A third group of parties retained their seats: the National Alliance from Latvia, Jobbik from Hungary, and the Freedom Party from the Netherlands. Wilders had been expected to lead the Freedom Party to great success, but the opinion polls proved wrong in this.

The election campaign for the EP had already begun when, in November 2013, Le Pen and Wilders announced they had teamed up together with the aim of forming a new joint party group – the *European Alliance of Freedom* (EAF) – after the election in 2014. 'We will liberate Europe from the monster of Brussels', declared Wilders as he described the project to bring together radical-right parties seeking to renationalize the EU (Reuters 2013). The member states would regain control of their borders, their currencies, and their economies. Lega Nord, Vlaams Belang, and the Freedom Party of Austria joined the new transnational radical-right alliance, and intensive work got underway to assemble a sufficient number of parties. Le Pen visited the Sweden Democrats in Stockholm, among other things, and the latter kept their door open initially. The Swedish party came in for heavy criticism for having met

Table 3.1 Election results for Eurosceptic and anti-immigration parties in 2014 and 2009, percentage (and number of seats); as well as party-group affiliation after EP elections of 2014 (and 2009)

Member state	Party	Party group 2014 (2009)	2014	2009	Difference
Belgium	VB	ENF (2015) (NI)	4.1 (1)	9.9 (2)	−5.8 (−1)
Bulgaria	Ataka	 (NI)	3 (0)	12 (2)	−9 (−2)
Denmark	DF	ECR (EFD)	26.6 (4)	14.8 (2)	+11.8 (+2)
Finland	PS	ECR (EFD)	12.9 (2)	9.8 (1)	+3.1 (+1)
France	FN	ENF (2015) (NI)	24.9 (23)	6.3 (3)	+16.6 (+20)
Greece	LAOS	 (EFD)	2.7 (0)	7.2 2	−5.52 (−2)
	XA	NI	9.4 (3)	0	+9.4 (−3)
Italy	LN	ENF (2015) (EFD)	6.2 (5)	10.2 (9)	−4.0 (−4)
	M5S	EFDD	21.2 (17)	0	+21.2 (+17)
Latvia	NA	ECR (ECR)	14.3 (1)	7.5 (1)	+6.8 (0)
Lithuania	TT	EFDD (EFD)	14.3 (2)	12.2 (2)	+2.1 (0)
Poland	KNP	ENF (2015)/ EFDD	7.2 (4)	0	+7.2 (+4)
Netherlands	PVV	ENF (2015) (NI)	13.3 (4)	17.0 (4)	−3.7 (0)
Romania	PRM	 (NI)	2.7 (0)	8.7 (3)	−6.0 (−3)
Slovakia	SNS	(EFD)	3.6 (0)	5.6 (1)	−2.0 (−1)
United Kingdom	UKIP	EFDD (EFD)	26.8 (24)	16.9 (13)	+9.9 (+11)
	BNP	 (NI)	1.1 (0)	6.0 (2)	−4.9 (−2)
Sweden	SD	EFDD	9.7 (2)	3.3 (0)	+6.4 (+2)

Table 3.1 (continued)

Member state	Party	Party group 2014 (2009)	2014	2009	Difference
Germany	NDP	NI	1		
			(1)	(0)	+1
	AfD	ENF/ECR	7.1	0	+7.1
			(7)		(+7)
Hungary	Jobbik	NI	14.7	14.8	−0.1
			(3)	(3)	(0)
Austria	FPÖ	ENF (2015)	19.7	12.7	+7.0
		(NI)	(4)	(2)	(+2)

Note: NI = Non-Inscrits, who are Non-Attached Members who do not sit in one of the recognized political groups. See Table 3.A3 in the appendix for a key to the party abbreviations used in this table.

with Le Pen. By cooperating with her highly xenophobic and anti-Islamic party – a party which furthermore had failed to renounce anti-Semitism in a credible manner – the party leadership had confirmed, according to critics, that the Sweden Democrats figured among Europe's highly rightist radical parties, and that its rejection of racism and extremism – epitomized in the 'zero tolerance' for extremist and racist statements enunciated by party leader Jimmy Åkesson – was cosmetic (Jungar 2015). The Danish People's Party, which is the party with which the Sweden Democrats' transnational contacts have been most extensive, also warned them against joining the EAF (*Dagens Nyheter* 2013-11-24). Such 'guilt by association' rhetoric, whereby a party's political values and legitimacy are called in question if it cooperates with parties deemed too extreme, is common in connection with radical-right parties (Almeida 2010; Jungar and Jupskås 2014).

The question was whether Le Pen would be successful in creating a large nationalist, Eurosceptic, and anti-immigration group in the EP – something that her father, former party leader Jean-Marie Le Pen, had failed to do earlier. Since the late 1990s, the founder of the Front National had tried to assemble the nationalist parties into a common party group. He met with no success in this endeavour until 2007, when Bulgaria and Romania joined the Union. On account of internal conflicts, however, the story of the party group in question – Identity, Tradition, Sovereignty – was a brief one. Among other things, Alessandra Mussolini spoke of the criminal proclivities of Romanians, prompting the Romanian members of the group to storm out. Conflicts of this kind, centred on national differences, have long posed an obstacle to the establishment of transnational ties among nationalist parties. But such ties have increased in recent years, not least through the opportunities for the creation of contacts afforded by the EP. First and foremost, however, it is due to their common resistance to immigration, to Islam, and to deeper European integration that these parties have been able to draw closer to one another.

When the results started streaming in on the night of the election, speculation intensified about which party groups would ultimately succeed in collecting the necessary 25 MEPs from at least seven member states. Such is the requirement for obtaining economic and administrative resources from the EP, as well as for securing rapporteurship and speaking time. It was clear that, due to their electoral success, all three of the party constellations comprising Eurosceptic and radical-right parties – the established EFD and ECR, as well as the EAF – had won a sufficient number of seats. The question was whether they would be able to assemble MEPs from at least seven member states.

As it turned out, the EAF had to throw in the towel after the EP elections of 2014: it had the necessary number of members, but it failed to assemble representatives from at least seven member states. After intensive negotiations, as well as regrouping within some of the parties, Le Pen and Wilders were able to present a new party group in June 2015: Europe of Nations and Freedom (ENF). In addition to the five original parties – Lega Nord, Vlaams Belang, the Front National, the Freedom Party, and the Freedom Party of Austria – the Congress of the New Right joined the group as well, as did Janice Atkinson, an MEP who had been expelled from UKIP. With representatives from seven member states, then, the group qualified to receive administrative support and financial resources (EUR 17 million), as well as more speaking time and rapporteurship. The formation of the party group was made possible in part by a split within the Congress of the New Right, in which the controversial party leader Janusz Korwin-Mikke, notorious for extreme utterances and open Holocaust denial (he had been fined for racist remarks during his first year in the EP), was replaced as chairman by Michal Marusik. Le Pen, who had purged anti-Semitic and other extremist groups from her own party, had refused to cooperate with the Congress of the New Right until the change in its leadership; now that Korwin-Mikke had left the Congress of the New Right, however, cooperation was possible. (The Congress of the New Right's second MEP, Robert Jaroslaw Iwaszkiewics, joined EFDD and saved that party group thereby; more on that below.) A conservative Romanian MEP joined ENF subsequently (in 2015), as did one of the remaining MEPs from Alternative for Deutschland (in 2016).

This made for a total of 39 members. (Alternative for Deutschland's second MEP, Beatrix von Storch, joined EFDD.)

The brief programme presented by the party group expresses support for democratic principles and for human rights and freedoms, and repudiates the authoritarian and totalitarian projects of former times. It also emphasizes the need to defend national sovereignty, both when it comes to the European project in general and when it comes to the right of member states to control their borders in particular.[2] The vice chairman of the group, Marcel de Graaff, identifies the threats against which the group's programme is aimed as follows: 'Our European cultures, our values and our freedom are under attack. They are threatened by the crushing and dictatorial powers of the European Union. They are threatened by mass immigration, by open borders and by a single European currency: one size does not fit all'.[3] The group has also taken positions favourable to Russia, calling among other things for an end to the EU boycott of that country.

The party groups EFD and ECR, which bring together Eurosceptic and anti-immigration parties, had already existed in the previous EP. They experienced both defections and an influx of new party members. EFD was founded in 2009 by parties from the Europe of Nations party group; in the summer of 2014, it changed its name to Europe of Freedom and Direct Democracy (EFDD). EFDD represents Eurosceptic parties that seek a return to a more intergovernmental type of European cooperation, as well as greater respect for Europe's history, traditions, and cultural values. ECR, a more moderate group, was also formed following the EP elections of 2009. The British Tories, together with a culturally conservative party from Poland, Law and Justice (PiS), left the European People's Party (EPP) group and formed a party group of their own. They saw the EPP as too well-disposed to further European integration. ECR describes itself as 'euro-realist', meaning that it opposes further development of the Union in a federal direction. It calls for a more flexible type of integration which takes national differences and the views of citizens into account.[4] The British Conservatives have a leading role in ECR, which stands for a more moderate Euroscepticism than does EFDD. The common platform of the party group, formulated in 2009, is the Prague Declaration. It sets out a 'euro-realist' position, meaning that its signatories seek neither to dissolve the Union nor to undermine European cooperation, but to reform the structures thereof.

It was unclear until the last minute whether EFD would survive. Despite UKIP's electoral success, Farage had to work hard to club together MEPs from a sufficient number of countries. Farage has been chairman of the group since its formation in 2009. Lega Nord had left the group for the EAF, the Slovak Nationalist party left as well, and the Danish People's

Party and the Finns party – to the great disappointment of the party group's leader – left to join ECR. The Five Star Movement joined the group after getting the cold shoulder from both the Greens and the Alliance of Liberals and Democrats for Europe (ALDE). The Five Star Movement reaches many of its decisions through internal referenda among its activists, and the latter gave their support in such a vote for joining EFD. The devotion of this party to direct democracy even left an imprint on the name of the party group, which was changed to Europe of Freedom and Direct Democracy (EFDD). The Five Star Movement's position on the EU is unclear: the party programme does not mention Europe, but party leader Grillo has repeatedly criticized the political establishment of the Union and EU's present structures.

The Sweden Democrats, who after warnings from the Danish People's Party deemed it best to decline Le Pen's overtures, received an invitation from UKIP at the last minute. The initial indications, however, had been that EFD would not admit them, due to their extreme past, as well as in view of the cooperation their youth league had established with its counterparts from the Front National and the Freedom Party of Austria. The party's MEPs had to submit a statement to the effect that the Sweden Democrats had repudiated its roots in racist and neo-Nazi organizations. Farage came in for a lot of criticism in the British media for admitting the anti-immigration party into the group, but doing so was necessary if a dissolution of EFD was to be avoided. For the Sweden Democrats – which is treated like a pariah in the Swedish parliament, where the other parties ban it from all cooperative efforts – it was a great achievement to be accepted as a member of EFDD. Belonging to an established party group in the EP rather than being non-attached grants a party greater legitimacy, and yields access to the resources possessed by the party group. EFDD, for its part, was able to assemble MEPs from the necessary number of countries because individual MEPs from the French Front National joined the group. This made it vulnerable, however, to defections. The group briefly seemed to face dissolution in October, when Iveta Grigule, a Latvian MEP, left its ranks. However, after negotiations with the Congress of the New Right, the libertarian and anti-establishment Polish party, one of that party's four members chose to join EFDD, and the group was able to form itself anew. EFDD was criticized for having accepted a representative from the new Polish party within its ranks, on account of the extreme statements made by its leader, Janusz Korwin-Mikke (see above). Finally, after the power struggle in Alternative for Deutschland – in which Petry, leader of the party faction strongly opposed to immigration, had taken over the party leadership – five of that party's seven MEPs left it. One of the two remaining members joined ENF; the other joined EFDD. These two members were excluded from ECR to which the AfD was admitted after the elections in 2014. Both of these party groups were thus able to muster enough MEPs from a sufficient number of countries.

Forming a group also proved complicated for ECR. The Danish People's Party and the Finns party left EFD for ECR; and it was, of course, a feather in the cap for these two Nordic radical-right parties to gain admission to a party group that had a more moderate image than EFD, and which was led by the British Conservatives (Jungar 2016). When the change in party-group membership went through, the top candidate of the Danish People's Party in the EP elections, Morten Messerschmidt, said the party was now 'joining a group in which the British Conservatives – the ruling party in the UK – are members', and that the influence of the party would grow with membership in a larger party group (Dansk Radio 2014).

Similar noises could be heard from the Finns party. Gaining admission to a more moderate party group in the EP granted greater legitimacy to the two parties, both of which have cited their admission to ECR in order to rebut criticism in their home countries concerning their radical character. More liberal ECR representatives criticized the immigration policies favoured by the two parties; Cameron, however, stressed the similarity of views about the EU. Alternative for Deutschland, the strongly Eurosceptic party from Germany, was also admitted to ECR. After Frauke Petry was elected party leader of the AfD in 2015 five of the seven MEPs left the party. The two remaining MEPs were expelled from ECR in 2016 as AfD had initiated cooperation with the Austrian FPÖ. They joined EFDD and ENF respectively. Lega Nord, on the other hand, got the cold shoulder. With the admission of the two new Nordic members, ECR took on a somewhat radical cast; however, the party group had already included parties with a nationalist ideology, such as the Latvian National Alliance. Finally, a regionalist and anti-immigration party from Belgium, NVV, was admitted to ECR in 2014, having been a member of the green party group during the previous parliament.

The three party groups described above hang by a fragile thread. Their future in both the short and long term is uncertain. Since they only meet the criteria for party-group status by a narrow margin (particularly in the case of ENF and EFDD), they run the risk of dissolution. Britain's imminent withdrawal from the Union will also affect the pattern of party-group formation among nationalist and Eurosceptic parties, inasmuch as UKIP has been dominant in EFDD and the Tories have been the leading force in ECR.

POLICIES: WHAT DO THEY WANT FROM THE EU?

The radical-right and Eurosceptic parties are united on one important point: they oppose the deepening of the Union, and its enlargement as well. The EU must not be allowed to develop into a federal state, and new members should only be admitted if they are culturally and socially compatible with the present member states. '*Hard*' Eurosceptics, however, need to be distinguished from '*soft*' ones (Szczerbiak and Taggart 2008). They call for the departure of their own country from the EU; or they demand that the Union be given a fundamentally different shape in terms of the powers invested in its institutions and the basic principles enshrined in the single market, the monetary union, and other areas of institutionalized cooperation. Hard Eurosceptics want to turn the clock back to a time when European cooperation was strictly intergovernmental, and the individual member states were sovereign. Soft Eurosceptics, on the other hand, do not oppose European integration in principle; nor do they take issue with their own country's membership in the Union. They take a critical view, however, of EU policies in one or more areas. This leads them to oppose some important aspects of European integration in its present form, and gives them a sense that the national interests of their own country are threatened.

Both hard and soft Eurosceptics can be found in the party groups studied in this chapter. Only UKIP, however, demands that its own country leave the Union. As UKIP's election manifesto puts it: 'All UKIP MEPs . . . have one over-riding goal: to make ourselves redundant, by getting Britain out, and returning to the UK the power to govern ourselves. We want our country back. Don't you?' (UKIP 2014). A referendum on Britain's membership topped UKIP's wish list, and the party welcomed Prime Minister Cameron's decision to allow the voters to decide the country's future relationship with the EU. Open borders, the EU bureaucracy, the constantly growing powers of the Union, and the violation of national sovereignty are the main reasons for UKIP's opposition.

Both harder and softer Eurosceptics can be found among the radical-right parties. The Sweden Democrats, for example, seek a renegotiation of Sweden's membership in the Union, as the result of a referendum in which citizens are to decide whether the country shall remain a member. The election manifesto of the EAF called for the decision-making powers of the EU's institutions to be renegotiated, and for the Lisbon Treaty to be abrogated in areas where it gave greater powers to the Union at the expense of the member states. The EAF also seeks restrictions on the free movement of EU citizens, as well as the reintroduction of border controls within the Union. Jobbik and Golden Dawn belong to the group of hard Eurosceptics too: Jobbik wants Hungary to rescind its ratification of the Lisbon Treaty, and Golden Dawn sees the EU as an illegitimate project. The Danish People's Party and the Finns party take a middle position between hard and soft Euroscepticism: both oppose a continued federalization of the EU; and, notwithstanding the declaration of the latter party that 'the EU is a political project and thus a fact which can be altered', the Finns party do not call for a Finnish exit from the Union. Both parties oppose the common currency in principle, but the Finns party do not call for a Finnish exit in that area either (Jungar 2016). The Baltic parties are fundamentally opposed to the Union's restrictions on national sovereignty: thus in Latvia, for example, the question of minority rights (which the EU has emphasized) has become a source of conflict, particularly in connection with the status of the Russian minority. Yet EU membership is perceived as largely positive, above all from the standpoint of national security. In its election manifesto from 2014, for example, the Latvian National Alliance stressed that 'there is no geopolitical alternative to a Latvian EU-membership', and declared that the party was determined that 'decisions made in the EU should be in the interest of Latvia' (National Alliance 2014). Alternative for Deutschland and the Five Star Movement can also be seen as soft Eurosceptics. Alternative for Deutschland opposes any further federalization of the Union, and turns a critical eye on the powers which EU institutions have amassed and on the policies that have been applied during the financial crisis. These, the party avers, pose a threat to the success which European integration has achieved in terms of prosperity and stability.

The democratic deficit. In their criticism of the democratic deficit, these parties weave populist and nationalist conceptions together. Populists paint the picture of a conflict between a unified and homogeneous people on the one hand, and a corrupt and unresponsive political establishment on the other. In such a picture, the EU makes an inviting target. Here the Union appears as an elite project with a large technocratic bureaucracy and few if any popular and democratic roots. Moreover, as the supranational features of the EU have grown more pronounced, popular influence has diminished and the member states have lost ever more autonomy. The EU's development in a federalist direction must be halted, and if possible the clock must be turned back. The right-wing populist parties also point out the lack of a common (national) identity as an obstacle to a European polity. The Sweden Democrats, for example, argue that the Union is too heterogeneous socially and culturally to form the basis for a state.

These parties also oppose further enlargement of the Union. Any new members will need to be stable economically and socially, as well as compatible culturally with the Union's fundamental values (the clear implication being that Turkey is not). The parties' strategy for reducing the democratic deficit is to restore decision-making powers to the member states. To prevent the transfer of any new powers to the Union, the populist parties call for new referenda to be held in the event of any changes in the treaties. Alternative for Deutschland proposes to deal with the democratic deficit by making it possible for individual national parliaments to veto proposals from the Commission. (Such an arrangement would ensure a much stronger position for the member states than does the present procedure for ensuring subsidiarity, according to which 11 national parliaments must be in agreement in asking the Commission to examine the subsidiarity of a bill.) Alternative for Deutschland also wants net economic contributors to the Union to be equipped with a veto, so that decisions are never taken that lack support from the states which are expected to bear the financial costs. The party also calls for a citizens' veto, to be structured along the lines of the European Citizens' Initiative.

The euro and solidarity. EU monetary policy and the single currency have reduced the self-determination of the member states still further, as the right-wing populist parties see it. The economic crisis that began in 2008 made this extremely clear. In the effort to save the euro, the influence of undemocratic institutions (the European Commission and the ECB) has been strengthened, and bodies with no basis in the treaties (the ESM and the banking union) have been established. In brief, the supranational features of the Union have been reinforced without the voice of the people having been heard. Moreover, the members of the eurozone are expected to show solidarity with the crisis-struck countries by transferring income to them, which the radical and right-wing populist parties oppose doing. In the electoral manifesto for the EP elections of 2014, Alternative for Deutschland 'insists on the responsibility of individual member states for their own economic and fiscal policies. It rejects any form of communitisation of debts – whether in the form of euro bonds or jointly financed institutions like ECB, ESM or the Banking Union'. The Finns party declares in its manifesto its opposition to guarantees and loan payments of an EU member state coming from the taxpayers of the other member states (Perussuomalaiset 2014). The eurozone should be dissolved, the rescue packages should be wound down, and it must be possible to leave the common currency. A social dimension for parrying the consequences of the common currency requires that a common fiscal policy be instituted. And the EU, the Finns party state in their election manifesto, should neither collect taxes nor establish its own social policy. The radical-right and extremist parties agree that the EU should not collect taxes, which would impart an ever more state-like character to the Union. The EU budget should be reduced, and it should consist only of contributions from the member states.

Stronger borders both internally and externally. Almost all of the populist parties, with the exception of the Five Star Movement, take a critical view of immigration, and this naturally affects their posture towards the EU. They pay lip service to the four freedoms of the single market, but it is more and more common among them to call for restrictions on general mobility within the EU. The Sweden Democrats and UKIP recommend that border controls be restored within the EU, and that visas be reintroduced for certain countries. This proposal is aimed at EU citizens from the newer member states, particularly Romania, Bulgaria, and Croatia. Its purpose is to make poverty-induced migration more difficult, that is, to prevent migrants from economically deprived regions from gaining access to social benefits in the richer member states. The German and British governments have also been concerned about the possibility of 'welfare tourism', and have sought to limit migrants' access to social rights. Freedom of movement within the EU must be limited according to this view and EU citizens cannot have an unconditional right to claim social benefits in other member states. The question of social Europe has also attracted attention from other political parties, as we shall see later in this chapter. With the rising tide of refugees from war-torn countries into Europe, the core issues of the radical-right parties – immigration and European integration – have come to dominate public discourse. The established parties have tightened their immigration policies to varying degrees, and reacted sceptically to the EU's proposal that the costs be shared out on a more solidaristic basis. However, notwithstanding the fact that these parties have to some extent embraced the policies recommended by their radical-right counterparts in this area, the carpet has not been pulled out from under the latter as far as continued electoral success is concerned. In the autumn of 2015, for example, the Swedish government tightened its immigration policies (which had been liberal by general European standards). It reintroduced border controls and began issuing residence permits on a temporary basis. The opposition parties in Sweden moved in the same direction, embracing more restrictive policies on immigration and adopting – to a degree – the kind of rhetoric regarding national values and identity associated with the Sweden Democrats. Yet these moves have made no dent in the popular support enjoyed by the latter party.

The right-wing populist parties also want to strengthen the EU's external borders. They urge that Frontex, the EU agency for securing the Union's external borders, be developed further, making it still more difficult for refugees to enter the EU. They also endorse – and seek tougher enforcement of – the Dublin Regulation, according to which asylum-seekers must apply for asylum in the EU member state in which they first arrive. Furthermore, in order to ensure that refugees do not arrive in their own backyard, the radical-right parties have suggested that internal refugee camps – 'safe havens' – be established within the EU. In sum, these parties are opposed to a common European immigration policy, which in practice would mean a more solidaristic sharing of responsibility for refugees.

HOW MUCH INFLUENCE? THE EUROPEAN PARLIAMENT AS AN ARENA FOR RIGHT-WING POPULIST PARTIES

The EP that convened after the elections of 2014 is a substantially more fragmented body than its predecessor. A total of 186 parties (37 of them altogether new) are represented in it, as compared with 170 in the previous legislature. The new EP is also more polarized, with fringe parties of both right and left having advanced. The two party groups of right-wing populist and Eurosceptic parties, ECR and EFDD, strengthened their representation. The proportion of non-attached members, many of them on the radical right, increased as well. The European United Left–Nordic Green Left (GUE/NGL) on the left increased its number of seats, the social democrats fell back slightly, and losses were sustained by the green party group EFA, the liberal group ALDE, and the conservative EPP. The situation changed further with the advent of ENF, which now has 39 members, most of whom had previously been non-attached.

The success of the fringe parties has implications for patterns of collaboration and decision making in the EP. Broad coalitions – consisting of the two largest party groups (EPP and the Progressive Alliance of Socialists and Democrats, S + D), together with a third party group – are necessary if the right-wing populist and radical-right parties are to be excluded from political influence. Since the EP is not headed by a government, new majorities are formed for each vote. Two different kinds of majority are needed in the EP. An absolute majority – 376 of the body's 751 members – is required to elect the President of the European Commission, as well as at the second reading of Commission proposals. To achieve such a majority, a broad coalition comprising the EPP and the social democrats, together with a third party group, must be formed. 'Euro-realist' ECR can furnish the needed number of votes, as can the liberal ALDE. A less likely outcome is that the two big party groups collaborate with EFDD or ENF, or with non-attached members. On the other hand, a simple majority (of those present at the plenary) is enough for resolutions, for ratifying international agreements, and at the first reading of Commission proposals. Various coalitions are possible in such cases, but their core is likely to consist of the EPP and the social

Table 3.2 Size of the different party groups in the European Parliament, percentage (and number of seats)

Party group	2014	2009	Difference
GUE/NGL	6.9 (52)	4.6 (35)	+2.3 (+17)
S + D	25.2 (189)	25.6 (196)	−1.4 (−7)
Greens/The Free Alliance	6.7 (50)	7.4 (57)	−0.7 (−7)
ALDE	9.3 (70)	10.8 (83)	−1.5 (−13)
EPP	28.9 (217)	35.8 (274)	−6.9 (−57)
ECR	9.7 (73)	7.4 (57)	+2.3 (+16)
EFDD	6.0 (45)	4.1 (31)	+1.9 (+14)
ENF	5.2 (39)	N.A	+5.2 (39)
NI	2.1 (16)	4.3 (33)	−2.2 (−17)
Total	751	766	

democrats. When the two big party groups cannot agree, party groups from left and right taken together can block the proposal or vote it down. Broad coalitions were already common in the EP earlier; but now, with the new parliamentary balance of forces, they supply the backbone of parliamentary cooperation. There is an obvious risk here that the parties taking part in such broad coalitions will do their deals behind closed doors, providing the populists with yet more grist to their mill regarding a closed and opaque EU.

Despite their gains in the EP elections, the extreme and radical-right parties can only exercise a limited direct influence. Their electoral successes, for one thing, were less impressive than expected. Furthermore, the differences between these parties on many issues, and their historical origins in different ideologies, continue to foster fragmentation among them. This may help to account for their inability to constitute a single party group in the EP. Furthermore, the ability of the existing party groups to exert influence – whether by blocking policies or by cooperating with other party groups – has been hampered by a below-average level of party discipline within their party groups, and by a historically high rate of absenteeism among their MEPs.

In addition, the established party groups in the EP started working together to limit EFDD's influence. The three biggest groups – the conservative EPP, the social democratic S + D, and the liberal ALDE – banded together to prevent EFDD from gaining any chairmanships on parliamentary committees (posts to which they would have been entitled under the principles of allocation that had applied previously). EFDD chairman Farage then received unexpected support from the green party group in his criticism of the cooperation among the three big party groups to exclude his party group from committee chairmanships. Speaking for the green group, MEP Margarete Auken argued that '[e]xcluding any political party group from a committee chairmanship to which it is due under the established system for fairly distributing these posts would be a blow to the democratic process in the EU parliament'. This case shows the inclination of the three major party groups to join together to prevent the right-wing populist party groups from gaining any influence.

However, the indirect influence of these parties on political processes within the EU has been – and will continue to be – greater than their direct influence. In many of the member states, radical-right parties have affected the posture taken by the established parties on their core issues. In some cases they have provided a support base in parliament for the government; in others they have even participated in the government outright. In Denmark and Finland, for example, parties opposed to immigration have been important for the actions of the respective national governments in the EU. As a support party for the government in parliament, the Danish People's Party exerted influence over the policies pursued by the Liberal–Conservative coalition government in the area of asylum and immigration. Denmark now stands outside the Union's common asylum policy, and the terms for family-reunion immigration have been tightened.

The sharp rise in voter support for the Finns party in the 2011 elections to the Finnish parliament, which was based on their criticism of the EU and particularly its defence of the euro, impelled the Finnish government to demand specific loan guarantees for Finland in connection with the financial support extended by the member states of the eurozone to the crisis-struck economies of Greece and Portugal.

Prime Minister Cameron's decision in 2013 to call a referendum on Britain's EU membership took place against the background of UKIP's success in gaining public support. Cameron hoped to halt the growth of the party thereby. The hard Euroscepticism championed by UKIP mainly took the form of a demand that a referendum be held on withdrawal from the EU (UKIP 2014). Economic arguments dominated the 'Remain' side's argumentation: the UK's economy would be adversely affected by a withdrawal from the EU and an exit from the single market, and London's role as a European financial centre would be weakened. The welfare-chauvinist rhetoric employed by the 'Leave' side bore the imprint of UKIP's policy positions: immigration – and in particular freedom of movement within the EU – posed a threat to British employment and welfare, while the process of European integration was eroding British sovereignty.

In certain member states, the refugee crisis served both to renew opposition to the EU and to strengthen it. Rhetoric resembling that of the radical-right parties is used by among others Viktor Orbán, the prime minister of Hungary and leader of the Fidesz Party (which is a member of EPP, the conservative party group). The targets of Orbán's disdain include Islam, immigration, freedom of movement, and the EU's efforts to coordinate the reception of refugees. When the European Council decided temporarily to reallocate 120,000 refugees to the member states where their applications for asylum ought to have been submitted, Orban announced a referendum on the Union's system for refugee reception. Hungary, the Czech Republic, Romania, and Finland(!) opposed the Council's decision on this matter (Balogh 2016).

The parties of the radical right, then, have exerted their influence over EU policies above all indirectly, by inducing the established parties to move towards positions which they themselves espouse. The processes that enable right-wing populist parties to make electoral gains, and possibly to exert influence over political decision making, are more dynamic than is sometimes supposed. The behaviour of the established parties has proven to be significant for the impact which the right-wing populist parties have had, both among voters and in political processes. In 'The Media and the Far Right in Western Europe: Playing the Nationalist Card', Antonis Ellinas (2010) argues that the established parties helped pave the way – by mobilizing voters on the basis of so-called identity questions (immigration and the status of minorities, for example) – for the successes of radical-right parties in the early 1990s. The right-wing populist approach to these questions gained visibility and legitimacy, because other parties were talking about them too.

There is no broad comparative research on how the actions of mainstream parties have affected the prospects of radical-right parties, but the fact that both Prime Minister Cameron and Chancellor Merkel called attention in 2013 to the 'problem' of welfare tourism likely contributed to UKIP's and Alternative for Deutschland's electoral success. The background to the statements by the two heads of government was the expiration of the exemption from freedom of movement which had previously applied for Bulgarian and Romanian citizens (who thus had not been able to move freely within the EU earlier). In an article in the *Financial Times* on 26 November 2013, Cameron called freedom of movement into question. The right to social welfare for migrant EU citizens, he argued, must be limited, and stricter conditions will have to be imposed for the payment of various social benefits to citizens from other member states. Freedom of movement within the Union cannot be an unconditional principle; instead it must be linked to a quid pro quo. Cameron elaborated on these views in later speeches, in which he claimed that immigration of this type (from poor member states like Bulgaria and Romania) imposes a burden on receiving societies in terms of costs for education, health care, and housing. Cameron's rhetoric was much like the formulations favoured by UKIP. His gambit represented a reaction to the popular support that UKIP had garnered, which had grown continuously since 2010. It is not unlikely, however, that it served as well to legitimize UKIP's increasingly anti-immigration rhetoric.

For her part Chancellor Merkel, who had said in a speech in 2010 that the multicultural project had failed, joined with the British prime minister in February 2014 in declaring that the EU is not and should not be a social union:

> [I]f we were to see that freedom of movement has, as a consequence, that each and every one who's seeking a job in Europe has the possibility to come to Germany, and will receive an equal amount of social benefits as someone who, for a long time, has been unemployed in Germany after 30 to 40 years of work, . . . then that would not be the interpretation of freedom of movement that I would have. (UK Government 2014)

The issue of the social costs of freedom of movement was also taken up in April 2013, in a joint letter to the European Commission from Britain, Germany, Austria, and the Netherlands. In all of these countries, with the possible exception of Germany, parties of the radical right were gaining in popularity and calling for restrictions on freedom of movement in Europe. The behaviour of the established parties can be seen as a reaction to this, but it is likely that their appeals in this area helped to publicize the fringe parties' favourite issues and to legitimize their rhetoric.

With the refugee crisis, the core questions of the radical-right parties – immigration and European integration – have come to dominate the political agenda. The scale of the refugee crisis and the rise in public support for the radical-right parties have left a deep imprint on the (ever more restrictive) policies pursued by European governments in these areas. However, the popular support garnered by the radical-right parties has not been affected by the fact that the established parties are now implementing policies closer to those they recommend. A possible explanation for this is that voters opposed to immigration perceive the radical-right parties as more credible on this matter than other parties – that is, the former parties 'own' this issue, as some political scientists have put it (Petrocik 1996). The perception among radical-right voters that the radical-right parties are more credible on the issue of immigration helps to account – together with the distrust felt by such voters for the established parties – for why public support for the radical-right parties has remained stable or even increased since 2014.

INCREASE THE RELEVANCE OF THE EU FOR THOSE WHO MISTRUST EUROPEAN INTEGRATION THE MOST!

As the successes of the radical-right parties have grown, various explanations have been put forward in public and academic debate for the increase in their voter support, parliamentary presence, and political influence (at times even as parties of government). In this chapter, I have stressed the centrality of supply and demand factors in this connection: simply put, the explanation for the growth of these parties is to be sought first and foremost in the desire among a section of the electorate to see anti-immigration and Eurosceptic policies implemented.

Now, it may be objected, we should take a few steps back and analyse the institutional and structural factors that might explain such a change in party sympathies. Political scientists speak of political opportunity structures – that is, factors which aid parties in their efforts to get a hearing for their proposals, to attract the sympathies of greater numbers of voters, and to gain access to arenas of political decision making. One precondition for the success of the parties examined in this chapter is that party loyalties have gotten weaker and that voting on the basis of social affiliations (such as class) has partly ceased. This is a trend that has proceeded for a long time, and which in some sense is irreversible. The convergence of the parties along the left–right axis is another factor, as among others Jens Rydgren (2012) has stressed. That is to say, parties of the radical right have successfully exploited the space which has opened up as the established parties have converged with one another along the conflict dimension which traditionally dominated most European political systems.

In the aftermath of the elections to both the EP and the Swedish national parliament, for instance, the claim has been made that revitalizing the old lines of political conflict – along the socioeconomic dimension – would pull the carpet from under the radical-right parties. More precisely, a stronger politicization of the traditional differences between left and right would move the policy framing away from identity politics and back to issues of economic justice, social welfare, and solidarity. The underlying assumption here is partly that those who vote for radical-right and Eurosceptic parties do so from a socioeconomically marginalized position, and partly that the other political parties would gain an advantage by shifting the political debate to their own favoured terrain, where they can discuss 'their' questions, and where they need not adjust to the right-wing populist framing of what challenges society is faced with and which solutions would be most suitable.

Political issues on the so-called post-materialist or liberal–authoritarian dimension have grown in prominence throughout Europe, which of course does not mean that socioeconomic questions have lost their relevance (such issues are still the most relevant ones for a majority of European voters). The increased centrality of sociocultural issues is intimately connected with broad societal changes such as globalization in general and European integration in particular, with the advancing denationalization of both economics and politics that they entail.

I began this chapter by asking whether the radical-right parties simply pose a threat, or whether they may actually offer a corrective by helping to make the project of European integration more credible and relevant for those European citizens who distrust it most. The voters who choose Eurosceptic, radical-right, and extreme right-wing parties feel homeless and anxious in our rapidly changing societies. The populism of the radical-right parties gives expression, in a paradoxical and contradictory way, to a nostalgic vision of society and the national community. It is a backward-looking political project. At the same time, as I pointed out earlier, it poses relevant questions about the legitimacy of European integration, as well as about the limits of global, European, and national solidarity in the distribution of economic and social resources. I have shown in this chapter that the radical-right parties contribute to an improved political representativity: in other words, our political systems now represent the diverse preferences of voters more effectively (in this case on matters of immigration and European integration). The future of the radical-right parties lies less in their own hands than in those of the other parties. The challenge for the established parties is to formulate answers – based on their own ideologies and visions – to the questions posed by supporters of the radical-right parties.

NOTES

1. The Finnish party name *Perussuomalaiset* literally means ordinary, regular, and basic Finns, translated into 'True Finns' as the official English name. After the party's electoral success in 2011, the board of the party decided to adopt 'The Finns' as the official English name. According to the party leader Timo Soini, the former name brought up incorrect associations with extreme nationalism, and referred to an essentialist rather than a cultural 'common' Finnishness.
2. See the ENF group's charter: http://www.enfgroup-ep.eu/charter/ (accessed 2016-09-22).
3. http://www.enfgroup-ep.eu (accessed 2016-09-22).
4. See the ECR group's policy: http://web.cor.europa.eu/ecr/Pages/Policy.aspx (accessed 2016-09-22).

REFERENCES

Albertazzi, D., and D. McDonnell (2015), *Populists in Power*, vol. 24. London: Routledge.

Almeida, Dimitri (2010), 'Europeanized Eurosceptics? Radical Right Parties and European Integration', *Perspectives on European Politics and Society* 11(3): 237–253.

Alternative for Deutschland (2014), 'Party Programme of the *Alternative für Deutschland* ("Alternative for Germany") (AfD) for the Election to the European Parliament on 25 May 2014 (Approved by the National Party Convention on 22 March 2014)', http://www.alternativefuer.de/wp-content/uploads/sites/7/2014/04/AfD-Manifesto-for-Europe.pdf (accessed 2016-09-19).

Bakker, R., E. Edwards, L. Hooghe, S. Jolly, G. Marks, J. Polk, and M. Vachudova (2014), *Chapel Hill Expert Survey*, Chapel Hill, NC: University of North Carolina.

Balogh, Peter (2016), 'The Hungarians Referendum in EU Migrant Quotas: Fidesz's Popularity at Stake', *Baltic Worlds* (2016-09-25), http://balticworlds.com/the-hungarian-referendum-on-eu-migrant-quotas/ (accessed 2015-09-26).

Brug, Wouter van der, Meindert Fennema, and Jean Tillie (2000), 'Anti-immigration Parties in Europe: Ideological or Protest Vote', *European Journal of Political Research* 37(1): 77–102.

Brug, Wouter van der, and Meindert Fennema (2003), 'Protest or Mainstream?: How the European Anti-immigrant Parties Developed into Two Separate Groups by 1999', *European Journal of Political Research* 42(1): 55–76.

Cameron, David (2013), 'Free Movement within Europe Needs to be Less Free', *Financial Times* (2013-11-26), https://www.ft.com/content/add36222-56be-11e3-ab12-00144feabdc0 (accessed 2017-11-01).

Canovan, M. (1999), 'Trust the People! Populism and the Two Faces of Democracy', *Political Studies* 47(1): 2–16.

Citrin, Jack, Morris Leavy, and Matthew Right (2014), 'Multicultural Policy and Political Support in European Democracies', *Comparative Political Studies* 47(11): 1531–1557.

Dagens Nyheter (2013), 'Dansk folkeparti varnar SD för le Pen' (2013-11-24), http://www.dn.se/valet-2014/dansk-folkeparti-varnar-sd-for-le-pen/ (accessed 2016-09-22).

Dansk Radio (2014), 'Ny gruppe giver oss mere magt' (2014-06-04), https://www.dr.dk/nyheder/politik/messerschmidt-ny-gruppe-giver-os-mere-magt (accessed 2016-09-22).

De Lange, Sarah L. (2007), 'A New Winning Formula? The Programmatic Appeal of the Radical Right', *Party Politics* 13(4): 411–435.

Ellinas, Antonis A. (2010), *The Media and the Far Right in Western Europe: Playing the Nationalist Card*, Cambridge: Cambridge University Press.

ESS Round 4: European Social Survey Round 4 Data (2008), Data file edition 4.4. NSD – Norwegian Centre for Research Data, Norway – Data Archive and distributor of ESS data for ESS ERIC.

ESS Round 7: European Social Survey Round 7 Data (2014), Data file edition 2.1. NSD – Norwegian Centre for Research Data, Norway – Data Archive and distributor of ESS data for ESS ERIC.

Ford, Robert, and Matthew Goodwin (2014), *Revolt on the Right Explaining the Support for the Radical Right in Britain*, London and New York: Routledge.

Heinisch, Reinhard, and Oscar Mazzoleni (eds) (2016), *Understanding Populist Party Organization: The Radical Right in Western Europe*, London: Palgrave Macmillan.

Ivarsflaten, Elisabeth (2008), 'What Unites Right-Wing Populists in Western Europe? Re-examining Grievance Mobilization Models in Seven Successful Cases', *Comparative Political Studies* 41(1): 3–23.

Jungar, A-C. (2015), 'Business as Usual: Ideology and Populist Appeals of the Sweden Democrats', in T. Pappas and H-P. Kriesi (eds), *Populism in the Shadow of the Great Recession*, Colchester, UK: ECPR Press, pp. 58–80.

Jungar, A-C., P. Henriksson-Timofejevs, and A. Backlund (2016), 'Explaining the Emergence of Populist Radical Right Parties in Latvia 2010–2015', paper presented at the First Annual Conference on Russian and East European Studies 'Europe under Stress: The End of a Common Dream' in Tartu, Estonia, 13 June 2016.

Jungar, Ann-Cathrine (2016), 'From the Mainstream to the Margin?: The Radicalisation of the True Finns', in Tjitske Akkerman, Sarah L. de Lange, and Matthijs Rooduijn (eds), *Radical Right Wing Parties in Western Europe: Into the Mainstream?*, London and New York: Routledge, pp. 113–143.

Jungar, Ann-Cathrine, and Anders Ravik Jupskås (2014), 'Populist Radical Right Parties in the Nordic Region: A New and Distinct Party Family?', *Scandinavian Political Studies* 37(3): 215–238.

Kitschelt, Herbert, with Anthony J. McGann (1997), *The Radical Right in Western Europe*, Ann Arbor, MI: University of Michigan Press.

Kriesi, Hanspeter, and Takis S. Pappas (eds) (2015), *European Populism in the Shadow of the Great Recession*, Colchester, UK: ECPR Press.

McLaren, Lauren (2012a), 'Immigration and Trust in Politics in Britain', *British Journal of Political Science* 42(1): 163–185.

McLaren, Lauren (2012b), 'The Cultural Divide in Europe: Migration, Multiculturalism, and Political Trust', *World Politics* 64(2): 199–241.

Mudde, Cas (2004), 'The Populist Zeitgeist', *Government and Opposition* 39(4): 542–563.

Mudde, Cas (2007), *Populist Radical Right Parties in Europe*, Cambridge: Cambridge University Press.

Mudde, Cas, and Cristóbal Rovira Kaltwasser (2012), *Populism in Europe and the Americas: Threat or Corrective for Democracy?*, Cambridge: Cambridge University Press.

National Alliance (2014), 'Election program' [Priekšvēlēšanu programma], http://www.nacionalaapvieniba.lv/velesanas-kampanas/12-saeimas-velesanas/#programma (accessed 2016-05-16).

Pauwels, Teun (2011), 'Explaining the Strange Decline of the Populist Radical Right Vlaams Belang in Belgium: The Impact of Permanent Opposition', *Acta Politica* 46(1): 60–82.

Perussuomalaiset (2014), 'The EU Parliament Elections Programme', https://www.perussuomalaiset.fi/wp-content/uploads/2013/04/EU_ELECTION_PROGRAMME_2014_v1.pdf (accessed 2017-01-25).

Petrocik, John R. (1996), 'Issue Ownership in Presidential Elections, with a 1980 Case Study', *American Journal of Political Science* 40(3): 825–850.

Reuters (2013), 'Le Pen, Wilders Call for Eurosceptic Bloc in EU Assembly' (2013-11-13), http://uk.reuters.com/article/uk-eu-vote-eurosceptics-idUKBRE9AC0HH20131113 (accessed 2017-01-25).

Rydgren, Jens (2012), 'Radikal högerpopulism: ett hot mot EU:s sammahållning i spåren av den ekonomiska krisen?', in A. Bakardjieva Engelbrekt, L. Oxelheim, and T. Persson (eds), *Arbetslöshet, Migrationspolitik och Nationalism: Hot mot EU:s sammanhållning?*, Stockholm: Santérus Förlag.

Schmitt, Hermann, Sara B. Hobolt, Sebastian A. Popa, and Eftichia Teperoglou (2016), *European Parliament Election Study 2014, Voter Study, First Post-Election Survey*, European Parliament, Directorate-General for Communication, Public Monitoring Unit. GESIS Data Archive, Cologne. ZA5160 Data file Version 4.0.0, doi:10.4232/1.12628.

Strömbäck, Jesper, Ann-Cathrine Jungar, and Stefan Dahlberg (2017), 'Sweden: No Longer a European Exception', in Toril Aalberg, Frank Esser, Carsten Reinemann, Jesper Strömbäck, and Claes H. de Vreese (eds), *Populist Political Communication in Europe*, London and New York: Routledge, pp. 68–85.

Szczerbiak, Aleks, and Paul A. Taggart (eds) (2008), *Opposing Europe?: The Comparative Party Politics of Euroscepticism*, Vol. 1, *Case Studies and Country Surveys*, Oxford: Oxford University Press.

The Economist (2014), 'Political Insurgency: Europe's Tea Parties' (2014-01-24), http://www.economist.com/news/leaders/21592610-insurgent-parties-are-likely-do-better-2014-any-time-second-world (accessed 2016-09-19).

UKIP (2014), 'Create an Earthquake', UKIP manifesto 2014.

United Kingdom Government (2014), 'David Cameron and Angela Merkel press conference: February 2014', 2014-02-17, https://www.gov.uk/government/speeches/david-cameron-and-angela-merkel-press-conference-february-2014 (accessed 2017-01-28).

Werts, Han, Peer Scheepers, and Marcel Lubbers (2013), 'Euro-scepticism and Radical Right-Wing Voting in Europe, 2002–2008: Social Cleavages, Socio-political Attitudes and Contextual Characteristics Determining Voting for the Radical Right', *European Union Politics* 14(2): 183–205.

APPENDIX

Table 3.A1 Change in mean positions and standard deviations for voter positions on European unification

Country	Country mean		Mean change	Std dev.		Std dev. change
	2008	2014	2008–2014	2008	2014	2008–2014
BE	5.4	5.1	−0.3	2.5	2.5	0.0
CH	5.1	4.6	−0.5	2.5	2.5	0.0
CZ	4.9	4.3	−0.6	2.6	2.5	−0.2
DE	52	5.4	0.2	2.8	2.7	−0.1
DK	5.7	5.4	−0.3	2.6	2.7	0.1
EE	5.5	4.8	−0.7	2.7	2.8	0.1
FI	4.5	4.4	−0.1	2.2	2.2	0.0
FR	5.0	4.9	0.0	2.5	2.6	0.1
IE	4.9	4.5	−0.4	2.1	2.3	0.2
NL	5.5	5.1	−0.5	2.3	2.3	0.1
PL	6.5	5.5	−1.0	2.4	2.6	0.2
SE	5.0	4.7	−0.2	2.2	2.2	0.0
SI	5.6	5.4	−0.3	2.4	2.5	0.2
Mean	5.3	4.9	−0.4	2.4	2.5	0.1

Note: 'Should European unification go further (0) or has it gone too far (10)?'

Sources: European Social Survey 2008; European Social Survey 2014.

Table 3.A2 Change in mean positions and standard deviations for voter positions on immigration

Country	Country mean		Mean change	Std dev.		Std dev. change
	2008	2014	2008–2014	2008	2014	2008–2014
BE	4.8	5.1	0.3	1.8	1.8	0.0
CH	4.0	4.6	0.6	1.7	1.7	−0.1
CZ	5.7	6.2	0.5	2.0	1.7	−0.3
DE	4.6	4.5	0.0	2.0	1.9	−0.1
DK	4.3	4.6	0.3	2.0	1.9	−0.1
EE	5.3	4.9	−0.4	2.0	1.7	−0.3
FI	3.9	4.4	0.5	1.6	1.6	0.0
FR	5.0	5.1	0.1	2.0	2.0	−0.1
IE	4.5	5.1	0.5	2.1	2.1	0.0
NL	4.5	4.8	0.3	1.6	1.5	−0.1
PL	4.0	4.6	0.6	1.8	1.7	0.0
SE	3.7	3.5	−0.2	1.9	1.8	0.0
SI	5.3	5.1	−0.3	2.1	1.8	−0.3
Mean	4.6	4.8	0.2	1.9	1.8	−0.1

Note: Three survey items combined in an additive index of opposition to immigration; most opposed=10. 'Immigration bad or good for country's economy', 'Country's cultural life undermined or enriched by immigrants', 'Immigrants make the country better or worse'.

Sources: European Social Survey 2008; European Social Survey 2014.

Table 3.A3 Party abbreviations

Abbreviation (country)	Full name
AfD (Germany)	Alternative for Deutschland
BNP (Great Britain)	British National Party
DF (Denmark)	Danish People's Party
FN (France)	Front National
FPÖ (Austria)	Freedom Party of Austria
Jobbik (Hungary)	Jobbik, the Movement for a Better Hungary
KNP (Poland)	Congress of the New Right
LAOS (Greece)	The Popular Orthodox Rally
LN (Italy)	Lega Nord
M5S (Italy)	Five Star Movement
NA (Latvia)	National Alliance
NPD (Germany)	National Democratic Party
PRM (Romania)	Greater Romanian Party
PS (Finland)	The Finns
PVV (the Netherlands)	Freedom Party
SNS (Slovakia)	Slovak Nationalist
SD (Sweden)	Sweden Democrats
TT (Lithuania)	Order and Justice
UKIP (Great Britain)	United Kingdom Independence Party
VB (Belgium)	Vlaams Belang
XA (Greece)	Golden Dawn

4. The prosperity gap and the free movement of workers

Joakim Ruist

INTRODUCTION

The free movement of workers has been a central part of the project of European integration for more than 50 years. It aims to improve the functioning of the economy by increasing the size of the labour market. In a larger market, each worker has a higher probability of finding a suitable employer, and vice versa. Hence temporary imbalances between worker supply and demand are mitigated and business cycle swings smoothened, in national economies as well as in specific industries. Long-term income differences between countries are also reduced, as workers move primarily from lower-income to higher-income countries.

Over the last 10–15 years, income differences between countries in the European Union (EU) have increased substantially. Since 2004 the Union has welcomed 13 new countries with lower average income levels than the previous 15 member countries. In addition, the economic crisis that began in 2008 and is still felt in some countries has increased the differences among these 15 countries. One of the many consequences of this is that the free movement of workers has been increasingly questioned. As economic inequality increases, mechanisms with a potential to reduce it become on the one hand potentially more important, and on the other hand more controversial. In the richer EU countries the fear has grown that immigration of people with low abilities to earn their own subsistence will place a heavy burden on their public welfare systems.

The aim of this chapter is to describe the economic consequences of the free movement of workers in the EU today. The first section describes the scale and main directions of intra-European migration. This is followed by an analysis of to what extent this migration at present levels may smoothen short-term business cycle swings within member states. The next section deals with receiving countries' public revenues and costs related to intra-European immigrants, primarily those from Eastern Europe. In short the economic consequences are found to be small at the national level, since intra-European migration remains low. However, migration may have more important consequences within certain industries where there is a shortage of domestic workers.

The fact that the economic consequences are small does not however seem to have sufficiently informed the public debate in several countries, where the economic crisis has been followed by increasing support for anti-immigration parties that have pushed governments into more restrictive positions on intra-European immigration. Yet the perception that this trend also mirrors trends towards more negative views on immigration among the general public is refuted in the last section of this chapter. It is shown, based on attitude surveys, that apart from in a few of the countries that were hardest hit by the economic crisis, public attitudes to immigration in Europe were generally more positive in the years after than in the years preceding the crisis. This result thus indicates that governments in several countries have been trying to adjust their policies to align with an opinion which they might not have interpreted correctly, and that the success of anti-immigration parties may be an indication of something other than increasingly negative public views on immigration.

OVERVIEW OF INTRA-EUROPEAN MIGRATION

In 2013 there were 16.4 million EU citizens living in an EU country other than the one in which they were born (Croatia, which became an EU member in 2013, is excluded from the statistics presented here). This is slightly above 3 per cent of the EU's total population. The largest share among these lived in Germany (3.6 million), followed by the UK (2.7 million). Intra-EU migrants' shares of the EU countries' total populations were in the range of 0–13 per cent in all countries except Luxembourg, where the share was 32 per cent. In the ten Eastern European countries the range was only 0–3 per cent. These ten countries are instead overrepresented as migrant-sending countries.

Approximately half of the migrants (there is no exact data) originate from one of these countries, although they make up merely one-fifth of the union's total population. Thus, intra-EU migration occurs primarily from countries with lower income levels to countries with higher income levels. In addition, migrants from lower-income countries on average stay longer in the destination country. Yearly migration between EU countries was around 1.6–1.8 million individuals, or merely 0.3 per cent of the population of the Union, in the years 2011–2013. Of these, approximately 700 000 people per year moved back to their country of birth.

Apart from income levels, the direction of migration flows is largely determined by geographic and linguistic proximity. Hence, for example, Belgium hosts the largest number of French emigrants, Germany the largest number of Austrian and Sweden the largest number of Danish. During the first two years after Romania's EU accession in 2007, approximately 700 000 Romanians moved to the linguistically closely related countries Italy and Spain, whereas probably fewer than 100 000 in total moved to any other EU country.

THE MIGRATION RESPONSE TO THE ECONOMIC CRISIS

A potential advantage of the free movement of workers, and an important reason for the existence of this institution, is its potential to smooth business cycle swings. This happens when workers move out of countries that are in an economic downturn and into countries with more favourable current economic conditions. This section analyses to what extent this potential was realized in the economic crisis that began in 2008, and whose consequences were highly unevenly distributed across Europe.

We thus aim to investigate to what extent people responded to the economic crisis by migrating from the worst hit to less severely hit countries. A suitable example is the migration from Greece to Germany. These two countries represent two opposing extreme cases. While Greece was hit hardest of all countries, Germany was the brightest shining star during the crisis. In addition, Germany has been an important receiver of Greek emigrants for decades, and alone hosts the majority of all Greek citizens who live in an EU country outside of Greece, that is, a full 300 000 persons. Hence to the extent that Greeks should respond to the crisis by emigrating, it should to a large extent be by emigrating to Germany.

The solid curve in Figure 4.1 shows how the number of Greek citizens in Germany developed from 1998 to 2013. The dotted curve shows the development of Greece's gross domestic product (GDP) per capita (measured on the right axis) during the same period. We see that economic growth was very strong in Greece during the first ten years of this period: on average 7 per cent per year. We also see that the number of Greek citizens living in Germany fell during these years. But from 2009, and more strongly from 2010, Greece was severely hit by the economic crisis, and the downward trend in the number of emigrants stopped and eventually turned upward instead. It thus appears clear that some Greeks responded to the economic downturn by moving to Germany. But how many? A rough answer to this question can be given by comparing the solid curve to the dashed line in

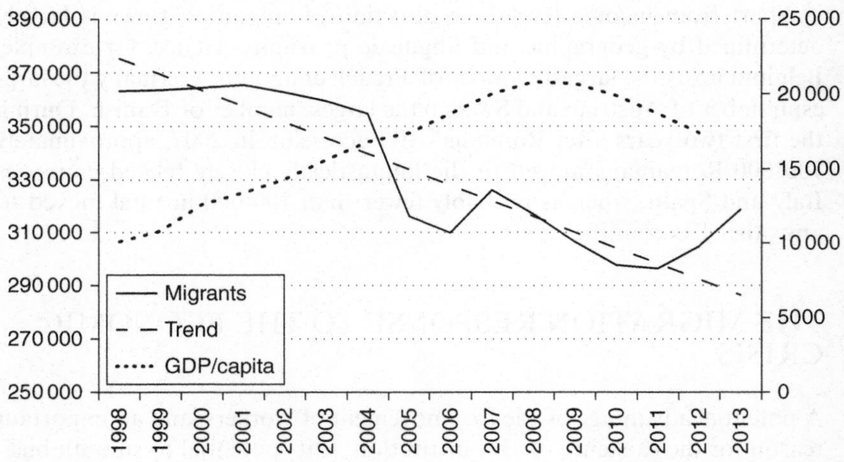

Note: The number of migrants and the trend are measured on the left axis. GDP/capita (in euros) is measured on the right axis. The trend line is fit to the years 1998–2008.

Source: Eurostat.

Figure 4.1 Numbers of Greek citizens living in Germany

Figure 4.1. This line represents the trend in the number of migrants in 1998–2008. Hence to the right of 2008 it represents a prediction of how the Greek population in Germany would have developed had their home country continued at an annual positive growth rate of around 7 per cent instead of swinging to a nearly as high negative rate. According to this prediction the number of migrants in 2013 would have been 286 000 persons instead of the factual 318 000 – a difference of around 30 000 individuals.

Although very rough, this analysis illustrates something important. Business cycle differences between European countries do create migration, but only to a very limited extent. In spite of the comparatively strong tradition of migration from Greece to Germany, not even a difference between extremely strong and extremely weak economic circumstances in Greece produced more than around 30 000 extra migrants, or nearly 0.3 per cent of the Greek population, after several years. From a perspective of business cycle smoothing, this is a negligible number.

A similar case is illustrated in Figure 4.2, which shows the number of Spanish migrants living in Germany. Spain was also among the countries most strongly affected by the crisis, and Germany is among the traditionally largest receivers of Spanish intra-European migration. The other two large receivers are France and the UK, but since these countries do not

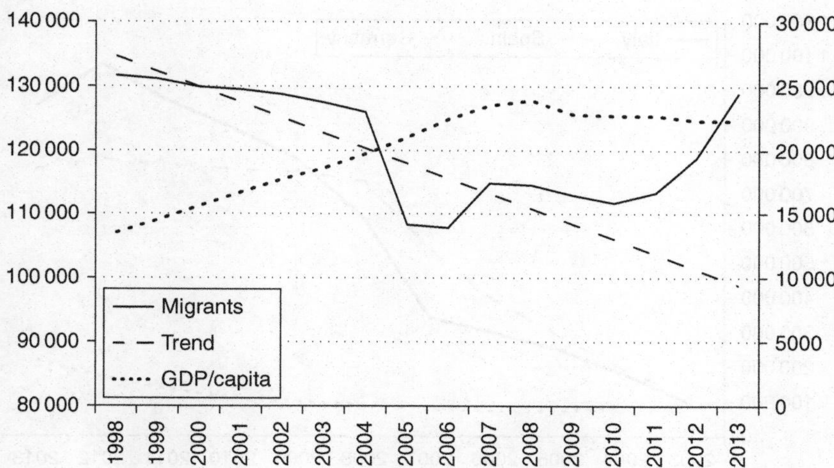

Note: The number of migrants and the trend are measured on the left axis. GDP/capita (in euros) is measured on the right axis. The trend line is fit to the years 1998–2008.

Source: Eurostat.

Figure 4.2 Numbers of Spanish citizens living in Germany

collect the necessary data, the analysis here is limited to Germany. The figure shows that Spain also had very strong economic growth from 1998 to 2008 (6 per cent per year), but in the Spanish case the initial drop in 2009 has only been followed by persistent stagnation and not by continued negative growth as in Greece. Also in this case the difference between the counter-factual trend and the factual number of migrants in 2013 is around 30 000 individuals. In the Spanish case this amounts to nearly 0.1 per cent of the population. It is reasonable that this number is smaller than the corresponding number for Greece since Spain was not hit as hard by the crisis and since Germany is not an equally dominant destination for Spanish emigrants as it is for Greek emigrants. Still the Spanish case confirms the conclusion from the Greek case, namely that emigration has been far too low to have any noteworthy impact on the business cycle.

During the particular period studied here, there is however one additional way in which intra-European migration may have had business cycle smoothing potential. The onset of the crisis happened only a few years after the Eastern European countries joined the EU, and fairly large migration started from these countries to the EU15 countries. Romania in particular is interesting in this respect. Romania has a large population of around 20 million, low income levels and high emigration rates (the highest

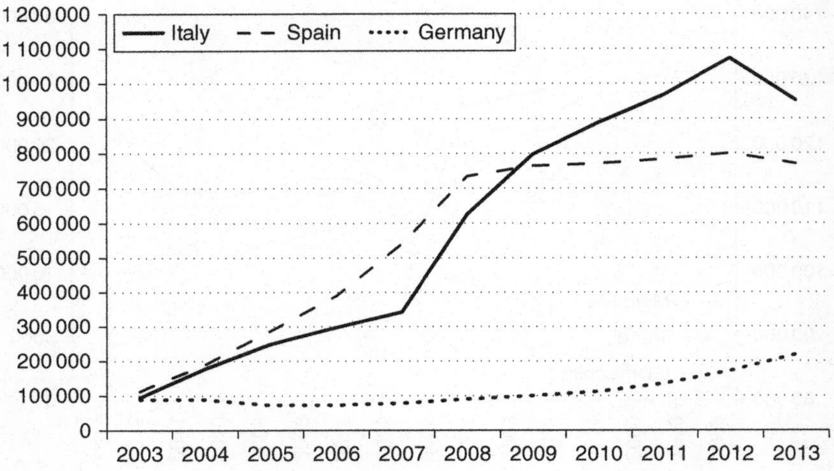

Source: Eurostat.

Figure 4.3 Numbers of Romanian citizens living in Germany, Italy and Spain

in the EU since its accession). Because of linguistic proximity, the main destinations for Romanian emigrants before and immediately after the EU accession were Italy and Spain. It is thus interesting to ask to what extent the economic downturn in these countries – in Spain in particular – may have redirected Romanian emigration to countries with more favourable economic development, such as Germany. A brief analysis of this question follows below (for a much more elaborate analysis, see Bertoli et al., 2016).

Figure 4.3 shows the numbers of Romanian citizens living in Italy, Spain and Germany in 2003–2013. It shows the large migration from Romania to Italy and Spain beginning around 2003–2004. In the Spanish case, net immigration from Romania halts almost completely at the onset of the crisis in 2008, as it amounts to a mere 35 000 individuals over the subsequent five years, compared with around 600 000 in the previous five. Also Romanian migration to Italy decreases, although it remains strong all the way up to 2012. In Germany the result is the opposite. Net immigration from Romania in 2003–2008 is practically zero, but over the subsequent five years it totals 130 000 individuals. From what is illustrated in the figure, there is reason to believe that the economic crisis has both reduced total emigration from Romania and redirected it primarily to Germany. However, the numbers are still not macroeconomically significant. The extra 130 000 Romanians in Germany that we may conclude are a hypothetical result of the economic crisis in the southern countries only amount to slightly more than 1 per cent of the German population. It is also important to note that the large Romanian emigration to the EU15 countries is probably to a large extent a one-time only phenomenon. Hence even if it had a smoothing impact this time, it is not likely to be there the next time different EU15 countries are hit by similar macroeconomic asymmetries.

The conclusion from this analysis is that the aggregate business cycle smoothing impact of intra-EU migration is negligible. The large majority of EU citizens do not exercise their right to apply for jobs anywhere in the Union. This is likely explained to a large extent by the linguistic, cultural and institutional differences across countries. For comparison we may look at migration between states in the US, across which such differences are much smaller. Every year approximately 1.5 per cent of the US population moves between states, as compared with the previously mentioned 0.3 per cent in the EU. Until 1990 the American figure was even twice as high. It is also not substantially higher in states with small surface areas on the east coast than in the rest of the country.

American interstate migration also responds strongly to business cycle asymmetries. A famous study by Olivier Blanchard and Lawrence Katz (1992) estimated that for every 100 jobs lost in one state, a full 65 individuals left the state within the first year thereafter. Hence in an economic downturn in one state (only), the number of unemployed in that state should rise by only around one-third of what it would have done had nobody emigrated.

Here we can directly compare how the asymmetric impact of the economic downturn in 2008–2009 affected interstate migration in the US and the EU. The horizontal axis in Figure 4.4 shows the percentage point change in the unemployment rate during 2008–2009 per state in the US. The vertical axis shows the population change in per cent by state in 2009–2010. The population change is measured one year after the unemployment rate change in order to give migration time to react to the downturn. It is measured for native-born Americans only, so as not to be contaminated by immigration from abroad. The figure clearly illustrates the high annual migration: in 9 of the 50 states the population size changed by more than 2 per cent up or down. We also see a strong relation with the unemployment rate change one year earlier. According to the regression line, every additional percentage point increase in the unemployment rate implies a population decrease one year later by on average 0.45 per cent.

The corresponding interstate migration in the EU, of EU citizens only, is shown in Figure 4.5 (there is data for all countries except Romania). Average migration levels are lower in this case: the population does not

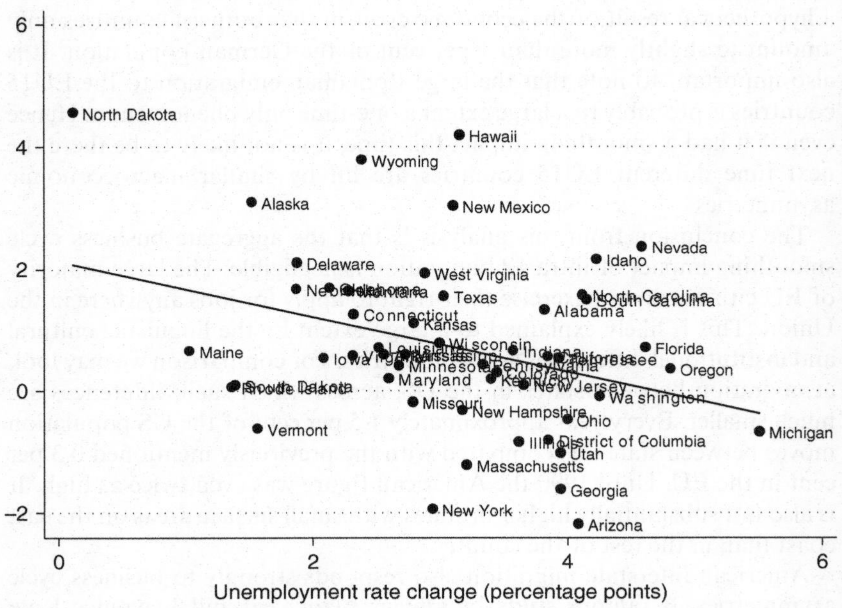

Note: The slope of the regression line is −0.45, with standard error 0.18. N=51.

Source: Own calculations based on American Community Surveys 2008–2010, obtained by Ruggles et al. (2010).

Figure 4.4 Change in unemployment 2008–2009 and population 2009–2010 per US state

change by as much as 2 per cent in one year in any of the 26 countries. We also see a weaker relation with changes in the unemployment rate. According to the regression line, every additional percentage point increase in the unemployment rate implies a population decrease one year later by on average 0.12 per cent. In sum we (very roughly) estimate that the aggregate business cycle smoothing impact of migration in the EU is only about a quarter of that in the US. Linguistic, cultural and institutional differences are likely explanations for this difference.

Business cycle smoothing by intra-EU migration may however be larger in certain industries. This is most clearly illustrated by the construction industry. When new countries joined the EU in 2004 and 2007, there was a shortage of construction workers in several EU15 countries. Hence the construction sector came to be the one most overrepresented among migrants from the new member states to the EU15. Here we report some

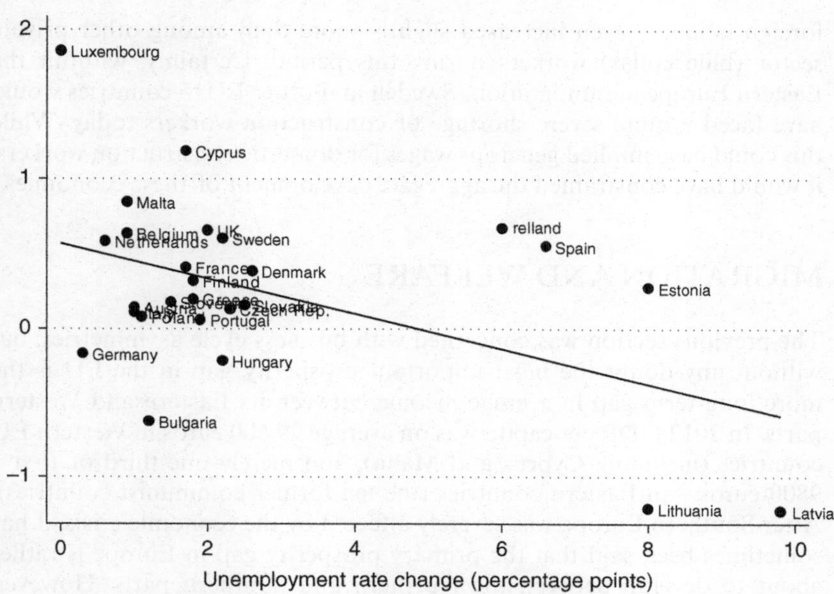

Note: The slope of the regression line is −0.12, with standard error 0.043. N=26.

Source: Eurostat.

Figure 4.5 Change in unemployment 2008–2009 and population 2009–2010 per EU country

example figures from Sweden, which has high-quality data: Among Eastern European migrants who arrived in Sweden after the EU enlargement and were employed in 2011, 18 per cent worked in the construction industry. In the total Swedish workforce this figure was 6 per cent. From a different angle, 1.4 per cent of all employees in construction were Eastern European immigrants; for employees in Sweden overall the figure was 0.6 per cent. In addition, the construction sector had almost twice as many mostly Eastern European posted workers, that is, persons employed in another EU country but working in Sweden (estimates from the Confederation of Swedish Enterprise and the Swedish Construction Federation; transformed into full-year worker equivalents). Hence in total around 4–5 per cent of all employees in construction in Sweden can be seen to be there as a direct consequence of the EU enlargement.

That this fairly large number of construction workers is a result of domestic supply being insufficient to meet demand is well illustrated by the fact that wages of construction workers – in spite of this inflow of foreign labour – even increased slightly more than among other private sector (blue collar) workers during this period. Certainly, without the Eastern European immigration, Sweden and other EU15 countries would have faced a quite severe shortage of construction workers today. While this could have implied generous wages for domestic construction workers, it would have constrained the aggregate development of these economies.

MIGRATION AND WELFARE

The previous section was concerned with business cycle asymmetries, but without any doubt the most important prosperity gap in the EU is the more long-term gap in average income between its Eastern and Western parts. In 2012 GDP per capita was on average 29 600 euros in Western EU countries (including Cyprus and Malta), and merely one-third of that – 9800 euros – in Eastern countries (the ten former communist countries). After Southern Europe was severely affected by the economic crisis, it has sometimes been said that the primary prosperity gap in Europe is rather about to develop between the Northern and Southern parts. However, in the EU's GDP per capita ranking we still find nine of the ten Eastern countries occupying the nine bottom positions, and the tenth of them ranking twelfth from the bottom.

In the last 10–15 years this gap, in combination with EU rules on the free movement of workers, has stirred much political anxiety in Western Europe. This anxiety stems largely from fears that the gap is so large that Eastern Europeans with a low probably of finding a job will find a life on welfare grants in the West more attractive than life at home. Hence they will move to the West and become a heavy burden on welfare systems in these countries. In response to this anxiety, temporary limitations to free movement were allowed when the Eastern countries acceded to the EU in 2004 and 2007 (the same happened earlier when Greece, Spain and Portugal joined the union). Each EU country was given the right to limit the access of citizens of the new EU countries to their labour markets and/or welfare systems for up to seven years. To varying degrees, all EU15 countries except Sweden came to exercise this right.

The last of these limitations expired on 1 January 2014 in the nine countries in which they were then still in place. In the meantime, in spite of the limitations, the number of Eastern European immigrants in the EU15 had increased from around two million in 2004 to around six million in 2014. This corresponds to a net emigration of approximately 4 per cent of the total population of these Eastern European countries, and a net immigration corresponding to approximately 1 per cent of the total population of the EU15. Emigration was highest from Romania: approximately 10 per cent of the total population.

If we wish to evaluate the proposition that unregulated immigration from Eastern Europe imposes a heavy burden on welfare systems in the EU15, Sweden is a suitable case for analysis. Sweden was the only EU15 country not to impose any limitations at all in labour market and welfare access. Hence the consequences of this policy, which today applies in all EU countries, have had sufficient time to become visible in Sweden. Furthermore, with Sweden being a country of high taxes, high levels of welfare support and high barriers to labour market entry, if the consequences of this free immigration would be negative anywhere it would plausibly be in Sweden.

The following analysis is based on data covering all individuals registered as living in Sweden. It thus excludes individuals who only exercise their right to stay in the country for up to three months with or without employment. Hence it excludes among others the small but well-known groups of individuals who stay in the country for the purpose of begging. These individuals are also not covered by the social rights that apply to those with a residence permit. Hence their potential impact on public finances is very small.

We first look at employment rates for migrants who arrived in Sweden from the EU12 (Eastern Europe + Cyprus and Malta) after the EU accession of their home countries (2005 for the countries that joined on 1 May 2004) and were still present in Sweden in 2011. Employment is defined as an annual income of at least 100 000 kronor (approximately 10 000 euros). With this definition the employment rate of the Swedish native-born population aged 15–64 was 74.4 per cent. The corresponding number for EU12 immigrants looks bleak at first: merely 44.4 per cent, that is, exactly 30 percentage points below the native born.

However, statistics that include very newly arrived immigrants always risk being misleading. Migrants who arrived in 2009–2011 have a strong negative impact on the average, since their employment rate is below 40 per cent. Yet the employment increase over the subsequent four years is strong, on average eight percentage points per year, and for those that have spent six years in the country employment reaches a full 68 per cent. As yet we do not know to what extent this impressive increase is due to non-employed people becoming employed versus giving up and returning to their home country (or moving on to a third country). But if this increase continues at the same rate for just one more year it will imply that those who immigrated in 2005 will be on a par with the employment rate for the native born after merely seven years.

Regardless, however, the conclusion remains that the average employment rate of EU12 immigrants is low. Hence the question of to what extent this low-employment group receives public welfare is a relevant one. It turns out that it does so to a quite limited extent. The average sum of social assistance, unemployment support, sickness support, parental leave support, early retirement, study grants and housing grants amounts to 13 540 kronor per EU12 immigrant aged 15–64. This is to be compared with the more than twice as high number of 29 116 kronor per native-born in the same age interval. The average sum is 2000 kronor in the year of arrival, but after six years it rises to around 26 000 kronor. Hence plausibly it will take EU12 immigrants seven years to also reach the native average in grant disbursements.

We proceed now to an analysis of to what extent EU12 immigrants impose a burden on Swedish public finances. We have seen that these immigrants on average have both low employment rates – and hence tax payments – and low welfare receipt levels. These two factors will work in opposite directions in determining their net impact on Swedish public finances. A summary of Swedish public revenues and costs per average inhabitant (of all ages) in 2011 is given in the first column of Table 4.1. 'Revenues' are mainly income, payroll and consumption taxes. 'Transfers' include the items listed in the previous paragraph. 'Other costs' are costs such as those for infrastructure, defence and central administration, which are distributed equally across the total population. On the last row we see that Swedish public finances made a surplus of 423 kronor per inhabitant, or 0.2 per cent.

The second column shows the corresponding revenues and costs per EU12 immigrant (for a more detailed description of the methodology applied here, see Ruist, 2014). These values exclude 2011 arrivals, for whom public spending cannot be satisfactorily accounted. The third

Table 4.1 Swedish public revenues and costs per inhabitant and per EU12 immigrant

	Total population	EU12 immigrant	Net gain EU12
Revenues	+182978	+126609	–56369
Transfers	–21513	–12516	+8 997
Pensions	–35582	–538	+35044
School and childcare	–21622	–20610	+1 012
Care	–35056	–16077	+18979
Other	–68782	–68782	0
Sum	+423	+8086	+7 663

Source: Own calculations based on data from Statistics Sweden.

column shows the difference between the first two, that is, the net contribution of the average EU12 immigrant to the public sector. We see that revenues have a negative sign in the third column, implying that the average EU12 immigrant contributes about 59 000 kronor less in public sector revenues compared with the average individual in the total population. Yet we see positive signs for all cost rows, implying that public costs are also lower for the EU12 immigrants. The difference is largest for pensions and care (i.e. hospital, elderly, and disability care), reflecting the fact that only 1.5 per cent of the EU12 immigrants (and their children) are 65 years of age or older. In fact a full 64 per cent are younger than 35, which is a high number also when compared with other immigrant groups.

Adding up all revenues and costs, we see that the average EU12 immigrant makes a small net contribution of approximately 8000 kronor per year to Swedish public finances. The low revenues are more than balanced by the low costs, most of all due to the economically beneficial age structure of the immigrant group. An obvious follow-up question is then whether this positive result will remain in the longer run, as the immigrants become old (assuming that they are still in Sweden at that point). Will they have had the time to 'pay for themselves' by then? We can see a fairly promising indication that they will, if we look at how their net contributions to the public sector vary with the number of years they have spent in Sweden. We then see that the net contribution from a person who has been in the country for six years is a full 30 000 kronor higher than that from a person who has only been there for one to two years.

Thus far the analysis has focused on the EU12 countries, since the general fears of economically costly intra-European immigration have primarily concerned this group. A similar analysis of immigrants who arrived in Sweden from the other EU15 countries during the same time period shows even more positive results. The net contribution of the average EU15 immigrant in Sweden is approximately 30 000 kronor. The difference from the EU12 group is mainly due to higher employment and salaries, and hence higher tax revenues.

The analysis presented here thus gives a positive image of the consequences of free labour immigration from Eastern Europe for Swedish public finances: the immigrants appear to put in slightly more to the welfare sector than they take out. How valid, then, is this conclusion for other EU15 countries, which more recently opened up for similarly free immigration? Probably most of these countries have reason to expect more positive results than the Swedish ones. Sweden is a country of compressed wages and a language that is not spoken outside the country's borders. Hence it is one of the countries in Europe where it is most difficult for an immigrant to enter the labour market and become self-sufficient, and hence also a net contributor to the public sector. We can illustrate this by showing that Sweden is the EU15 country with the largest negative employment gap between EU12 immigrants and natives: a full 6.7 percentage points. In the average EU15 country on the other hand, there is a *positive* gap of 1.0 percentage points. (Due to data limitations, these numbers refer to all EU12 immigrants and not only those who arrived after the EU accessions of their home countries. However, they should paint a fairly correct picture also for the latter group, which on average makes up at least two-thirds of the former one.) One could imagine the absence of limitations to free movement being an important factor in explaining this result, but this is not likely to be the case. In the UK there were only marginal limitations concerning workers from all EU12 countries except Romania and Bulgaria (which make up only 10 per cent of the EU12 group in the country). In spite of this, EU12 immigrants' employment rate in the UK is a full 5.9 percentage points above that of natives, that is, one of the most positive gaps in the EU15. A more plausible explanation for the differences is instead that the gaps are most negative in the countries with the highest thresholds to enter the labour market.

Another reason why other EU15 countries may have reason to expect more positive results than the Swedish ones is migrant selection. Sweden is above the EU15 average in both the degree of progression in income taxation and the size of the welfare sector. Compared with countries like the UK, Ireland and Luxembourg in particular, Sweden should thus reasonably attract migrants with lower expected income. Migrants with higher expected income should have relatively more reason to choose a country of destination with less progressive taxation and less redistribution through the welfare sector.

All the reasons listed here – language, labour market entry and redistribution through the public sector – clearly point at two countries having more reason than others to expect a positive net contribution of EU12 immigration to the public sector: the UK and Ireland. For the UK this is also the conclusion of a study by Dustmann, Frattini and Halls (2010). They studied public revenues and costs in a way similar to that presented here, but only for immigrants from the countries for which the UK did not impose substantial entry limitations. Fully in line with the theoretical predictions outlined here, their results showed a more positive net contribution from the average Eastern European immigrant in the UK than in Sweden. In spite of all this, the UK has become the country where opposition to the free movement of workers has grown the strongest. Officially, protecting public finances has been stated as a main rationale for this opposition. But it is clear that this logic lacks empirical support.

HAS EUROPE HAD ENOUGH OF IMMIGRATION?

The UK is, however, only one among several EU15 countries where the official support for free worker mobility has recently been waning. And this is in spite of leading politicians being well aware of the research results in this area. Plausibly several among them are driven by the recent successes of political parties that firmly oppose immigration, in elections both to national parliaments and to the European Parliament. Parties strongly critical towards immigration received more seats in the European Parliament than ever before in both the 2009 and 2014 elections (see also Chapter 3 in this book written by Ann-Cathrine Jungar). The UK Independence Party (UKIP) became the largest party in the UK and Front National the second largest in France in the 2014 elections.

It is of course easy to interpret these successes in the same way that these parties themselves do: the people of Europe have had enough of immigration at current levels. Yet others claim that this is not so, but that anti-immigrant parties are rather fuelled by a more general dissatisfaction with politics and politicians, which has also increased due to the economic crisis. Have the people of Europe become more negative to immigration? In this section I answer this question by looking at responses from the attitude survey European Social Survey, which is performed biannually in most European countries. One of the questions asked in the survey is 'Is [country] made a worse or a better place to live by people coming to live here from other countries?'

The answers are coded from 0 (worst) to 10 (best). In Figure 4.6 I compare the average numerical response by country in the years 2004/06, that is, before the economic crisis and the general rise in support for anti-immigration parties, with those in 2010/12, that is, after these occurrences. Only responses from native-born respondents are included. We see that there was a trend towards more negative attitudes in only 8 countries, whereas the trend was positive in 14 countries.

The most visible exceptions from the trend towards more positive attitudes can be seen in Ireland, Greece and Cyprus. These are three of the countries that were hardest hit by the economic crisis. This is indicative of a correlation between business cycle movements and attitudes that is visible also among the other countries: attitudes have changed in a more positive direction in countries less affected by the crisis. For a full analysis of this pattern, see Ruist (2016).

The analysis shown here thus paints a different picture to the common one regarding trends in how the peoples of Europe look upon immigration. Beyond the successes of certain movements that want to strongly reduce immigration, the attitudes of the majority of the European popula-

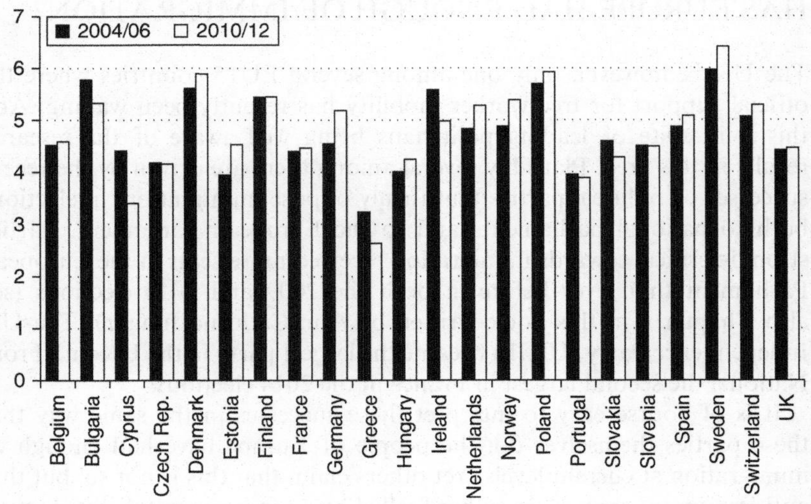

Note: The figure shows the average response by country and year to the question on whether immigration makes the country a better or worse place to live in, with 10 being the most positive response and 0 the most negative.

Source: Own calculations based on data from the European Social Survey.

Figure 4.6 Average native attitudes to immigration 2004/06 and 2010/12

tion appear to be moving in the opposite direction. If this picture is true, it implies that several European governments misjudged the situation when they choose to copy parts of the anti-immigrant rhetoric.

STAND BY FREE MOVEMENT

The free movement of workers in the EU has never been as threatened as it is today. The main argument for limiting it is that it is not compatible with the welfare regimes of the higher-income countries in combination with the income gap between these and the lower-income countries of the Union. Yet as has been shown in this chapter, there is no empirical support at all for this argument. Against this conclusion, pragmatic politicians might respond that it does not matter much that research shows that immigration does not harm societies, as long as voters *believe* it does and act accordingly. But this argument also appears weak in the face of what has been shown in this chapter.

One important advantage of free movement that has been stressed in this chapter is that it helps to reduce labour shortages in specific sectors in specific countries, although intra-European migration is not large enough to significantly smooth business cycles at the national level. However, we must conclude that the most important economic consequence of free movement is the income gain it implies for the migrants themselves, when they are given the opportunity of moving to a country with several times higher average income, as has been the case with much of the European East–West migration. This chapter has focused on evaluating the economic consequences of migration for European countries. But even if we cannot show that migration has substantially helped reduce income inequality between European countries, it has certainly done so between European individuals. But then again, defending free movement should not require proving the presence of economic *gains*. The basic human stance should be that if one person wishes to move from one country to another and there is no important argument *against* this, then they should be allowed to do so.

REFERENCES

Bertoli, Simone, Herbert Brücker and Jesús Fernández-Huertas Moraga (2016), 'The European crisis and migration to Germany', *Regional Science and Urban Economics*, 60: 61–72.

Blanchard, Olivier and Lawrence Katz (1992), 'Regional evolutions', *Brookings Papers on Economic Activity*, 1992 (1): 1–75.

ESS Round 2: European Social Survey Round 2 Data (2004), Data file edition 3.5. NSD – Norwegian Centre for Research Data, Norway – Data Archive and distributor of ESS data for ESS ERIC.

ESS Round 3: European Social Survey Round 3 Data (2006), Data file edition 3.6. NSD – Norwegian Centre for Research Data, Norway – Data Archive and distributor of ESS data for ESS ERIC.

ESS Round 5: European Social Survey Round 5 Data (2010), Data file edition 3.3. NSD – Norwegian Centre for Research Data, Norway – Data Archive and distributor of ESS data for ESS ERIC.

ESS Round 6: European Social Survey Round 6 Data (2012), Data file edition 2.3. NSD – Norwegian Centre for Research Data, Norway – Data Archive and distributor of ESS data for ESS ERIC.

Dustmann, Christian, Tommaso Frattini and Caroline Halls (2010), 'Assessing the fiscal costs and benefits of A8 migration to the UK', *Fiscal Studies*, 31: 1–41.

Ruist, Joakim (2014), 'Free immigration and welfare access: the Swedish experience', *Fiscal Studies*, 35: 19–39.

Ruist, Joakim (2016), 'How the macroeconomic context impacts on attitudes to immigration: evidence from within-country variation', *Social Science Research*, 60: 125–134.

Ruggles, Steven J., Trent Alexander, Katie Genadek, Ronald Goeken, Matthew B. Schroeder and Matthew Sobek (2010), *Integrated Public Use Microdata Series: Version 5.0* [Machine-readable database], Minneapolis: University of Minnesota.

5. The political challenge of austerity politics

Pär Nyman

INTRODUCTION

In the countries most affected by the Great Recession, public finances had developed structural weaknesses well before the crisis hit. The fiscal situation in countries such as Greece, Italy, and Portugal, and the austerity policies that have followed in its wake, have had dramatic consequences. To a clearly higher degree than countries with stronger public finances, these countries have seen rising unemployment, increasing poverty, and deteriorating public services. Moreover, economic and social challenges were already more prominent in these countries before the crisis. Recent developments, accordingly, have widened the prosperity gap in Europe.

The political consequences of this development are far-reaching. To restore market confidence and to comply with fiscal regulations like the Stability and Growth Pact, many countries have implemented large programmes of fiscal consolidation. Austerity, however, often meets with public resistance, so most of these countries have also experienced a reduction in political stability (Armingeon et al. 2016). Trust in mainstream parties has declined, and newly established parties with a populist agenda have enjoyed tremendous electoral success. In the words of the Irish political scientist Peter Mair (2009, 2013), we are witnessing an increasing tension between responsiveness (listening to the people) and responsibility (in this case, complying with fiscal rules and agreements with lenders).

The situation is most alarming in the countries of southern Europe, where we find the greatest fiscal problems and the most dramatic changes in domestic political systems. Figure 5.1 shows average levels of public debt and of trust in the government for six groups of European Union (EU) member states between 2007 and 2015. While debt levels have risen in all of the country groups, and trust in the national government has shrunk in all of them save eastern Europe, the trajectory is clearly most dramatic in southern Europe. A similar picture emerges if we look not at trust in the

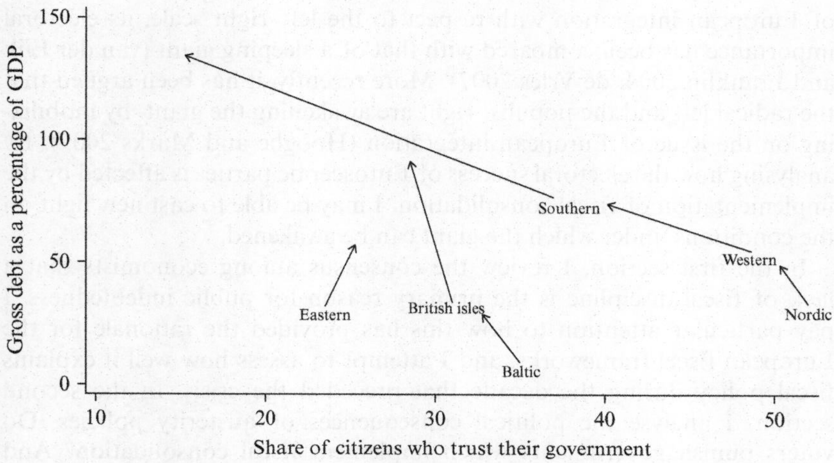

Note: Each arrow shows how the average level of trust in the government and the average size of government debt have developed in a group of countries between 2007 and 2015. The six country groups are the Baltic countries (Estonia, Latvia, and Lithuania); the British Isles (Ireland and the United Kingdom); eastern Europe (Bulgaria, Croatia, Czechia, Hungary, Poland, Romania, Slovakia, and Slovenia); the Nordic countries (Denmark, Finland, and Sweden); southern Europe (Greece, Italy, Portugal, and Spain); and western continental Europe (Austria, Belgium, France, Germany, Luxembourg, and the Netherlands).

Sources: The data are from Eurostat and the Eurobarometer.

Figure 5.1 Change in debt and in trust in the government, 2007–2015

national government but at electoral volatility, the share of the vote going to populist parties, or levels of support for the EU.

In this chapter, I ask how we can improve fiscal performance without putting political stability at risk. By analysing the tension between the need for constraints on fiscal policy, on the one hand, and the political consequences of reduced responsiveness, on the other, I try to shed new light on the prospects for long-term fiscal discipline. My main conclusion is that we need to increase public support for fiscal prudence. If we fail to accomplish that, and instead rely exclusively on fines and external enforcement to achieve fiscal discipline, the chances are that the political system in the worst-affected countries will be weakened for decades to come. The results in this chapter thus contribute both to the political economy literature concerned with fiscal sustainability and the literature on EU issue voting (de Vries 2007). For a long time, attitudes towards the EU played but a minor role in both national and European elections (Reif and Schmitt 1980; Mair 2000). However, due to the orthogonality of the issue of European integration with respect to the left–right scale, its electoral importance has been compared with that of a sleeping giant (van der Eijk and Franklin 2004; de Vries 2007). More recently, it has been argued that the radical left and the populist right are awakening the giant, by mobilizing on the issue of European integration (Hooghe and Marks 2009). By analysing how the electoral success of Eurosceptic parties is affected by the implementation of fiscal consolidation, I may be able to cast new light on the conditions under which the giant can be awakened.

In the first section, I review the consensus among economists that a lack of fiscal discipline is the primary reason for public indebtedness. I pay particular attention to how this has provided the rationale for the European fiscal frameworks, and I attempt to assess how well it explains fiscal policy during the decade that preceded the crisis. In the second section, I analyse the political consequences of austerity policies. Do voters punish governments which implement fiscal consolidation? And if so, to which parties do the voters go? Is it correct that fiscal austerity leads to an increase in support for populist and Eurosceptic parties? I conclude the chapter by discussing the prospects for fiscal discipline in view of prevailing conditions. In my policy recommendations, I focus on how we can reduce the risk of future debt crises, on how we can mitigate the electoral costs of fiscal consolidation, and most importantly on what we can do to reduce the tension between fiscal responsibility and electoral responsiveness.

FISCAL DISCIPLINE AND THE DEFICIT BIAS

Over the last three decades, the dominant explanation for public indebtedness has been based on the idea that a deficit bias is inherent in political decision making (Debrun et al. 2009). The story goes like this: unless they are restrained in some way, governments have a tendency – especially if they are responsive to the demands of voters – to spend beyond their means. The research literature has identified a number of possible reasons for such a bias.

For a number of reasons, governments may have an electoral incentive to run larger deficits than they would have done had they not cared about being re-elected. First, if voters are poorly informed about the nation's fiscal stance, but observe how much they pay in taxes and what they get in return, the incumbent government can gain popularity by cutting taxes and raising spending (inasmuch as voters do not observe the long-term consequences of the deficit). A 'fiscal illusion' of this kind may also arise if voters do not fully understand that the public debt must eventually be repaid (Rogoff and Sibert 1988). Second, if voters are less concerned about the welfare of future generations than they are about their own, they will reward governments that give higher priority to current consumption and punish those that save for the future (Bowen et al. 1960; Cukierman and Meltzer 1989). Third, similar incentives can arise if voters are short-sighted or put disproportionate weight on their current situation (Buchanan and Wagner 1977).

Other accounts too portray governments as tempted to run deficits. First, while government expenditures are often targeted on concentrated minority interests, it is unclear when or by whom the public debt will be repaid. According to Olson (1982), therefore, concentrated minority interests are more influential than diffuse majority interests, which can cause debts and deficits to be larger than any single actor would prefer (Velasco 2000). Second, if an incumbent government expects to be replaced after the next election, it can use debt strategically to constrain the policy options of its successor. By running a deficit, it can spend additional money on tax cuts or on expenditures of its preferred type, while forcing its successor to repay the debt instead of implementing reforms of its own (Persson and Svensson 1989; Alesina and Tabellini 1990). Third, fiscal policy may suffer from a time-inconsistency problem (Kydland and Prescott 1977), meaning that the optimal fiscal policy from the perspective of the government changes over time, in a predictable manner. In the short run, the incumbent government has the ability to increase output by increasing aggregate demand more than expected. For example, a not previously announced tax cut would increase economic activity, until wage levels have adapted to the increased demand. However, because rational agents realize that governments have an incentive to 'surprise' the labour market, they expect this to happen, and adjust their wage expectations accordingly. This possibility would then simply result in larger deficits without any output benefits. Fourth and finally, the deficit bias may be aggravated in monetary unions or other situations where the costs of fiscal laxity spill over to entities outside the fiscal jurisdiction in question (Eichengreen and Wyplosz 1998; Faini 2006; Basso and Costain 2016).

The idea, then, is that unconstrained democratic governments – operating under no other limits than those imposed by their national electorate – are characterized by a lack of fiscal discipline. This idea has provided the rationale for the Stability and Growth Pact, as well as for the domestic fiscal frameworks of the member states (Morris et al. 2006). The policy recommendations concern three areas: fiscal transparency, fiscal rules, and fiscal councils.

Fiscal transparency means that budgets are presented in a way that makes it easy for citizens to assess the nation's financial position, as well as the economic and social implications of government activities (Kopits and Craig 1998). By reducing the information advantage that policy-makers have over voters, this approach makes it less attractive for the incumbent government to increase current public consumption by issuing debt (Alt and Lassen 2006). Fiscal transparency can also prevent governments from using creative accounting in order to comply with fiscal rules (Milesi-Ferretti 2004).

Fiscal rules are constraints on fiscal policy, expressed as numerical ceilings or targets for budgetary aggregates. Their main objective is to limit deficit bias (Debrun et al. 2008). The best-known fiscal framework is the Stability and Growth Pact, which requires deficits to be kept within 3 per cent of gross domestic product (GDP), and gross government debt within 60 per cent of GDP.

Fiscal councils are independent institutions with a mandate to monitor the government's fiscal policy. They are seen today as a complement to fiscal rules, rather than as a substitute. It has been suggested that decisions affecting the budgetary balance be delegated to such institutions, or even that the setting of specific tax rates be assigned to experts (Blinder 1997). However, all existing councils of this kind are merely advisory, and their most common tasks are forecasting, assessing fiscal policy, and evaluating fiscal sustainability (Calmfors and Wren-Lewis 2011).

Over the last few decades, Europe has seen an increase in fiscal transparency, a greater number of fiscal councils, and the introduction of fiscal rules on both the national and the Union level. Yet, such efforts notwithstanding, public debt has risen in virtually all European countries. Current debt-to-GDP ratios are shown in Figure 5.2. The horizontal line is drawn at 60 per cent of GDP. Debt levels above this line constitute violations of the Stability and Growth Pact, unless they are falling by at least five percentage points per year. The highest debt levels are found in Greece, Italy, and Portugal.

The Stability and Growth Pact, clearly, did not prevent public debt from soaring. Many economists have therefore concluded that Europe still suffers from fiscal indiscipline. Their policy prescriptions for dealing with this range from fine-tuning fiscal rules (Bergman et al. 2016) and strengthening fiscal councils (Calmfors 2015) to delegating decisions on the issuance of debt to an independent supranational authority (Basso and Costain 2016). Can we be so sure, though, that it was a lack of fiscal discipline which made public finances so vulnerable?

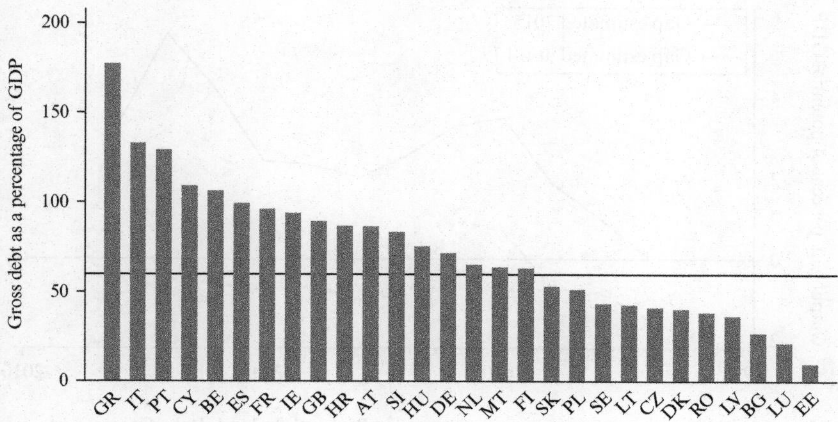

Note: The figure shows debt-to-GDP ratios according to the Maastricht definition. The horizontal line, drawn at 60 per cent, corresponds to the debt ceiling in the Stability and Growth Pact.

Source: The data are from Eurostat.

Figure 5.2 Gross public debt in EU member states, 2015

Does Fiscal Indiscipline Explain the Current Problems?

In retrospect, the decade preceding the Great Recession was a golden opportunity to consolidate public finances. Partly thanks to real-estate bubbles, the economy was booming and unemployment rates were below their equilibrium level. Looking back at such beneficial conditions, it is easy to interpret the loose fiscal policies pursued during this period as a lack of fiscal discipline. But can we be so sure fiscal policy would have been different if independent experts had decreed it or a fiscal rule decided it?

Many economists have a naïve notion of what fiscal policy would look like if it had to follow set targets, or if it were conducted by benevolent independent experts. It is not surprising, then, that fiscal problems are blamed so readily on the lack of fiscal discipline in politics. However, when the financial crisis struck the world in 2007, fiscal policy in most European countries fell within the bounds set by the Stability and Growth Pact and accorded with the advice given by the International Monetary Fund (IMF), the European Commission, and other international organizations.[1] There are two reasons why fiscal policy could be too lax despite the comparative concordance among governments, rules, and experts.

The first reason why public finances could be so vulnerable is that the

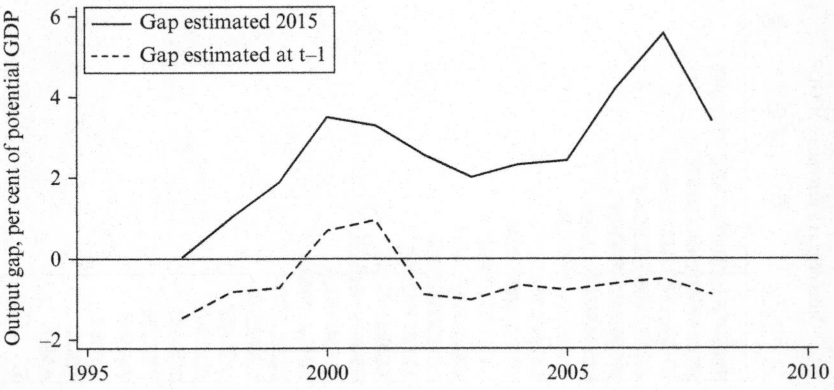

Note: Both lines show the average output gap for Portugal, Ireland, Italy, Greece, and Spain. The solid line is derived from output gap estimates published in November 2015, while the dashed line shows the forecast made one year before the year concerned.

Source: OECD Economic Outlook.

Figure 5.3 Output gap estimates 1997–2008, PIIGS

Stability and Growth Pact did not require member states to maintain large enough safety margins. While there had been a large number of violations of the pact a few years earlier, there were 'only' three countries which breached the pact in 2007 (Calmfors and Wren-Lewis 2011). However, when deficits soared because of the weak labour market, and some countries had to pump money into the financial sector, levels of debt rose quickly. Pre-crisis debt levels in many countries would have needed to be much smaller than the 60 per cent of GDP stipulated in the Stability and Growth Pact for the financial markets not to lose confidence in the solvency of said countries.

The second reason is that the business cycle was systematically misperceived. Figure 5.3 shows the average output gap for Portugal, Ireland, Italy, Greece, and Spain.[2] The solid line represents the estimates published by the Organisation for Economic Co-operation and Development (OECD) in November 2015. Surely, with such large and positive output gaps, the decade preceding the crisis was a good opportunity to consolidate public finances. However, when we examine how the economy was perceived at the time budgets were passed, a different picture emerges.

The dotted line in Figure 5.3 represents projections made during the autumn before the year concerned. It is intended to approximate the perceptions of policy-makers when they passed their budget bills. As the figure shows, the governments in these countries were repeatedly told they were in the midst of an economic downturn, with output running below long-run potential. They wrongly believed, therefore, that there was a need to stimulate the economy, and that the budget balance would improve as soon as the economy bounced back.

Moreover, a quick analysis of the advice given by the IMF and the European Commission shows that it was not just politicians who perceived things this way. Consider Ireland, for example. Recent estimates by the IMF indicate that, just before the crisis struck, Ireland was running a structural primary deficit of close to 12 per cent of potential GDP (IMF 2015). It is not surprising, then, that the country's lax fiscal policy has been criticized by both the IMF and the European Commission (IMF 2009; European Commission 2011). At the time these budgets were passed, however, the IMF described Ireland's fiscal position as sound (IMF 2006); and the EU Council concluded that 'the medium-term budgetary position is sound and the budgetary strategy provides a good example of fiscal policies conducted in compliance with the Stability and Growth Pact' (Council of the European Union 2007).

So, how important were these misperceptions for the fiscal outcomes? According to my estimates, biased projections weakened annual budget balances in OECD countries by approximately 1 per cent of GDP (Nyman 2016b). It is possible that the decade preceding the Great Recession was a unique period, but there are indications that perceptions of the business cycle were biased throughout the post-war period. For example, the OECD has presented economic analyses in its Economic Outlook since 1967, but only during the last years of the 1980s did they state that the economy was in an upturn.

WHAT HAPPENS TO GOVERNING PARTIES THAT CONSOLIDATE?

Europe has not seen the end of austerity policies. Many countries have already taken dramatic measures to improve their structural budget balance, but it will take both time and additional fiscal adjustment before debt rates return to their pre-crisis levels. As argued above, moreover, public debt can increase rapidly even under fiscally disciplined governments. We can therefore rest assured that similar situations will also arise in future.

But what happens to governments that implement fiscal consolidation? Do they lose votes in subsequent elections? And if so, where do their previous voters go? Do the latter vote for established opposition parties, or do new parties emerge? Is it correct, as suggested in Chapter 3, that fiscal consolidation has led to an increase in the share of the vote gained by populist parties? Before examining these questions empirically, I will briefly discuss why governments that implement fiscal adjustment may be at an electoral disadvantage.

Why Would Voters Punish Governments?

At first sight, it is unclear why we should expect voters to punish governments for austerity policies. After all, governments do not implement fiscal consolidation because they are evil or incompetent, but because they believe it will lead to a more efficient inter-temporal allocation of public resources. Nevertheless, we can imagine two situations where a majority of citizens will oppose fiscal adjustment.

In the first situation, voters reward or punish governments in proportion to how expansive or contractionary their fiscal policy is. Other things being equal, voters will act *as if* they prefer lower taxes and higher spending today, even if it means greater austerity in future. The possible reasons for this are the same as those described earlier. In short, fiscally disciplined governments may be at an electoral disadvantage, because voters suffer from a fiscal illusion (Rogoff and Sibert 1988), because they are short-sighted (Buchanan and Wagner 1977), or because they are willing to exploit future generations (Bowen et al. 1960; Cukierman and Meltzer 1989).

In the second situation, voters react asymmetrically to fiscal expansion and contraction. In other words, they may punish governments for carrying out fiscal consolidation, even if they have nothing against fiscal discipline in general. Borrowing from the 'new-politics' approach in welfare-state research (Pierson 1996), according to which retrenchment in the welfare state follows a different political logic than expansion of the same, we can imagine two explanations for such a bias. First, the costs of retrenchment are concentrated, immediate, and well defined, as compared with the future benefits made possible by fiscal consolidation. And it is widely held that concentrated interests have more political influence than diffuse and scattered ones (Olson 1965; Wilson 1973; Lohmann 1998). Second, voters may exhibit a negativity bias, which means they react more strongly to losses and negative risks than to corresponding positive experiences. The literature on retrospective voting (Bloom and Price 1975; Lewis-Beck and Paldam 2000) confirms the existence of this bias, and experiments on the psychological bias known as loss aversion (Kahneman and Tversky 1979, 1984) – that is, people's tendency to prefer avoiding losses to making equivalent gains – have given it further empirical support.

What Do the Data Say?

To analyse the electoral consequences of fiscal adjustment, I have combined economic data from the OECD with data on vote shares and party characteristics from the Parlgov database (Döring and Manow 2016). My dataset covers 244 national elections between 1972 and 2016. The empirical results presented in this chapter consist of graphs and correlations. See Nyman (2016c) for a more formal analysis of the same questions.[3]

To define the fiscal policy conducted during each election period, I have used the OECD's measure of cyclically adjusted net lending. This is a measure of the budget balance, adjusted for temporary costs and revenues associated with the business cycle. In this chapter, I will refer to this as the structural budget balance. If the adjustment is correctly estimated, changes in the structural budget balance will reflect discretionary actions. An increase in the structural budget balance, for example, will correspond to spending cuts, to tax hikes, or to a mixture of the two. I define fiscal expansion as an election period during which the structural budget balance diminishes; *small-scale* fiscal consolidation as an election period during which it improves, but by *less* than 5 per cent of GDP; and *large-scale* fiscal consolidation as an election period during which it improves by *more* than 5 per cent of GDP.

Figure 5.4 shows the average decrease in the share of the vote going

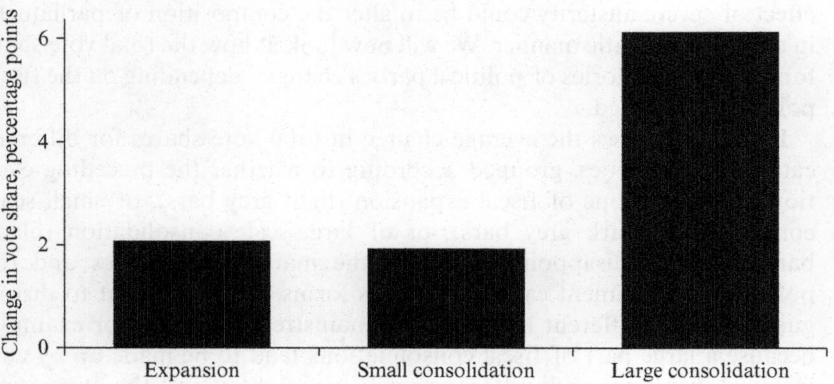

Note: Each bar represents the average vote loss for a party which spent most of the election period in government. From left to right, the election periods are divided into periods of fiscal expansion (a weakened structural budget balance), of small-scale consolidation (the budget balance is improved, but by less than 5 per cent of GDP), and of large-scale consolidation (the budget balance is improved by more than 5 per cent of GDP). The bars contain 269, 253, and 27 observations, respectively.

Figure 5.4 Average decrease in vote share for governing parties

to governing parties, according to the fiscal policy conducted during the election period. After periods of both fiscal expansion and of small-scale consolidation, governing parties have on average lost approximately two percentage points. This tendency is sometimes referred to as the cost of ruling (Nannestad and Paldam 2002). Following periods of large-scale fiscal consolidation, however, the loss in vote share has been much greater. On average, governing parties of this category have lost six percentage points in the subsequent election. Moreover, the size of the vote loss tends to grow with the size of the fiscal adjustment (Nyman 2016c). This finding – that the vote loss does not differ between periods of fiscal expansion and of small-scale consolidation, but that governing parties can expect severe electoral punishment after periods of large-scale consolidation – strongly supports the idea that voters react asymmetrically to fiscal expansion and contraction.

But which are the parties that gain votes after periods of fiscal consolidation? If voters switch their support to the main opposition parties, the electoral punishment for fiscal consolidation will only result in an increase in government turnover. The expected vote loss will probably deter the incumbent government from implementing such a policy, and this will affect budget discipline; but at least fiscal consolidation will not influence what kinds of parties are in power (i.e., all will be conventional established ones). However, if voters lose trust in all of the established parties, the effect of severe austerity could be to alter the composition of parliament in a more systematic manner. We will now look at how the total vote share for different categories of political parties changes, depending on the fiscal policy implemented.

Figure 5.5 shows the average change in total vote shares for different categories of parties, grouped according to whether the preceding election period was one of fiscal expansion (light grey bars), of small-scale consolidation (dark grey bars), or of large-scale consolidation (black bars). Because disappointment with the mainstream parties and the political establishment can take various forms, it is important to distinguish between different kinds of non-mainstream parties. For example, because a large part of fiscal consolidations tend to be made up by cuts in social insurance and welfare services, we might expect the opposition towards these policies to result in an ideological shift towards the left. On the other hand, if general anti-establishment sentiments are the primary consequences of austerity policies, we might expect populist and radical parties to rise on both sides of the ideological spectrum. From left to right, the figure shows the results for parties without cabinet experience, for radical-left parties, for radical-right parties, for Eurosceptic parties, and for populist parties. These categories are positively correlated, so

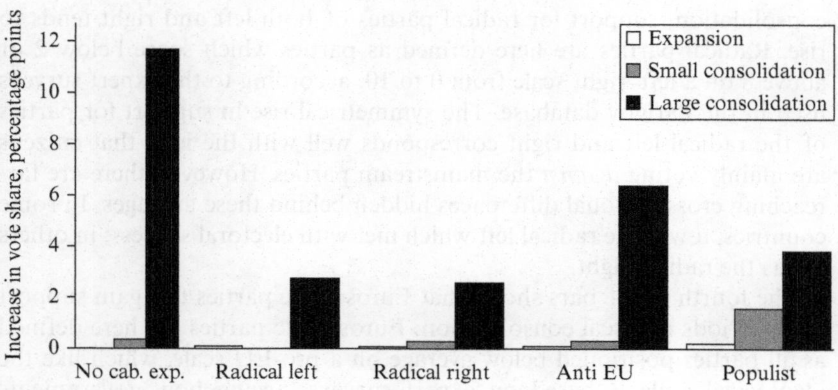

Note: From left to right, the figure shows the average change in percentage of the vote cast for parties without cabinet experience, for radical-left parties, for radical-right parties, for Eurosceptic parties, and for populist parties. Election periods are divided into periods of fiscal expansion (a weakened structural budget balance), of small-scale consolidation (the budget balance is improved, but by less than 5 per cent of GDP), and of large-scale consolidation (the budget balance is improved by more than 5 per cent of GDP). Something not shown in the figure is that parties without cabinet experience have on average experienced a small reduction in their vote share during periods of fiscal expansion (−0.7 percentage points).

Figure 5.5 Change in vote shares for different kinds of parties

it is not unusual to find that the same party belongs to several of these categories.[4]

As shown by the black bars, all of these categories of parties have gained votes following periods of large-scale fiscal consolidation. Parties without previous cabinet experience have experienced the greatest changes. On average, when the structural budget balance has improved by more than 5 per cent of GDP, their share of the vote has increased by almost 12 percentage points. This is a clear sign that fiscal consolidation causes citizens to vote for parties other than those which traditionally compete for government office. In many cases, these parties were not even represented in parliament when they broke through electorally. The 'Five-Star Movement' in Italy, for example, was only founded in 2009, by the comedian Beppe Grillo. In its first election, this party received 25.6 per cent of the vote. Much the same happened in the case of the Spanish party Podemos: in the 2015 election, just one year after being established, it got 20.7 per cent of the vote. Similar growth trajectories can be seen in the case of Syriza in Greece, of Jobbik in Hungary, and of 'Action of Dissatisfied Citizens' in the Czech Republic.

The second and third sets of bars show that, following periods of fiscal consolidation, support for radical parties of both left and right tends to rise. Radical parties are here defined as parties which score below 2 or above 8 on a left–right scale from 0 to 10, according to the expert surveys used in the Parlgov database. The symmetrical rise in support for parties of the radical left and right corresponds well with the idea that citizens are mainly voting *against* the mainstream parties. However, there are far-reaching cross-national differences hidden behind these averages. In some countries, it was the radical left which met with electoral success; in others it was the radical right.

The fourth set of bars shows that Eurosceptic parties too gain support after periods of fiscal consolidation. Eurosceptic parties are here defined as all parties positioned below average on a pro-EU scale, which like the ideological scale is based on expert surveys. Seeing how governments often blame the EU for unpopular domestic policies, it is perhaps not surprising that fiscal consolidation increases the vote share for Eurosceptic parties. The correlation between unpopular fiscal policies and support for parties with Eurosceptic views could reflect a reduced legitimacy for EU institutions (Wyplosz 2016), or it may mean that slumbering Eurosceptic attitudes have become salient (van der Eijk and Franklin 2004).

As shown by the last set of bars, the share of the vote cast for populist parties has also increased after election periods marked by fiscal consolidation. On average, such parties have increased their share of the vote by 1.6 percentage points after periods of small-scale consolidation, and by 3.9 percentage points after periods of large-scale consolidation. There is an ongoing discussion about how populism can be defined and measured, but most scholars would agree that populist parties can be found anywhere on the left–right scale. The categorization used here comes from Inglehart and Norris (2016), and includes both left- and right-wing populist parties.

In Chapter 3, Ann-Cathrine Jungar discusses whether people vote for populist parties to protest against the political establishment or because such parties better represent their political preferences. Her conclusion is that populist parties are on the rise because of a congruence between their policies and the preferences of their voters. Moreover, she argues, these parties strengthen the political system, because they provide previously unrepresented voters with a political alternative. However, the fact that support for populist parties grows during times of austerity is hard to explain in terms of 'enlightened'[5] preferences against immigration or the EU. The fit is better with a picture of what happens when governments – instead of doing what the electorate demands – do what they believe to be right, or what they are required to do according to the fiscal framework. In the next section, I discuss why populism and other challenges to a well-functioning democracy can be expected to grow when governments are forced to be unresponsive to the demands of voters.

RESPONSIBILITY, RESPONSIVENESS, AND THE QUALITY OF DEMOCRACY

Even if the debt problems were not caused primarily by fiscal indiscipline, there is more or less a consensus among economists that everyone is better off if fiscal policy is not too responsive to the demands of voters. This does not have to be a democratic problem; after all, every contemporary democracy uses non-majoritarian institutions in policy fields where it is important to isolate decision making from fickle mass opinion (Majone 1996). The rationale for constraining fiscal policy is that, if policy-making is encumbered by a deficit bias, then constraining the government's policy options can lead to better fiscal outcomes.

But in addition to its formal institutions, a well-functioning representative democracy involves democratic ideals like enlightenment, legitimacy, and responsibility. If voters' opinions are based on misconceptions or psychological bias, or citizens do not trust their political representatives, or political parties are unable to take responsibility for the greater good, then the democratic process is unlikely to yield desirable outcomes. In the area of fiscal policy, it will probably lead to higher debts and deficits. However, such aspects of democratic decision making scarcely figure at all in the economic literature on fiscal discipline.

In this literature, both voter preferences and party characteristics are usually assumed to be stable. But what happens when the distance between the popular will and the policy which is implemented becomes too large? What does this do to the political system, and to our democratic ideals? Below, I discuss why we should expect enforced fiscal discipline to have implications for how voter preferences are formed, for how legitimate the political system is, and for how responsible the parties in parliament will be. (By enforced, I mean policies which are explicitly required by lenders or by EU fiscal frameworks.)

In an ideal democracy, the behaviour of voters reflect their 'enlightened preferences'. Or in the words of Jane Mansbridge, we want citizens' policy demands and voting choices to reflect 'the preferences that people would have if their information were perfect, including the knowledge they would have in retrospect if they had a chance to live out the consequences of each choice before actually making a decision' (Mansbridge 1983, p. 25). In the realm of fiscal policy, we would like voters to have information about the budget balance and the long-term consequences of government debt.

Survey data have shown, in fact, that well-informed citizens are more likely to support deficit reduction (Althaus 1998).

Is this just wishful thinking, or are there things we can do to make preferences better informed? Beginning with Plato and Aristotle, political philosophers have repeatedly argued that enlightenment emerges from discussion and contention among a diversity of ideas (Barabas 2004). This position is also dominant among less esoteric democratic theorists (Föllesdal and Hix 2006). And while it might be naïve to believe the deficit bias can be eliminated through education, it stands to reason that discussions about the budget balance and fiscal sustainability will make people more aware of the need for fiscal discipline. Unfortunately, when it comes to austerity and other unpopular decisions, governments tend to resort to various strategies of blame avoidance, rather than promoting public debate (Weaver 1986; Pierson 1996). Economists and politicians alike have sought to supply governments with strategies for avoiding blame, so as to reduce the electoral costs for unpopular policies (Vreeland 2003). Indeed, the need to create a scapegoat for the pursuit of restrictive fiscal policies is often cited as one of the main reasons behind the Maastricht Treaty (Rotte and Zimmermann 1998). One aspect of such strategies, however, is often overlooked: they are likely to have repercussions on the opinions and preferences of voters. How can citizens adopt informed opinions if there is no debate? And why should they support fiscal discipline when the government itself cannot argue for its merits?

If fiscal rules are repeatedly used as scapegoats, the effect may be to undermine their legitimacy, as well as that of the government. Ultimately, legitimacy is required if a democracy is to survive (Lipset 1959). Until things get really critical, however, there are more pressing concerns. If governments on the national level are forced to implement policies that lack public support, they may appear powerless or unresponsive to popular demands. Either way, their democratic legitimacy is likely to take a knock.

On the European level, the scapegoat function of the Commission and of other EU institutions raises further concerns about legitimacy. The classic scapegoat for unpopular economic policies is the IMF. Unlike the institutions of the EU, however, the IMF has only a temporary presence in its mission countries. A build-up of resentment against permanent institutions like the European Commission is much more dangerous, because the legitimacy of European integration and of the Union's institutions can be undermined thereby (Wyplosz 2016). Survey data from the Eurobarometer suggest there is cause for concern on this point. For example, in the countries of southern Europe, where the sharpest fiscal consolidation has been carried out, the percentage of the population reporting an inclination to trust the EU fell from around 60 per cent in 2009 to approximately 25 per cent in 2012 (Guiso et al. 2016). This trend echoes the above-mentioned finding that Eurosceptic parties gain support during periods of austerity.

The last democratic ideal I will discuss here is the need for responsible parties. To begin with, political parties should contribute to public debate, by showing honesty, sharing knowledge, and presenting rational arguments. This will enable voters to bring their opinions into line with their enlightened preferences. Populist parties, by contrast, deliver messages that appeal more to voters' wishes and emotions than to their enlightened preferences. Such parties are also likely to make promises that they cannot keep. To be sure, democracy is ultimately about the rule of the people. As Rousseau noted, however, 'the people cannot be corrupted, but they are often deceived, and it is only then that they seem to wish for what is bad' (Rousseau 1968 [1762]).

Responsible parties must also balance their desire to maximize their vote share against the need to make decisions for the common good. Mair (2009, 2013) describes macroeconomic policy-making as a conflict between responsibility (meaning both policy efficiency and commitment to agreements and accepted procedures) and responsiveness (meaning the degree to which the actions of the government follow the salient preferences of the electorate). According to Katz and Mair (2008), the growing tension between responsibility and responsiveness has led to a bifurcation in many party systems, whereby established parties are joined by a new type of opposition. According to the two authors, the new opposition parties as characterized by a strong populist rhetoric and a tendency towards irresponsible opposition and a politics of outbidding. Their explanation for the emergence of these parties is that the established parties have become more responsible than responsive – in part because of the increased importance of fiscal frameworks, of obligations to international organizations, and of commitments to prior agreements. Or as Wolfgang Streeck (2011) puts it, 'citizens increasingly perceive their governments not as their agents, but as those of other states or of international organizations, such as the IMF or the European Union'. This gap between the voters and their government may explain why support for newly established and populist parties increases after periods of fiscal consolidation (Figure 5.5), as well as why levels of trust in the government have fallen in countries with fiscal problems (Figure 5.1).

To sum up, there is a risk that fiscal discipline will damage our democratic ideals if it deviates so much from the popular will that it must be externally enforced. For example, if a government uses the Commission or the Stability and Growth Pact as a scapegoat for its policies, instead of defending said policies in public, the effect may be to damage the legitimacy of European institutions and to undermine the formation of enlightened preferences among citizens. On the other hand, if established parties are not responsive enough to voters' demands, we may see them get replaced by less responsible parties.

HOW TO INCREASE FISCAL DISCIPLINE WITHOUT PUTTING POLITICAL STABILITY AT RISK

The simultaneous rise of public debt and of political dissatisfaction, as manifested in growing support for populist parties, in reduced trust in national governments, and in higher rates of electoral volatility, is one of the most worrying trends in Europe. Over the last decade, in the member states of the EU, the debt-to-GDP ratio has increased by 25 percentage points on average. Forcing debts back to their pre-crisis levels is an important challenge that requires fiscal discipline. Meanwhile, alarming developments in the domestic politics of many countries raises questions about how unresponsive governments can be before the political cost becomes too large.

While each of these developments is of great concern on its own, finding a solution becomes difficult indeed when they appear simultaneously. If austerity policies have contributed to political dissatisfaction, additional fiscal consolidation will probably make things even worse. And how can fiscal discipline be enforced if citizens elect parties that oppose fiscal rules and previous agreements with lenders? This dilemma is confirmed by the empirical findings in this chapter. When fiscal adjustment is implemented, voters desert established parties in favour of Eurosceptic parties without previous government experience. To a great extent, moreover, these parties can be characterized as populist parties. While it is not possible to test directly whether such parties are also less concerned about fiscal discipline, their other traits clearly indicate that they probably are. Besides, dramatic change in the party composition of a nation's parliament can be problematic in itself.

The situation is most alarming in the countries of southern Europe. Here we find the worst fiscal problems, as well as the greatest political instability. In Spain and Italy, the two dominant parties have together lost 33 and 25 per cent of the vote respectively to newly established parties. In Greece, the ruling party PASOK was virtually eliminated when it went from 44 per cent in 2009 to 5 per cent in 2015. The new ruling party, Syriza, received 36 per cent of the vote in the 2015 elections. Now, in late 2016, after continued cooperation with the European Central Bank (ECB), the IMF, and the European Commission, the latter party is down to 20 per cent in the opinion polls. The conflict between responsibility and responsiveness could not be more obvious.

While the fiscal problems in these countries have already had dramatic consequences, and further widened the social and economic gap between European regions, I believe we have reached the end of the road in what can be accomplished through fiscal rules and institutions that aim directly at enforcing fiscal discipline.[6] Unless we can increase public support for fiscal discipline, we will find it very difficult to achieve fiscal sustainability in any way which is also politically sustainable. This approach stands in sharp contrast to recent reforms in European fiscal frameworks, where the focus has been on strengthening the enforcement of rules (by increasing the number of situations where the Commission and the Ecofin Council can impose fines), as well as on changing voting rules (so that a qualified majority is no longer needed for new steps in the excessive-deficit procedure).

There are two reasons why 'forcing' fiscal discipline on incumbent governments cannot solve these problems. First, the fiscal problems were not primarily caused by fiscal indiscipline. During the decade before the Great Recession, most countries conducted a fiscal policy in line with recommendations from the European Commission and other monitoring bodies. The problem during those years was that analysts mistakenly perceived economic output to be below its capacity, which caused fiscal policy as well as advice from independent experts to be overly expansive. This, together with the fact that the Stability and Growth Pact did not require large enough safety margins to cope with the expenditures directly related to the Great Recession, is a better explanation than fiscal indiscipline for the gloomy situation of public finances in Europe.

Second, even if established parties can agree on a trajectory for fiscal policy over the medium term, there will always be other parties that do not abide by such an agreement. If there is a wide gap between public opinion and the policies which are implemented, dissatisfied citizens may vote for unestablished parties which promise an end to austerity policies, even at the cost of breaking with the fiscal framework or with agreements with the EU. Indeed, this is exactly what has happened in countries such as Hungary, Greece, Spain, and Italy, where Jobbik, Syriza, Podemos, and the Five-Star Moment have come out of nowhere and gained 20–35 per cent of the vote.

I have divided my policy recommendations into three parts, structured after what they are meant to achieve. The recommendations in the first part concern how we can minimize the risk of sovereign debt crises in the future. The second part is focused on lowering the electoral costs of fiscal consolidation, while the third set of recommendations are meant to reduce the tension between responsibility and responsiveness.

Let me begin with the first set of recommendations. In order to reduce the risk of future debt crises, we must acknowledge that public debt can rise rapidly, even without a lack of fiscal discipline. It used to be costly wars that put unexpected pressure on public finances: at the end of World War II, for example, many countries had a government debt of 100 to 200 per cent of GDP. During this last recession, by contrast, the causes lay in a combination of bank bailouts, expenditures directly related to the weakening labour market, and systematic misperceptions of the business cycle (Nyman 2016b). Moreover, public debt tends to rise during economic downturns, when both the economic and the political costs of fiscal consolidation are large. Governments should therefore try to establish safety margins during upturns in the business cycle, so that they are not forced to implement austerity policies in the midst of economic downturns.

I have two suggestions for how to secure such safety margins. The Stability and Growth Pact requires gross debts to be smaller than 60 per cent of GDP. This ceiling should be combined with a more ambitious *target* at which countries should try to aim, in order to create a large enough safety margin when the next crisis hits. The operationalization of this target should be decided by the individual member states. Moreover, fiscal policy has been made increasingly dependent on structural indicators – that is, estimates of what the economy would look like if it were operating at full potential. If the calculation of such indicators is biased, a similar bias will inflect fiscal policy. This is an argument for using backward-looking criteria when evaluating compliance with fiscal policy rules. If fiscal policy has been too expansive over a given period, compliance with backward-looking criteria will require the government to compensate for past errors.

The second set of policy recommendations is meant to make it less costly for governments to implement fiscal consolidation. One such strategy would be to reduce the salience of this issue, by making the adjustment automatic instead of discretionary. If nominal expenditures do not automatically increase in line with rising wages or prices, the budget balance will improve without discretionary actions, since tax revenues tend to rise as wages increase. However, such a solution will cause economic growth to reduce levels of public spending automatically (Nyman 2016a). To counteract this political bias, a reduced level of indexation should be combined with other measures, such as a floor for tax revenues or a medium-term target for the tax ratio.

When implementing unpopular policies, governments can also use scapegoating tactics – that is, they can blame their policies on someone else. Or they can try to reduce the salience of the issue. However, it is probably a wise long-term strategy to avoid such tactics – partly because they damage the legitimacy of the scapegoat, and partly because they make voters less informed about why fiscal discipline can actually be a good thing.

In a situation as extreme as the one in which we now find ourselves, it is hard to see how certain countries will be able to repay their debt without dramatic consequences for their political system. One solution to this problem could be some form of collective debt restructuring, whereby the creditor countries agree to write off a portion of the debt (Wyplosz 2016). In practice, this has already happened in the Greek case. Naturally, however, this is a politically contested topic, with many more aspects than I can cover here.

My third set of policy recommendations concern the most important challenge – but also the most difficult one – which is how to increase public support for fiscal discipline. In the end, the only way to enhance fiscal responsibility without reducing policy responsiveness is by increasing the salience of the country's fiscal position, by changing voters' preferences, and by making citizens better informed. The idea is to move the expressed wishes of citizens closer to their enlightened preferences.

Perhaps it is not surprising that the European Union has failed in this regard. According to public-choice theory, international organizations are created in part because they benefit incumbent national governments (Vaubel 1986). For example, international agreements can enable national policy-makers to implement unpopular domestic policies without taking the blame for them. Instead of having to argue that such policies are beneficial in the long run, policy-makers can use the international agreement as a scapegoat. And while fiscal rules can be introduced (formally speaking) on the national level, the creation of the Economic and Monetary Union (EMU) opened a window of opportunity, allowing the political elite to introduce fiscal frameworks that would had been difficult to implement in the national political arena (EEAG 2003; Baimbridge and Whyman 2005).

However, using an external agent as a scapegoat is dangerous, especially when it is a permanent institution like the EU (Wyplosz 2016). As argued above, the legitimacy of the scapegoated institution can be damaged, and the quality of citizens' preferences as well. If the institution lacks legitimacy, it may also be less effective as a scapegoat. Furthermore, if the country in question receives bailout loans from the ECB or from other member states, the domestic fiscal policy pursued can get entangled in conflicts of interest between member states. As such, it may contribute to a deterioration in relations between countries.

It may be a bit naïve to believe that fiscal sustainability will be achieved if only public discourse is guided by rational arguments. But even should it prove impossible to increase sincere public support for fiscal discipline, we should at least strive to increase the legitimacy of the fiscal frameworks and institutions. This will probably require that they be created on the national level and exposed to national debate. There is also evidence to indicate that national fiscal frameworks are more effective than their supranational counterparts. For example, Bergman et al. (2016) find that national fiscal rules increase fiscal discipline; by contrast, they find no such effect on the part of the Stability and Growth Pact. It bears noting that the Fiscal Compact requires member states to introduce balanced-budget rules on the national level. If they do not comply, they can be brought before the Court of Justice of the European Union, and ultimately fined. However, forcing countries to implement certain rules is not likely to solve the problem of legitimacy.

This leads to my last two policy recommendations. First, to the extent possible, fiscal frameworks and fiscal councils should be designed in such a way that they increase public support for fiscal discipline. They can do this by enhancing fiscal transparency, increasing the salience of the country's fiscal position, and contributing to the public debate on fiscal policy (whether by participating actively or by providing a point of reference to which prevailing policies can be compared). Other discipline-enhancing methods, like a resort to scapegoating or a strict enforcement of rules, should be used with care. Second, national fiscal rules and fiscal councils have often been introduced in response to a public debt crisis. In the wake of a fiscal crisis, the public is more aware of the negative consequences of fiscal indiscipline and can be expected to be more positive towards institutions of this kind. Governments ought, therefore, to use the opportunity created by the current crisis to create or modify national fiscal frameworks.

Until we find ways to increase public support for fiscal discipline, we will be caught in a difficult dilemma. If we make fiscal policy more responsive to popular wishes, the chances are that debt levels will continue to increase and that more countries will suffer dramatic sovereign debt crises. And if we make policy-making less responsive, trust in established parties will likely keep falling and populist parties will continue to rise. Since the countries with the worst fiscal problems to a large extent also have the most vulnerable political systems, an increasing tension between responsiveness and responsibility is likely to widen the prosperity gap in Europe.

NOTES

1. Greece stands out as a clear exception and an obvious example of fiscal indiscipline.
2. The output gap is the most common measure of the business cycle. It measures the estimated difference between actual and potential output, usually expressed as a percentage of potential GDP. The output gap is negative during bad times and positive during good times.
3. Previous research has found that fiscal adjustment does not affect the likelihood that a government will be re-elected (Alesina et al. 1998, 2012; Brender 2003; Brender and

Drazen 2008); nor does it influence a government's expected vote share (Peltzman 1992; Lowry et al. 1998; Drazen and Eslava 2010). I argue (Nyman 2016c) that these studies underestimate the effects, because of two identification problems.

4. For four of these categories of parties, the change in vote share is positive during periods of fiscal expansion as well, although it is very close to zero. This means their vote shares have increased over time. It is only the vote share for parties without cabinet experience that has decreased on average during periods of fiscal expansion (−0.7 percentage points, not shown in the figure).
5. That is, informed, deliberate, and considered. See the words of Jane Mansbridge, quoted below.
6. By this I mean rules and institutions that affect policy, but not the information available to policy-makers or the public support for fiscal discipline.

REFERENCES

Alesina, A. and Tabellini, G. (1990). 'A positive theory of fiscal deficits and government debt'. *Review of Economic Studies*, *57*(3), 403–414.

Alesina, A., Carloni, D., and Lecce, G. (2012). 'The electoral consequences of large fiscal adjustments'. In: Alesina, A. and Giavazzi, F. (eds), *Fiscal Policy after the Financial Crisis* (pp. 531–570). Chicago, IL: University of Chicago Press.

Alesina, A., Perotti, R., Tavares, J., Obstfeld, M., and Eichengreen, B. (1998). 'The political economy of fiscal adjustments'. *Brookings Papers on Economic Activity*, *1998*(1), 197–266.

Alt, J. E. and Lassen, D. D. (2006). 'Fiscal transparency, political parties, and debt in OECD countries'. *European Economic Review*, *50*(6), 1403–1439.

Althaus, S. L. (1998). 'Information effects in collective preferences'. *American Political Science Review*, *92*(3), 545–558.

Armingeon, K., Guthmann, K., and Weisstanner, D. (2016). 'How the Euro divides the union: The effect of economic adjustment on support for democracy in Europe'. *Socio-Economic Review*, *14*(1), 1–26.

Baimbridge, M. and Whyman, P. (2005). *Fiscal Federalism and European Economic Integration*. London: Routledge.

Barabas, J. (2004). 'How deliberation affects policy opinions'. *American Political Science Review*, *98*(4), 687–701.

Basso, H. S. and Costain, J. (2016). 'Fiscal delegation in a monetary union with decentralized public spending'. *CESifo Economic Studies*, *62*(2), 256–288.

Bergman, U. M., Hutchison, M. M., and Jensen, S. E. H. (2016). 'Promoting sustainable public finances in the European Union: The role of fiscal rules and government efficiency'. *European Journal of Political Economy*, *44*, 1–19.

Blinder, A. S. (1997). 'Is government too political?'. *Foreign Affairs*, November/December, 115–126.

Bloom, H. S. and Price, H. D. (1975). 'Voter response to short-run economic conditions: The asymmetric effect of prosperity and recession'. *American Political Science Review*, *69*(4), 1240–1254.

Bowen, W. G., Davis, R. G., and Kopf, D. H. (1960). 'The public debt: A burden on future generations?'. *American Economic Review*, *50*(4), 701–706.

Brender, A. (2003). 'The effect of fiscal performance on local government election results in Israel: 1989–1998'. *Journal of Public Economics*, *87*(9), 2187–2205.

Brender, A. and Drazen, A. (2008). 'How do budget deficits and economic growth affect reelection prospects? Evidence from a large panel of countries'. *American Economic Review*, *98*(5), 2203–2220.

Buchanan, J. M. and Wagner, R. E. (1977). *Democracy in Deficit*. New York: Academic Press.

Calmfors, L. (2015). 'The roles of fiscal rules, fiscal councils and fiscal union in EU integration'. IFN Working Paper No. 1076, Research Institute of Industrial Economics, Stockholm.

Calmfors, L. and Wren-Lewis, S. (2011). 'What should fiscal councils do?'. *Economic Policy*, *26*(68), 649–695.

Council of the European Union (2007). 'Council Opinion of 27 February 2007 on the Updated Stability Programme of Ireland, 2006–2009'. Vol. 2005. *Official Journal of the European Union*, 1055.

Cukierman, A. and Meltzer, A. H. (1989). 'A political theory of government debt and deficits in a neo-Ricardian framework'. *American Economic Review*, *79*(4), 713–732.

de Vries, C. E. (2007). 'Sleeping giant: Fact or fairytale?'. *European Union Politics*, *8*(3), 363–385.

Debrun, X., Hauner, D., and Kumar, M. S. (2009). 'Independent fiscal agencies'. *Journal of Economic Surveys*, *23*(1), 44–81.

Debrun, X., Moulin, L., Turrini, A., Ayuso-i-Casals, J., and Kumar, M. S. (2008). 'Tied to the mast? National fiscal rules in the European Union'. *Economic Policy*, *23*(54), 298–362.

Döring, H. and Manow, P. (2016). 'Parliaments and governments database (ParlGov): Information on parties, elections and cabinets in modern democracies'. Development version.

Drazen, A. and Eslava, M. (2010). 'Electoral manipulation via voter-friendly spending: Theory and evidence'. *Journal of Development Economics*, *92*(1), 39–52.

EEAG (2003). *Report on the European Economy*. European Economic Advisory Group, CESifo, Munich.

Eichengreen, B. and Wyplosz, C. (1998). 'The Stability Pact: More than a minor nuisance?'. *Economic Policy*, *26*, 65–113.

European Commission (2011). *The Economic Adjustment Programme for Ireland*. European Economy Occasional Papers. Directorate-General for Economic and Financial Affairs, Brussels.

Faini, R. (2006). 'Fiscal policy and interest rates in Europe'. *Economic Policy*, *47*, 443–489.

Föllesdal, A. and Hix, S. (2006). 'Why there is a democratic deficit in the EU: A response to Majone and Moravcsik'. *JCMS: Journal of Common Market Studies*, *44*(3), 533–562.

Guiso, L., Sapienza, P., and Zingales, L. (2016). 'Monnet's error?'. *Economic Policy*, *31*(86), 247–297.

Hooghe, L. and Marks, G. (2009). 'A postfunctionalist theory of European integration: From permissive consensus to constraining dissensus'. *British Journal of Political Science*, *39*(1), 1–23.

IMF (2006). *Staff Report for the 2006 Article IV Consultation*. International Monetary Fund, Washington, DC.

IMF (2009). *Staff Report for the 2009 Article IV Consultation*. International Monetary Fund, Washington, DC.

IMF (2015). *Staff Report for the 2015 Article IV Consultation*. International Monetary Fund, Washington, DC.

Inglehart, R. and Norris, P. (2016). 'Trump, Brexit, and the rise of populism: Economic have-nots and cultural backlash'. HKS Working Paper RWP16-026.

Kahneman, D. and Tversky, A. (1979). 'Prospect theory: An analysis of decision under risk'. *Econometrica, 47*(2), 263–292.

Kahneman, D. and Tversky, A. (1984). 'Choices, values, and frames'. *American Psychologist, 39(*4), 341–350.

Katz, R. S. and Mair, P. (2008). *MPs and Parliamentary Parties in the Age of the Cartel Party*. ECPR Joint Sessions, Rennes.

Kopits, M. G. and Craig, M. J. (1998). *Transparency in Government Operations* (No. 158). International Monetary Fund, Washington, DC.

Kydland, F. E. and Prescott, E. C. (1977). 'Rules rather than discretion: The inconsistency of optimal plans'. *Journal of Political Economy*, *85*(3), 473–491.

Lewis-Beck, M. S. and Paldam, M. (2000). 'Economic voting: An introduction'. *Electoral Studies*, *19*(2), 113–121.

Lipset, S. M. (1959). 'Some social requisites of democracy: Economic development and political legitimacy'. *American Political Science Review*, *53*(1), 69–105.

Lohmann, S. (1998). 'An information rationale for the power of special interests'. *American Political Science Review*, *92*(4), 809–827.

Lowry, R. C., Alt, J. E., and Ferree, K. E. (1998). 'Fiscal policy outcomes and electoral accountability in American states'. *American Political Science Review*, *92*(4), 759–774.

Mair, P. (2000). 'The limited impact of Europe on national party systems'. *West European Politics*, *23*(4), 27–51.

Mair, P. (2009). 'Representative versus responsible government'. MPlfG Working Papers. Max Planck Institute for the Study of Societies, Cologne.

Mair, P. (2013). 'Smaghi versus the parties: Representative government and institutional constraints'. In: Schäfer, A. and Streeck, W. (eds), *Politics in the Age of Austerity* (Chap. 6, pp. 143–168). Cambridge: Polity Press.

Majone, G. (1996). 'Regulatory legitimacy'. In: Majone, G. (ed.), *Regulating Europe* (pp. 284–301). London: Routledge.

Mansbridge, J. J. (1983). *Beyond Adversary Democracy*. Chicago, IL: University of Chicago Press.

Milesi-Ferretti, G. M. (2004). 'Good, bad or ugly? On the effects of fiscal rules with creative accounting'. *Journal of Public Economics*, *88*(1), 377–394.

Morris, R., Ongena, H., and Schuknecht, L. (2006). 'The reform and implementation of the Stability and Growth Pact'. ECB Occasional Paper No. 47.

Nannestad, P. and Paldam, M. (2002). 'The cost of ruling: A foundation stone for two theories'. In: Dorussen, H. and Taylor, M. (eds), *Economic Voting* (pp. 17–44). London: Routledge.

Nyman, P. (2016a). 'Economic growth is deflating the welfare state'. In: *Austerity Politics: Is the Electorate Responsible?* Doctoral dissertation, Acta Universitatis Upsaliensis.

Nyman, P. (2016b). 'Politics or perceptions?'. In: *Austerity Politics: Is the Electorate Responsible?* Doctoral dissertation, Acta Universitatis Upsaliensis.

Nyman, P. (2016c). 'Punished for austerity?'. In: *Austerity Politics: Is the Electorate Responsible?* Doctoral dissertation, Acta Universitatis Upsaliensis.

Olson, M. (1965). *The Logic of Collective Action: Public Goods and the Theory of Groups*. Cambridge, MA: Harvard University Press.

Olson, M. (1982). *The Rise and Decline of Nations: Economic Growth, Stagnation, and Social Rigidities.* New Haven, CT: Yale University Press.

Peltzman, S. (1992). 'Voters as fiscal conservatives'. *Quarterly Journal of Economics*, *107*(2), 327–361.
Persson, T. and Svensson, L. (1989). 'Why a stubborn conservative would run a deficit: Policy with time-inconsistent preferences'. *Quarterly Journal of Economics*, *104*(2), 325–345.
Pierson, P. (1996). 'The new politics of the welfare state'. *World Politics*, *48*(2), 143–179.
Reif, K. and Schmitt, H. (1980). 'Nine second-order national elections – a conceptual framework for the analysis of European election results'. *European Journal of Political Research*, *8*, 3–44.
Rogoff, K. and Sibert, A. (1988). 'Elections and macroeconomic policy cycles'. *Review of Economic Studies*, *55*(1), 1–16.
Rotte, R. and Zimmermann, K. F. (1998). 'Fiscal restraint and the political economy of EMU'. *Public Choice*, *94*(3–4), 385–406.
Rousseau, J. J. (1968 [1762]). *The Social Contract.* Translated by Maurice Cranston. London: Penguin.
Streeck, W. (2011). 'The crises of democratic capitalism'. *New Left Review*, *71*, 5–29.
van der Eijk, C. and Franklin, M. N. (2004). 'Potential for contestation on European matters at national elections in Europe'. In: Marks, G. and Steenbergen, M. R. (eds), *European Integration and Political Conflict* (pp. 33–50). Cambridge: Cambridge University Press.
Vaubel, R. (1986). 'A public choice approach to international organization'. *Public Choice*, *51*(1), 39–57.
Velasco, A. (2000). 'Debts and deficits with fragmented fiscal policymaking'. *Journal of Public Economics*, *76*, 105–125.
Vreeland, J. R. (2003). *The IMF and Economic Development*. Cambridge: Cambridge University Press.
Weaver, R. K. (1986). 'The politics of blame avoidance'. *Journal of Public Policy*, *6*(4), 371–398.
Wilson, J. Q. (1973). *Political Organizations*. New York: Basic Books.
Wyplosz, C. (2016). 'The six flaws of the Eurozone'. *Economic Policy*, *31*(87), 559–606.

6. The Social Dialogue in Europe 1985–2014: has it been played out?

Lars Magnusson and Sofia Murhem

INTRODUCTION

It was no coincidence that the meeting where the Social Dialogue was founded took place in Val Duchesse, in what was then called the European Economic Community (EEC). It was meant to symbolize the significance of such a dialogue and the importance that its founders attached to it. Val Duchesse is a beautiful castle just outside of Brussels, which started as a convent in 1262. Since World War II it has been used for various important meetings. For example, the discussions which led to the institution of the Rome Treaty in 1957 were held here, as were the ones which led to the foundation of the EEC and Euratom the following year. Moreover, the first formal meeting of the Hallstein Commission (later the European Commission) was held at the castle. In placing the set up of the Social Dialogue in January 1985 in the magnificent halls of the castle, the significance of instituting a social dialogue for the future development of the European Union (EU) was signalled.

Jacques Delors, then about to take office as Chair of the European Commission, summoned the chairs and secretary generals of the organizations within the EEC representing the labour market parties: for the employees ETUC (the European Trade Union Confederation), for the private employers UNICE (Union des confédérations de l'industrie et des employeurs d'Europe, since 2007 BusinessEurope) and for the public employers CEEP (Centre européen des entreprises à participation publique et des entreprises d'intérêt économique général). It was common knowledge that Jacques Delors himself had high ambitions with regard to the integration of the social dimension into the European construction. For Delors, the labour unions, the farmers' organizations and the employers' organizations represented vast parts of the grass roots in Europe, which the European project needed to connect to. At play was also the Social Dialogue as an offset to the open market and free trade, the economic freedoms enacted already in the Rome Treaty. Delors also talked at this time of what was widely called 'A Social Europe'. This could counterbalance an absolute, primarily Anglo-Saxon 'pure' market economy, he thought. The social deficiency possibly brought about by free trade would be counterbalanced by a social dialogue.

Delors' role in establishing the Social Dialogue should not however be exaggerated. Without doubt he had great influence and vast opportunities to exert this influence. He was indisputably a strong chairman, with a stubbornness that often resulted in him having his way. He also got to stay for two terms of office, 1985–1995. But the social partners also played a part in setting up the dialogue. The ETUC was especially keen to try this new route. It would mean a step forward, they believed. At the same time the unions of northern and southern Europe disagreed on what role the Social Dialogue should have. Throughout the history of EU collaboration runs the dividing line between those who propose supranational legislation and those who rather suggest soft agreements and benchmarking (so-called Open Method Coordination, OMC). The labour market is no exception to this and neither was the Social Dialogue. In southern Europe the member states were particularly keen to introduce various types of minimum legislation throughout the EU, to regulate wages, social conditions and workplace issues. In the Scandinavian countries, and also in Germany, the unions were less enthusiastic about too much supranational legislation in the form of EU directives – they safeguarded their labour market models. They could, however, imagine collective agreements between parties at the EU level. Sweden was of course not yet a member of the EU, but it was a member of the ETUC, and thereby had an interest. Representatives from Sweden, as well as from other European non-member countries, were also present at the meeting in Val Duchesse. Perhaps the importance of Jacques Delors starting the Social Dialogue rested in his ability to balance the unions in the north and the south. In retrospect, he, a Social Democrat, was probably most impressed by the collaboration between the parties in northern Europe (perhaps particularly in Sweden), but he never closed the door on legislation. It is said that he made many trips to Sweden to study the labour market parties' work and organization.

The opposing party – the employers – instead agreed to uphold an undecided attitude. They were generally sceptical towards the centralization that the Social Dialogue might lead to – they wanted wages and working conditions to be decided at the most decentralized level possible. On top of that they feared that the unions would strengthen their position. This incongruity has been a constant phenomenon in the Social Dialogue: the European unions wish to develop the dialogue (albeit in somewhat different ways) whereas the employers rather resist it.

At the meeting in January 1985, the participants agreed on the promotion of a continued social dialogue. It was also agreed that two working groups would be set up, one that focused on macroeconomic issues, and one on how the parties should deal with new technology and work organization in working life. At the beginning the Dialogue led to three joint statements, two from the macroeconomic group (1986 and 1987) and one from the group on new technology: a joint declaration on education and motivation and also on information and consultation (1987). It was however difficult to come up with more tangible proposals or reach (collective) agreements. As pointed out earlier, there was also a disagreement within the ETUC. At the same time, such agreements had been made possible from 1987 through the Single European Act, which aimed to establish a common market. Within this there existed an opportunity for employees and employers to set up common agreements at EU level, if they so wished. Such agreements were not, however, to be seen for another decade. The difficulties in this field did not diminish when Great Britain on the whole objected to the development of a social dimension in EU cooperation. After numerous negotiations a compromise was reached with regard to improvements in the work environment that regulates health and safety among employees. The decision was taken by a qualified majority, that is, without Great Britain.

At the same time, the Single European Act can be seen as the first regulation of a dialogue between the 'Social Partners', which the labour market parties came to be called. No direct rules regarding how to manage the Dialogue were agreed on, and there was no regulation of the legal status and the extent of agreements reached within the Dialogue.

During the first years that followed the conclusion of the Single European Act, a dozen joint opinions were agreed upon. The opinions, which dealt with further education, mobility and so on, were perhaps not significant as separate documents, but they became important in that they created a way of working within the Social Dialogue. The employers saw the agreements as important signals that Europe's Social Partners could sit at the negotiating table and set up mutual goals, while the employees – with varying enthusiasm in the north and south of Europe – longed for more rapid strides towards European legislation and collective agreements. This divide between employers and employees, where the employers were more cautious and the employees wished to move forward faster and further, continued all through the development of the Social Dialogue, as will be discussed later in the chapter.

THE ROAD TO VAL DUCHESSE

Val Duchesse was far from the first time the labour market parties discussed the social area within the European cooperation. Following the establishment of the European Coal and Steel Community in 1952, a lively debate took place regarding the objectives of further European integration and how the European structure should turn out. Two alternatives were discussed: one vertical, which meant the creation of multiple sectorial unions, and one horizontal, which saw a common union containing a number of vertical groups (Zeitlin et al. 2006; Marlier and Natali 2010; Magnusson 2004). The treaty that established the Community contained text suggesting the setting up of a consultative committee, consisting of equal numbers of producers, workers, consumers and tradespeople. The representatives of workers and producers were appointed by the Council of Ministers from their respective organizations. The Consultative Committee had a unique position, unlike anything seen before or after. It was always to be consulted on general goals and programmes, and be informed of what was going to be done within the area of competition. In 1955 two new committees were established, one for the coal industry and one for steel: the so-called joint committees for the harmonization of working conditions and standards of living. The labour unions had the ambition of reaching European collective agreements in this way. That ambition never came to be realized, but both the thought and the ambition lived on. Instead, the steel committee devoted years to collecting data on wages and social insurance conditions, while the coal committee tried to carry out negotiations in the mining field, which eventually broke down. Despite this, the committees can be seen as the beginnings of the Social Dialogue in Europe. After six countries formed the EEC, the coal and steel committees were followed by five joint committees for social problems – within agriculture; road transportation; water transportation, excluding sea transports; fishing; and railways. These were established between 1963 and 1972. They, in turn, were followed by four more committees during the 1980s and 1990s: sea transports, civil aviation, telecommunications and postal services. The first sectorial dialogues after the original ones were then set up within transport and communications.

Parallel to this, through the Rome Treaty of 1957, the European Economic and Social Committee (EESC) was founded to engage economic and socially interested parties in the creation of the common market and provide the Commission and the Council of Ministers with valuable information. The EESC had representatives of employers, employees and farmers. Its role can be seen as a continuation of the earlier ambitions to involve the labour market parties in the work of the Community, although its focus was more on economic rather than social cooperation. Today, the third group of representatives, the farmers, has been broadened to represent more interests, and it is therefore labelled 'other' interests. Here we find representatives for groups of all sorts of economic and social interests besides the labour unions and the employers. The Committee has 353 members that are elected by the member states every five years. It works as a consultative organ and has gained an important role within the social field, above all through Europe 2020, which will be shown later. The EESC is always consulted when larger projects are planned and new strategies established. The Social Committee is also an important resource in relation to the European Parliament, the Commission and the European Council when the views of various interested parties within the EU are required for specific issues.

WHAT IS THE SOCIAL DIALOGUE?

The EU defines the Social Dialogue as the consultative process carried out with the labour market parties to defend the member's interests. This process has been the subject of extensive research (see e.g. Branch 2005; Dölvik 1997; Mailand and Due 2004; Streeck 1994; Dufresne et al. 2006). The Social Dialogue in the EU can be carried out between the employees' and the employers' organizations, that is, what we in Sweden know as dialogue between the parties. It can also be carried out between these and the European institutions as a three-party dialogue, which for Swedish ears may sound strange, in that for the Swedish the opinion of the state should normally be left out. In the EU an institutionalized form of corporatism exists, which is embedded in the form of labour market parties' collaboration. Such an ideology has moreover been a guiding-star of cooperation within the EU dating back to the days of the coal and steel community. Three-party collaboration is carried out at, for instance, summit meetings on economic growth and employment. The Social Dialogue in the EU is performed at two levels: on the one hand professionally all-embracing, that is, comprising all workers; and on the other hand at sector level, that is, comprising all workers within a particular sector or branch. The former takes place in the earlier-mentioned three-party summits and in the committee for the Social Dialogue and the latter in the social sector dialogue (Dölvik 1997, Part II).

If we look at the parties' own definitions, these are more in accordance with established Swedish concepts. The parties themselves normally label the independent two-party dialogue as social dialogue, whereas the three-party dialogue is called tripartite consultation. The social dialogue can result in joint opinions, joint declarations, joint statements that are not binding, or agreements which are binding. The joint opinions are usually agreed upon when dealing with complex areas or issues, where negotiations and compromises are necessary. When preparing for a bill on employment and social issues the Commission has to confer with the labour market parties. The parties may themselves, after such consultation, negotiate an agreement that is implemented by them at national level or, alternatively, demand that the agreement gets executed by a decision in the European Council. If binding agreements are made at the EU level, they can be called either agreements, which means that they get implemented at EU level, or autonomous agreements, which replace legislation and are implemented nationally in accordance with the principle of subsidiarity.

After 1998, when the Commission adopted new guidelines to form new and more Sectorial Social Dialogue Committees (SSDCs), the number of sectorial dialogues increased markedly. From primarily taking place within the basic industries (coal, steel, agriculture and fishing) and transport and communications (railways, postal services and telecommunications), the sectorial dialogues now exist in almost all areas.

In 2014 there were 43 sectorial dialogues of varying sizes, ranging from professional football players and the metal industry, to hospitals and health services. The scope is, in other words, significant, whether we look at the impact in terms of economics or employment. The purpose of the social sectorial dialogues is for them to function as central organs for consultation, joint initiatives and negotiations. They comprise over 145 million employees, and more than 500 joint texts of varying types and importance have been adopted. More than three quarters of all employees in Europe are thereby covered by a social sectorial dialogue. How active the various sectorial dialogues are differs significantly. Some have produced a large number of joint texts and have made significant progress in their work, whereas others are less active. Many national organizations, irrespective of whether they are labour unions or employer organizations, take part in multiple sectorial dialogues. The SSDCs should, according to their rules, meet at least once a year. The chair is either a representative of the parties or someone from the Commission. The Commission always supplies the committees with a secretariat. The secretariat usually has responsibility for preparing meetings, setting the agenda and following up on meetings, and in this it is not an outright collaboration between the parties according to the Swedish view, since here the Commission takes an active part and can, through the secretariats, influence the agenda.

Obviously, there are problems embedded in the Social Dialogue. Perhaps the most important is the way in which the parties themselves are responsible for implementing the agreements entered upon. This evidently becomes problematic in cases where national parties do not exist or are weak, which as we will see later is by no means unusual. The dialogues of course also get weaker and less legitimate if many countries and large groups of employees or corporations are not represented. As the sectorial dialogues increase in number, it gets increasingly difficult for the representatives of unions and employers to attend them all. The fact that an increasing number of other interested parties also take part in the dialogues means that the labour market parties do not dominate them as they once did.

A trend towards less implementation than before is also clearly visible. For example, in 2002 the Commission warned that a majority of the non-binding texts – that is, the ones that put forward some kind of joint statement or joint opinion – did not contain any directives regarding implementation or enforcement. As pointed out by the Commission, their efficiency could therefore be questioned. The risk is that they become only words on paper. This development has undoubtedly strengthened since 2002.

MAASTRICHT AND AMSTERDAM

In the small city of Maastricht, right on the Dutch-Belgian border, an agreement was signed on 9–10 December 1991 which was subjoined to the Rome Treaty in the form of a social protocol. It had been preceded by a lively discussion, and the employers' union, UNICE, had been far from enthusiastic. UNICE's members from Great Britain, Portugal and Greece had been particularly sceptical. The scepticism of the British employers' organization towards greater responsibility within the social area of the European Community (EC, the new name for the EEC following the Maastricht Treaty) was seconded by the country's political leadership, and an exception was made for Britain in the amendment. The European Social Partners received through the social protocol an institutionalized role in the EC legislative process, wherein the European Social Dialogue was inserted. The Maastricht Treaty was implemented on 1 November 1993 and meant a deepening and a sort of constitutionalization of the Social Dialogue within the EU collaboration.

There is no denying that the Maastricht Treaty broadened the area of competence of the EU in labour market and social policy matters. According to the Maastricht Treaty, one task of the Community is to support full employment and social protection, but it is in the social amendment that we find the parts that have later come to lay the foundations for continued work on a social Europe. The protocol declares that both the Community and its member states are to promote employment, better living and working conditions, social protection and dialogue between the labour market parties. Exclusion from the labour market should also be counteracted. In striving to achieve this, consideration should be taken of distinctive national patterns and the need to uphold competitiveness. There thus existed two reservations that came to greatly influence the continuation of the work.

The Community's areas of competence were health and safety for employees, working conditions, information and consultation, equality, and integration of persons outside the labour market. The Council could, by means of a qualified majority, pass directives in the form of minimum standards. In decisions concerning, among other things, social insurances and social protection, as well as the representation and collective safeguarding of employees' and employers' interests, unanimous decision-making is required as well as consultation with both the European Parliament and the EESC. Exempted from the protocol are decisions regarding wages, freedom of organization, the right to strike and the right to issue a lock out.

The Amsterdam Treaty, which was signed six years later, in October 1997, meant yet another step forward for the Social Dialogue, since the earlier amendment to the Maastricht Treaty now became an integrated part of the treaty. This was made possible since Great Britain, under Labour and Tony Blair's leadership, had changed its views in comparison to those of the earlier Tory governments under Margaret Thatcher and John Major. In the Amsterdam Treaty the member states for the first time declared that employment was of common concern. Since the role of the Social Partners was now written down in the treaty, the interference of the Commission in the Dialogue decreased. The new text declared that the Commission was to 'facilitate' the Social Dialogue, whereas earlier it had the task of 'developing' it.

In practice, the Social Dialogue now had its real breakthrough. The numerous sceptics, who had seen the employers' resistance as a real hindrance, were surprised to see three new joint agreements during the latter part of the 1990s: 1995 on parental leave, 1997 on part-time work and 1999 on temporary employment. These, of course, did not come about without difficulties. UNICE refused to discuss the introduction of information and consultation as an obligation for employers in 1998, and the unequal power balance to the advantage of the employers became ever more visible as we approached the year 2000. Earlier the power balance had been more even, thanks to bonds between certain senior officials in the Commission and the ETUC; but as time passed, these for various reasons decreased and the employers showed their unwillingness to negotiate if there were no direct threats of legislation. The Social Dialogue was increasingly used by the employers as a lobbying device rather than as a means of negotiation, which led to the agreements being signed as voluntary and not binding.

Finally, in the so-called Lisbon Strategy agreed in March 2000, the Social Dialogue gained an even more important role within the EU, partly because of the economic and social modernization that was part of the strategy established by the prime ministers of the member states in Lisbon, but also as part of the democratic control aimed at by the Commission. In proud proclamations it was laid down that by 2010 Europe (the EU countries) should be the world's most modern economy through offensive investments in education and innovation, aiming towards the establishment of an overachieving knowledge sector. In the strategy it was also laid down that full employment should be an overall objective in the European collaboration. In the EU summit in Barcelona in 2002, against this background, government leaders emphasized that the Social Partners ought to have a greater say in the modernization of working life and its qualities, and that they had a joint responsibility for finding a balance between flexibility and employment security, which came to be called flexicurity. They also had a responsibility for securing full employment through increased flexibility and increased learning (much was said about life-long learning during these years). In 2003 the earlier mentioned three-party summits were introduced so that the Social Partners could contribute to the social strategy and the strategy for sustainable development. It seems as if the government leaders and the Commission now wished for the Social Partners to have a greater responsibility for dealing with complex and sensitive issues. Everyone needed to help out in creating beneficial conditions for increased flexibility in the labour market, which the Lisbon Strategy presupposed, as well as in changing from an 'old' industrial economy to a knowledge-based one (on the Lisbon Strategy, see Bruun et al. 2012; Rodrigues 2004).

A TOUGHER CLIMATE

At this time many believed in a further development and coordination of the European labour market models through the Social Dialogue. The phenomenon even got its own name as a Europeanization of the labour market models was talked about. The most extreme advocates saw in this a standardization across the member states, whereas the more down to earth pointed to the large differences that still existed and rather saw a harmonization with preserved diversity. Both groups were, however, too optimistic. The European development had been focused upon too much and the strength of national models had been underestimated. Although the formal significance of the Social Dialogue continued to increase, its practical importance was to diminish.

Parallel to the widening of the Social Dialogue (particularly after Amsterdam in 1997), through a more formal role and more instruments, such as the above-mentioned three-party summits, its role paradoxically became less important in practice during the decade following the year 2000. It became increasingly hard to reach agreements of the type that were decided on at great speed at the end of the 1990s. It is true that three such agreements were signed (2002: teleworking; 2004: work-related stress; and 2007: harassment and violence at work), but they did not really deal with the most sensitive issues between the parties. The latest collective agreement at the European level was signed in 2010 (inclusive labour markets). The writings are general, and it is a known fact that it was hard to agree.

Of course, the reasons for the increasing difficulties are numerous. *First*, this is part of a more general change within the EU since the start of the Lisbon Strategy in 2000. Viewed in a long-term perspective the EU Commission was unusually strong from 1985 and at least ten years onward. As we have seen, the Social Dialogue was to a large extent promoted by the Commission, and particularly so due to its strong chair during this period, Jacques Delors. The Maastricht and Amsterdam treaties as well as the Euro were to no small degree the result of a both strong and highly regarded Commission. The fall of the Soviet Union and the Berlin wall, as well as the establishment of a unified Germany after 1990, overturned the old balance of power in the EU – particularly the balance between Germany and France. For the Commission this opened up a window of opportunity to push towards a deepening of EU collaboration. Slowly but steadily the member states have however regained their influence. Intergovernmental work has come increasingly to the fore while the Commission has come to play a minor role. The European Council, but also the economic Ecofin, where the Ministers of Finance meet and negotiate, today seem more important than the Commission. The Commissions that have served since the mid-1990s have been visibly weaker than under Delors' presidency.

One could also argue that the strategy established in 1997, which came to be called the Luxembourg strategy, to streamline European labour market policy towards more job creating measures, which at the time was regarded as a sign of a potent EU, in fact was the first step towards an increasingly intergovernmental collaboration. The Luxembourg strategy had been patched together in the Swedish archipelago during 1996 by Allan Larsson, then director-general of the Directorate of Labour Market and Social Issues (DG 5), and Jean-Claude Juncker, then prime minister in Luxembourg and now Chair of the Commission after José Manuel Barroso, and it contained a number of pillars and concrete commitments by the member states to boost employment in the EU. The strategy was heavily influenced by the Scandinavian work-line policy that Allan Larsson in particular was schooled in, which undeniably also comprised – according to its critics in, particularly, southern Europe – elements of a less socially generous 'workfare' or 'work first' attitude, to be achieved with the aid of the stick. In countries like Spain and Portugal it was not unusual to view the work first policy as right wing or even as a policy with a Fascist touch.

The Luxembourg strategy was nevertheless the first of several similar strategies launched in various areas from the end of the 1990s onwards, based on the idea of the so-called Open Method of Coordination (OMC). It meant that Brussels was not to legislate in matters of the labour market and social and welfare policy by issuing directives. Instead soft policies were to be implemented in the form of benchmarking and recommendations put forth by the Commission, and the member states were to report what had been done to implement these recommendations in national reports. There were no means of sanction besides a scrutiny of the national reports and a follow-up leading to positive or negative comments. Without doubt this made it possible for the member states to interpret the recommendations in various ways – which they often made the most of. The recommendations were often vague, and in national reports a flattering description could be given which included exaggeration, or failings could be toned down or even omitted.

Whether OMC has been a success or not has been animatedly discussed in recent years (Zeitlin et al. 2006). There is no consensus on this issue. Some have argued to its merit that the Luxembourg strategy in particular was successful in creating consensus regarding the need for a labour market policy and more explicit employment goals. It has even been argued that the increase in employment in the first years of the twenty-first century (before the crisis in 2008) was due to the Luxembourg strategy. Others claim that the effects of the strategy on increased employment can be discounted and that soft policies create political opportunism: the member states pretend to implement all recommendations, but in real life they take the best plums and ignore the others. Moreover, the drawback is that the method allows countries to emphasize areas they are already good at and where there exists national acceptance, at the expense of other – but for the Community perhaps no less important – more controversial areas.

Another area that also has seen the development of intergovernmental cooperation rather than binding directives is monetary collaboration. The countries that introduced the Euro in January 1999 at the same time solemnly signed a pact on stability and economic growth that most observers agreed was necessary for the project's realization. Above all it was here prescribed that no single country's national deficit could exceed

60 per cent of gross domestic product (GDP). The inherent danger in countries that were extremely different in economic structure and other matters – that is, were not what economists called an 'optimal currency area' – was meant to be counteracted by this pact. The member states also promised transparency and openness towards each other. In retrospect, a 'soft' legislation did not succeed in preventing a number of countries from tampering with these rules as times got tough in the early twenty-first century. This also applied to large countries such as Germany and France. When these countries ignored the rules, why would smaller countries not do the same? Without getting into detail, this was one of the prime reasons behind the budget crisis, with ensuing cut backs that took place after the financial crash in 2008 and that even today is highly noticeable in Europe's economies (Magnusson and Stråth 2001).

Doubtlessly this development has also interfered with the possibility of maintaining and developing the Social Dialogue. When the member states are left to decide for themselves, it is less likely that they will be enthusiastic in streamlining their own labour market models with those of the others. A weaker Commission has also had difficulties in pushing the development of Social Dialogue and creating 'better conditions' for the parties to cooperate, as promised in the Amsterdam Treaty of 1997.

Second, the Social Dialogue has not been favoured by the general decline that the Social Partners have seen in the member countries, not least visible in declining membership particularly among the trade union organizations. For British trade unions, the EU – paradoxically enough, considering the large degree of EU scepticism among both British politicians and the general public – acted as a lifeline and power basis after their catastrophic decline in the 1980s. In countries where the so-called Ghent system does not exist (the Ghent system being the system whereby the labour unions administer unemployment benefit funds), the rate of unionization usually declines when unemployment rises. This has been the case during the latest crisis, with a few exceptions (as for instance in Spain, where union membership has slightly risen).

The declining rate of unionization is, however, not the result of the latest economic crisis. Not counting Spain, we have seen declining rates in the EU's member countries during the last 30 years. Also, in Spain the rise is modest: we are talking about a unionization rate of approximately 20 per cent. To some degree the change in unionization rate can be explained by general employment difficulties, but also by the restructuring that has taken place during several decades, from employment being dominated by industrial jobs, to the service sector dominated economy we have today. The rate of unionization is lower in the service sector, due both to tradition and to a larger proportion of smaller firms. The unions are present to a lesser extent in small firms, which lowers the rate of unionization. The transfer of public sector undertakings to private enterprises – a result of the so-called Cardiff process, which was launched in the mid-1990s and aimed to dismantle state monopolies particularly in energy and electricity, but also in postal services, railways and so on – has also contributed to lowering the rate of unionization. So has the increasing numbers of people in precarious or atypical employment. In Sweden the development has been similar, with a general declining trend, which was further accentuated in the rising costs of the unemployment benefit funds since 2007. In several of the new member states, such as the Baltic countries, the trend in growing labour movements has been halted. Declining unionization rates have led to a number of problems for the Social Dialogue. A changed balance of power makes it increasingly difficult to reach agreements, and it may cause problems for the implementation when this is to be done voluntarily. The legitimacy of the Social Dialogue may decrease, both if the organizations in themselves are regarded as less legitimate representatives since they only represent a small portion of the employees, and if the organizations cannot nationally implement the results obtained. It may also become harder for the trade union representatives to engage themselves at the EU level if membership is declining. The engagement is then perhaps directed primarily at national level.

Third, the extension of the EU to ever more countries over the last ten years has hardly benefited the Social Dialogue. There was a general enthusiasm when the EU in 2004 brought in ten new members and later an additional three (Magnusson et al. 2004). Without doubt this can be seen as a strengthening of the thought of a cohesive Europe. On the other hand, the experience of earlier expansion shows that processes to deepen the collaboration easily come to a halt when new members are accepted. This is perhaps not strange. If it was hard to reach agreements between 15 members it hardly got easier when the EU all at once increased to 25 member states. The new members also had some difficulties with the thought of strong Social Partners. Irrespective of the large differences in labour market models between the earlier 15 member states, they all had a tradition of free and democratic employers and trade unions. But in the former Eastern European countries the trade unions were part of the party apparatus and there were no independent employer organizations. Following the introduction of a market economy, free organizations have been established, but many are still weak and have low unionization rates. A lingering disbelief in trade unions is present in many places, sometimes combined with a new scepticism towards organized interests due to a strong belief in the functioning of the market economy.

The result is that in many cases there exist weak organizations with low unionization rates and limited resources, which makes participation in the Social Dialogue problematic. The EU finances the actual dialogue meetings, but nothing else (permanent offices etc.). The implementation, which to an increasing degree is entrusted to the labour market parties, also becomes hard when the parties are weak and in many cases lack legitimacy. This means that the employees in these countries can benefit from the results of the Social Dialogue to a far lesser degree than in the old member states.

Fourth, and finally, since autumn 2008 the world has been struggling to cope with an unusually deep and severe economic crisis. After 15 September 2008, when Henry Paulson, Minister of Finance in the Bush administration, allowed Lehman Brothers to go bankrupt, the financial sector almost ceased to function and was only saved because states put liquid capital into their banks. During 2009 the reaction came in the form of a substantial fall in the real economy. The following year it became evident that the capitalization of the banks, together with a drop in GDP and rising unemployment, had led to rising budget deficits in both the US and Europe (Shiller 2008; Krugman 2008).

It also became increasingly clear that some countries, especially the so-called PIGS countries in southern Europe (Portugal, Italy, Greece and Spain; sometimes PIIGS with the addition of Ireland), had amassed large deficits over a long period of time which were now becoming too much of a burden. This further deepened the problems. Within the monetary union, states like Greece and Italy had been borrowing money at low rates. This was because these loans were regarded as without risk – not least since the EU in the end was expected to pay the bill. This of course was not true as there are no mechanisms in place for an institution such as the European Central Bank (ECB) to function as a 'lender of last resort'. When a banking union and increased possibilities for the ECB to act are talked about today, it is the need for such security that is under discussion. It is however uncertain whether these proposals will be carried through, and they are met with scepticism from different directions. In any case, this issue transformed the financial crisis into one involving both the real economy and EU budgets. The result has been that many countries have worked to stabilize their finances at the same time as they do not have low rates as a tool to boost the economy. This has led to high unemployment and poor economic growth in Europe.

The consequences have also become significant at the political level. This applies to EU collaboration as well, which is our prime concern here. It is hardly an exaggeration to claim that new initiatives to develop European cooperation have been conspicuous by their absence over these last few years. An exception is the finance and banking sectors where it seems that greater cooperation is desired. Here there are signs of a return to an increased role for 'hard' legislation, for example in the form of the above-mentioned bank union. There is however vast disagreement as to how such a union should be constructed and financed. Some claim that such a union – in practice a fund to be used in crises – should be financed through common European taxes, while others strongly defend themselves against such a scenario. What role Brussels is to play in this as opposed to the member states is still unclear.

In other political areas initiatives have been rather absent, as said earlier. This is especially the case in the social area. Within the EU, the ETUC for one is deeply disappointed at the development, but the same also applies to the unions in many member states.

WHAT FUTURE?

Seen from Brussels' perspective, the importance of the Social Dialogue is still important. The question is, however, how much of this is mere lip service. According to the Lisbon Strategy agreed upon in 2000 the social parties were recognized as vital for the modernization of the European economy. The Lisbon Strategy was continued after 2010 with Europe 2020. Out of five goals outlined in the Europe 2020 strategy, three are about the Social Dialogue's areas of competence: employment, education and social participation. The remaining two are innovation and climate and energy. The EESC was entrusted with the task of establishing guidelines for how the social parties were to participate in the Europe 2020 strategy. Within the respective goals, seven main initiatives were established, of which one was an agenda for new competence and employment opportunities. The initiative thus broadened the goal to also comprise working conditions and job quality, job creation and flexicurity.

In 2004 came the report from the first five years of the Lisbon Strategy. The report had been worked on by a group led by former Dutch prime minister Wim Kok, and it consisted of politicians, researchers and representatives of the social parties, among them Wanja Lundby-Wedin, then Chair of the Swedish Trade Union Confederation, LO, and later (2007–2011) Chair of the ETUC. The group reached the conclusion that the reason for the failure of the Lisbon Strategy to make Europe competitive through sustainable economic growth, good jobs and greater social cohesion was due to a lack of political will and action. The social parties also needed to assume responsibility for the failure, and one means to come to terms with the labour market problems was to establish partnerships for growth and employment. Again, collaboration by the various parties was pointed to as an important solution to Europe's problems.

The Lisbon II Strategy from 2010 (Europe 2020) therefore contains clear indications of the importance of a social dialogue. The writings are however vague and mostly deal with flexicurity, which was the big in-word used in the strategic report of suggested measures put forward by the Commission when the Lisbon Strategy became the Lisbon Treaty in 2009. The enthusiasm from some of the unions in particular has been modest. Flexicurity, at least as seen in the developments of the last decade, in more atypical and insecure temporary employment, which has increased substantially in Europe, is something many unions are against. How an alternative measure should be created to gain the legitimacy of the European unions is something neither the Commission nor others involved have had much to say about during recent years. At the same time, employers are fairly passive – as usual – and pursue a wait-and-see policy, even if they show quite a lot of enthusiasm for the flexicurity concept – but then rather of the very sort the unions are sceptical of. The Social Dialogue, which at present is making no progress, has become the victim of this lessened legitimacy and wait-and-see attitude.

IS THERE A NEED FOR THE SOCIAL DIALOGUE?

From what can be seen today, there is reason to be pessimistic about the future of the Social Dialogue – at least in its present form. It is clear that its main successes have come about during periods when European cooperation in general has been deepened and steps have been taken towards increased supranationalism. The Social Dialogue can obviously not be left to evolve on its own, but needs political will to flourish. The shift during recent years towards increased intergovernmental cooperation has not been good for the development of the Social Dialogue. The member states have instead kept to national models for welfare, taxes and labour market, which OMC has also favoured.

At the same time the development is not unambiguous. In places where the social model has had difficulties at central level, cooperation between various national unions and employer organizations has been successful. This is not least the case in industry where parties in the metal and engineering industry continuously develop their collaboration. Actual collective agreements at branch level between different EU countries have perhaps not come thick and fast. Bilateral agreements of various sorts have however been reached which deal with wages and working conditions. A few steps are being taken towards a more cohesive labour market in EU. The development is slow and we should not exaggerate what has been achieved so far. In many cases implementation of the agreements is lacking and the gaps between sectors is large.

Considering cooperation seems to be developing mainly at the industry and branch levels, and combined with the increased difficulties experienced at central level, one can wonder whether there is any need for a social dialogue which is pursued at central level by the EU. Has the Social Dialogue had its day?

Again, the answer depends on what one wishes for in terms of EU cooperation. If the aim is increased federalism and a deepened collaboration, a harmonization of the social institutions in the different member states is necessary. Something of that sort demands a social dialogue between those that are concerned – the citizens in the member states but also the social parties that make up the various national systems of labour relations. Such a dialogue cannot be held at the sector level but has to be held at the central level. At the same time much has happened since the end of the 1990s. It is an obvious problem that unions and employers within the EU have been weakened in most countries over the last twenty years. This weakening is a result of the EU's extension eastwards, where the new countries lack well-developed parties, as well as a loss of members in almost all EU countries. Besides a strong will on the part of the EU's institutions, strong social parties are needed to establish a social dialogue.

On the other hand, if one considers the EU's future more in terms of international cooperation – and not necessarily in terms of a deeper and more harmonized social area for instance – it may seem less important to push for a renewed and strong social dialogue. Cooperation between the social parties could remain at current levels: at industry and branch level; but the earlier mentioned reservations with regard to the strength and representativeness of the parties at branch level would still apply. To hurry a harmonization of rules and conditions in the social area and on the labour market is hardly something one wishes for in the first place.

For the time being enthusiasm is sparse for a development towards more federalism (perhaps with the exception of the finance sector). Many EU countries have a growing share of Eurosceptics in their electorates, and these would rather see an exit from the EU than increased federalism. The election of Jean-Claude Juncker as the new Chair of the Commission could perhaps be looked upon as a move – albeit small – in a federal direction. At the same time it is clear that new questions arise which demand the participation of many more participants than before – single companies, non-governmental organizations (NGOs) but also the social parties – maybe in the form a reformed social dialogue that concerns social problems of different sorts but where the solution ought to lie in increased cooperation within the EU rather than increased nationalism.

THE SOCIAL DIALOGUE AS A PATH TO COHESION WITHIN THE EU

Social dialogue can provide a path to cohesion within the EU by promoting consensus and participation. Through dialogue, more people would be able to influence the EU and consider it a common project. This is particularly important from three perspectives, as outlined below.

First, from a long-term perspective, what is at stake is the legitimacy of the whole EU project and its support among the citizens. After Lisbon 2000 many claim that Europe has developed in a direction which favours employers and the wealthy as opposed to the less well-to-do employees. Many argue that the gap is widening and that Europe is being pulled apart. The earlier proud declarations of a 'social Europe' are no longer to be heard. The halted Social Dialogue strengthens the view that there is an imbalance between labour and capital in the EU.

Second, a number of other problems are also building up which undoubtedly demand an increased dialogue, and where the European Social Partners can play an important role. When employment is on the rise in most EU countries but unevenly, there is a need for a discussion of increased mobility of employees between countries. Here we see that the development in many countries goes in the opposite direction. In many places demands are being made for decreasing rather than increasing mobility within Europe. Increased mobility undoubtedly demands harmonization, not least of retirement and social insurance systems. An increased dialogue is also required to manage increasing migration from countries outside of Europe. Today, xenophobia and hostility towards foreigners thrive in Europe. Many wish to fence off the labour market from persons coming from outside of Europe. This is a worrisome development that calls for more cooperation and dialogue within the EU.

Finally, it is important to point out a factor that will affect most countries of the world in the long run, but affects Europe in the short run as well: the ageing society. Today, we see a clear development towards a situation where ever fewer persons support an ever increasing share of the population. The so-called dependency ratio is steadily increasing. This undoubtedly puts pressure on Europe's welfare systems. The remedy may be for us to work longer or to increase immigration. It would be a clear advantage if EU member states had the possibility to cooperate in the search for solutions. Every solution in its turn demands legitimacy, and this could be achieved by means of a dialogue where large parts of society feel that they have the opportunity to have their say. Here, too, is an argument for a continued social dialogue in Europe.

REFERENCES

Branch, Ann (2005), 'The evolution of the European social dialogue towards greater autonomy: challenges and potential benefits', *International Journal of Comparative Labour Law* 21(2): 321–346.

Bruun, Niklas, Klaus Lörcher and Isabelle Schömann (2012), *The Lisbon Treaty and Social Europe*. Brussels: ETUI.

Dölvik, Jon Erik (1997), *Redrawing Boundaries of Solidarity. ETUC, Social Dialogue and the Europeanisation of Trade Unions in the 1990s*. FAFO report no. 238. Available at http://www.fafo.no/index.php/en/publications/fafo-reports/item/redrawing-boundaries-of-solidarity.

Dufresne, Anne, Christophe Degryse and Philippe Pochet (eds) (2006), *The European Sectoral Social Dialogue: Actors, Developments and Challenges*. Brussels: PIE Lang.

Krugman, Paul (2008), *The Return of Depression Economics*, 2nd edition. London: Penguin Books.

Magnusson, Lars (2004), 'A political economy for Europe', in: *Markets and Embeddedness: Essays in Honour of Ulf Olsson*. Publications of the Department of Economic History, Göteborg University, no. 21.

Magnusson, Lars and Bo Stråth (eds) (2001), *From the Werner Plan to EMU*. Brussels: PIE Lang.

Magnusson, Lars, Celine Lafoucriere and Bela Galgoczi (eds) (2004), *The Enlargement of Social Europe*. Brussels: ETUI.

Mailand, Mikkel and Jesper Due (2004), 'Social dialogue in Central and Eastern Europe: present state and future development', *European Journal of Industrial Relations* 10(2): 179–198.

Marlier, Eric and David Natali (eds) (2010), *Europe 2020: Towards a More Social EU?* Brussels: PIE Lang.

Rodrigues, Maria João (2004), *European Policies for a Knowledge Economy*. Cheltenham, UK and Northampton, MA, USA: Edward Elgar Publishing.

Shiller, Robert J. (2008), *The Subprime Solution*. Princeton, NJ: Princeton University Press.

Streeck, Wolfgang (1994), 'European social policy after Maastricht: the Social Dialogue and subsidiarity', *Economic and Industrial Democracy* 15(1): 151–177.

Zeitlin, Jonathan and Philippe Pochet with Lars Magnusson (eds) (2006), *The Open Method of Co-ordination in Action. The European Employment and Social Inclusion Strategies*. Brussels: PIE Lang.

7. Youth, labour law, and European economic crisis*

Jenny Julén Votinius

INTRODUCTION

In the aftermath of the global financial crisis of 2008 and the ensuing euro crisis, unemployment among young people rose rapidly in the European Union (EU). By 2013, youth unemployment had reached alarmingly high levels in many member states. Moreover, large numbers of jobless youth were not engaged in any other type of occupation either, such as education or training. Youth unemployment has slowly fallen from 2014 onwards, but it remains at a high level. In many member states, the economic recovery has been too weak to bring youth unemployment back down to the levels seen before the financial crisis (OECD, 2017). The problem is particularly severe in the countries hardest hit by the crisis, such as Spain, Greece, Croatia, and Italy; but it is in no way limited to those countries. In Belgium and France, for example, many young people are out of work. One striking feature of youth unemployment in the EU is its variation from country to country. In Greece, more than half of all employable persons aged 15–24 were jobless in 2015; in Germany, the figure was one in 15 (Eurostat, 2016).

Youth unemployment figures centrally in the debate on the prosperity gap in Europe. Not only do the member states suffering the most economically also have the highest levels of youth unemployment; equally important is the rapidly widening prosperity gap between the different generations in the Union. When young people lack access to the labour market on the same terms as their elders, significant prosperity gaps arise. Young people without work have a weak economic position; they find it hard to obtain housing and to establish an adult life; and they enjoy but limited opportunities to save or invest. A delayed career start also leads to weaker private finances over the long run, due to the lower lifetime earnings and lower pensions that it entails.

Finding strategies to fight youth unemployment is a high priority for the Union. In this chapter, I focus on the way in which youth unemployment has been dealt with in Europe during the years of economic crisis, and I consider what can be done to close the prosperity gap that is now appearing between the generations. I describe and analyse EU policies to curb youth unemployment in light of the Europe 2020 growth strategy, the economic crisis, and the increased emphasis on fundamental social rights. In order to explore these questions in greater detail, moreover, I look at national labour-law reforms aimed at facilitating labour-market entry for young people specifically.

In this discussion, the economic crisis constitutes an important background factor. The strained budgetary situation has had significant implications for national labour law in many EU member states, particularly in countries on the receiving end of International Monetary Fund (IMF)–EU bailouts. The labour-market reforms introduced as a result of these bailouts have involved a far-reaching reassessment of accepted ideas about reasonable levels of job security, about the pain threshold for cuts in public spending, and about the distribution of responsibility and risk between employees and employers (Barnard, 2012; Koukiadaki and Kretsos, 2012; Clauwaert and Schömann, 2013; Moreira et al., 2015). Austerity measures introduced in the wake of the crisis have created a profound need for policies that take a holistic approach to the problem of young people's vulnerability in the labour market.

In 2012 and 2013, when youth unemployment peaked in the EU, the European Commission took a number of initiatives. Most important among them were the 'Youth Opportunities Initiative', the 'Youth Employment Initiative', and the 'Youth Guarantee', adopted in December 2012, March 2013, and April 2013 respectively. For their part the member states introduced various measures at the national level, including educational programmes, apprentice systems, and subsidies to employers. Given the theme of this volume – the prosperity gap – it is of particular interest that some member states have decided to address youth unemployment by adopting legislative reforms weakening employment protection specifically for young employees (a group which, in Spain for example, is defined as all employees under 30 or sometimes 35). Reforms of this kind have exacerbated the prosperity gap between generations, since they mean that younger employees receive lower salaries and enjoy less job security than their older counterparts.

While youth unemployment in Europe increased dramatically in the wake of the crisis, the vulnerability of young people in the labour market can only be partly explained by economic hard times. In the EU, as in many other regions, unemployment has always been higher among youth than among workers on average. Young people typically have a weaker status in working life, due to an actual or presumed lack of knowledge and experience, and also as a consequence of the role that age plays as a basis for social hierarchy. Moreover, the vulnerability of young people – like that of other weaker groups in society – is intensified by the general trend towards a more market-oriented approach to employment policy, labour law, and welfare that has long characterized the debate in Europe. This market-oriented approach has been operationalized in the deregulation of employment protection, as a stage in the introduction of *flexicurity*. The dire economic situation in many EU member states has helped to impart greater legitimacy to deregulatory policies of this kind. The shift of focus characterizing reforms in labour law and social security in crisis countries – from job security and employees' rights to austerity measures and increased individual responsibility – can thus be found in some degree throughout the EU, even in countries that have not been hit very hard by the economic crisis.

This chapter is structured as follows. In the first section, I describe the group of young workers in the Union today. In addition, I examine certain traits of these employees – and assumptions held about them – which serve in various ways to worsen the vulnerability of young people in the labour market, and which thereby help to increase the intergenerational prosperity gap. In the next section, I describe the broader employment-policy context in which the issue of youth unemployment is handled at the EU level. My focus here is on the labour-law aspects of employment policy, especially those relating to the debate on the flexibilization of working life. Then, in the section after that, I discuss the status and treatment of young people in EU employment policy. (NB: the concepts of employment policy and of labour-market policy are used interchangeably in this chapter.) I explore how young employees have become an increasingly visible and delimited target group for EU employment policy, and how the focus in this area has shifted from youth policy to employment policy. The emphasis here is on the concrete initiatives taken in recent years at the Union level in the fight against youth unemployment. The next section discusses certain labour-law reforms that have been introduced at the national level, with an eye to improving young people's access to the labour market. The focus here is on reforms that worsen working conditions for young employees – above all in connection with wage levels and job protection – in order to make young job-seekers more attractive in the labour market. The section that follows thereupon ties the discussion to the national reforms described earlier. I consider how special and disadvantageous terms of employment for young people can be understood (and questioned) from the perspective of fund-mental social rights – especially in view of the EU Court's stance against age discrimination. In the last section of the chapter, finally, I look at the measures that will be needed to halt the increase in the generation gap that threatens to follow from high unemployment among European youth.

YOUNG PEOPLE – A VULNERABLE GROUP IN THE LABOUR MARKET

In 2013, youth unemployment rates in the EU peaked. Although the numbers have seen a modest decrease since then, they are still high in many countries. They range from under 7 per cent in Germany to almost 50 per cent in Greece and Spain. The average for the Eurozone is just above 21 per cent; that for the EU as whole is just below 19 per cent. In six EU member states, the average is close to or exceeds 30 per cent. (Figures are for January 2017, from Eurostat data.)

In addition, high youth unemployment figures are just *one* expression for the special vulnerablity of young people in the labour market. Among the group of young Europeans actually in work, many hold poor-quality jobs with little security. For example, almost 44 per cent of young employees in the EU held fixed-term contracts in 2015, compared with only 11 per cent of the entire workforce. A young employee is thus four times as likely to have a fixed-term job as the average employee. It is also increasingly common for young employees – especially young women – to work part-time (European Commission, 2016b).

In this context, it should be noted that a policy which fastens solely on age has always been considered a blunt tool in the search for ways to raise youth employment levels. There are far-reaching differences between different groups of young people. For a long time, women have been clearly overrepresented among jobless youth in the EU. It soon became clear, however, that young men were being hit harder by the financial crisis. Another important factor is education. Young people who have finished no more than their compulsory schooling are among those who have struggled the most in the labour market during the crisis. It is thus an important problem that 11 per cent of the EU's young people leave the educational system having completed at most a lower secondary education. The national numbers here range from less than 3 per cent in Croatia to 20 per cent in Spain (Eurostat, 2016). However, the financial crisis has also brought reduced opportunities for highly qualified young people – not only by compelling such persons to take unqualified work, but also by creating an artificially high threshold for qualification to entry-level positions. Persons with low qualifications, it has often been pointed out, face difficulties in entering the labour market which are rooted at least partly in their lack of the right qualifications. Yet highly educated youth face the same problem. In many cases their qualifications, while high, are not in demand in the labour market (European Commission, 2012a). A further problem is that youth unemployment rates in most EU countries are higher for foreign-born young people. Other important aspects here include social status and personal situation, for example in terms of family responsibilities, access to housing, and state of health.

The importance of providing a detailed picture of young people, in terms of their varying position in the labour market, is well established in social-science and economics research. Legislation intended to promote youth employment does not usually focus on specific subgroups, even if this does happen from time to time. For example, the French law on work for the future – *emploi d'avenir*, passed in 2012 – emphasizes the importance of supporting young people with low educational levels in particular (law 2012-1189 of 26 October 2012). In this regard, however, the French legislation is an exception to the rule. The laws of most EU member states mention only age. Yet, notwithstanding its lack of precision, this broad definition of the target group has worked up to this point, at least on a political level. Furthermore, while a more nuanced approach would have been more suitable, this rough definition does correspond fairly well to reality: during the financial crisis, high levels of unemployment have affected nearly all groups of young people.

Young workers typically lack much experience of working life or of concrete work tasks, just as their life experience in general is limited. This normally results in a weaker position in working life. However, this weaker status reflects the expectations of young people held by the established older generation, as well as society's understanding of what young people are, what they do, and in what social contexts they belong. In research on ageism – that is, prejudices or preconceived notions based on a person's age – significant concrete evidence has been found for how age-related perceptions are used to justify less advantageous treatment of young persons. For example, young people are not always considered to have the same needs as older people, because they are not yet fully engaged in adult life. In addition, disadvantages for young people are often seen as justified, because young people will eventually grow older and then receive the same rights as the rest of the adult population (Loretto et al., 2000; Snape and Redman, 2003). The perception of younger people as having fewer needs or otherwise being less deserving than their older counterparts finds expression in the notion that employment conditions need not meet as stringent requirements for young people as for their elders (cf. Knijn, 2012).

Both of these aspects of the situation of young workers – both their young age as such and the view that they can fairly be offered less advantageous terms of employment – contribute to their vulnerability in the labour market. Against this background, labour-market measures and labour law have great potential to work as a counterweight, by serving as a protective barrier for young people. Still it is clear that, depending on their specific nature, labour-market measures and labour law can have the opposite effect – increasing youth vulnerability and thus worsening the gap between generations. This double-edged sword, in terms of the effects on young workers, is inherent in the employment policies that the EU has promoted over the past 20 years, which have sought to bring about increased flexibilization in working life.

THE EMPLOYMENT-POLICY CONTEXT: FLEXIBILIZATION AND FLEXICURITY

EU employment policy is based on continuous cooperation between the Commission and the member states. The Commission sets guidelines for employment policy and recommends certain labour-market measures, which the member states are then expected to implement in their national action plans. Each year, moreover, the member states submit a progress report to the Commission. This approach is called the open method of coordination (for more on this method see, among others, Armstrong, 2010).

Ever since its adoption in 1997, the European employment strategy has rested on the assumption that increased flexibility in the labour market is necessary to stave off unemployment, to meet global structural changes, and to ensure a proper balance between labour supply and demand. The employment strategy was founded on four pillars: employability, entrepreneurship, adaptability, and equal opportunity (Biagi, 2000; Goetschy, 2001; Ashiagbor, 2005). The first two pillars focused on ensuring that tax frameworks and educational systems serve to promote employment, as well as on improving the business climate by making it easier to start and run a business. Equal opportunity initially was mainly a matter of improving the position of women in the labour market and of increasing people's opportunities to combine family duties and work. For the theme of this chapter, the adaptability pillar is of particular interest. Improved adaptability, often expressed as flexibility, is a key concept in employment policy at the Union level, where an important goal has been to meet the demand for labour in a rapidly changing labour market.

Since increased flexibility normally means reduced employment protection, a one-sided focus on flexibility will not only be difficult to justify; it can also be expected to lead to greater social exclusion over the long term. The notion of flexicurity, however, offers a way out of this seemingly irresolvable dilemma (Wilthagen, 2002; European Commission, 2006).

In the EU context, flexicurity contains four components (European Commission, 2007):

- Flexible and reliable employment agreements
- Comprehensive strategies for lifelong learning
- Effective active labour-market policies
- Modern social-security systems that provide adequate compensation during periods of unemployment.

Flexicurity strives to create a balance between employers' need for flexible labour and employees' need for security. This balance is achieved by locating part of the employee's security outside the employment relationship. Traditionally, employee security in working life and in the labour market has been ensured through collective bargaining and extensive labour legislation. In a labour market increasingly characterized by flexicurity, society shoulders a greater responsibility for economic security on the one hand, while emphasizing the employee's individual responsibility on the other.

When implementing flexicurity strategies, the legislator increases flexibility in the employment relationship by moving away from employment-protection legislation. Instead, the employee is to be protected by relevant social policies providing income support in times of temporary unemployment; and the employee is to increase his or her value in the labour market by engaging in lifelong learning and taking advantage of effective active labour-market measures. Ensuring that flexicurity provides the intended advantages requires that the active participation of the social partners be emphasized. A less clearly expressed but nonetheless obvious feature of the flexicurity approach is that it entails expansion of the employee's own responsibility to remain employable – for example by choosing the right education, acquiring the right experience, adapting to labour-market requirements, and continuing training and learning (Julén Votinius, 2012).

In the mid-2000s, the measures stemming from the European employment strategy became more and more an express strategy of encouraging flexicurity, with the Netherlands and Denmark serving as forerunners. It is primarily up to the individual member states to determine how flexicurity shall be achieved in their case. However, a set of common principles was adopted in 2007 by the Council of Europe. In connection with this, ideas were also advanced concerning ways to achieve flexicurity, taking into account the special circumstances faced by different categories of member states. Today flexicurity measures are a central method for achieving the goals set out in the Europe 2020 strategy: employment, growth, and social participation. These measures also make up much of European employment policy and of the employment guidelines.

The flexicurity model has not escaped criticism, however. One important reason for this is that flexicurity is a visionary model for how a well-functioning labour market should be designed. This visionary model is based on the existence of an extensive and well-developed social safety net – one far more extensive than has ever existed in many member states. In the actual implementation of flexicurity in the member states, the expansion of the social safety net has taken a back seat, rarely being realized to the degree required by the model (Heyes, 2011; Laulom et al., 2012). As a result, the politically sanctioned concept of flexicurity has been used to describe what in reality has consisted largely of flexibilization, with the element of security being very limited or even completely absent. In this context, it has been suggested that an accurate term would be 'flexiprecarity' (López et al., 2014) or 'flexinsecurity' (Suárez Corujo, 2014).

An important part of the criticism thus focuses on the failure to convert theory into functioning practice. It is also frequently noted that these failures have led to a form of societal development more in line with capitalist ideology. Connected to this criticism are arguments based on the observation that trade unions have become increasingly unwilling to accept the seemingly unceasing pursuit of flexibilization through flexicurity (see also Chapter 6 by Lars Magnusson and Sofia Murhem in this book). As it is quite urgent that the social partners cooperate in implementing flexicurity, it is indeed a serious state of affairs when employee representatives wish to abandon the model and to return to previous frameworks (Auer, 2010).

Yet another criticism is that the flexicurity model has not survived the stresses placed on it by the financial crisis. During the crisis, unemployment increased faster in some countries with a high degree of flexicurity (such as Denmark and Sweden) than, for example, in Germany, where employment protection is essentially unchanged (Tangian, 2010a and 2010b; Capaldo and Izurieta, 2013). Nevertheless, there are those who support the opposing view – that well-implemented flexicurity mitigates the societal effects of financial downturns (Caspar et al., 2012; Chenic, 2012).

In my own research, I too have criticized the concept of flexicurity. I consider it instrumentalist and simplistic, since it defines security only in terms of compensation for income loss and support for competence development (Julén Votinius, 2014). The traditional protection for employees in an employment relationship cannot be neatly replaced with protection provided through an expanded social-security system. It is true that such a system can compensate for income loss; however, traditional legal employment protection has more functions than just providing economic security. For example, employment protection offers security in terms of occupational identity and one's relationship with colleagues. Even more important, from a structural perspective, is the function of labour law to intervene and in some degree even out the power imbalance that exists in the employment relationship, and which manifests itself in the managerial prerogative. This makes the role of labour law in ensuring self-determination, dignity, and integrity in the employment relationship essential for employees.

If flexibility in working life is increased through labour-law deregulation and reinforced managerial rights, then the employer's power increases. This means that the employee's influence diminishes in corresponding measure. A loss of security for the employee in the employment relationship, as a consequence of increased flexibility in working life, cannot be mitigated through more generous social-security systems designed to compensate for income loss upon dismissal. The structural changes imposed on everyday workplace relations by labour-law deregulation – and the subsequent loss of security – disappear from view in an analysis based on the concept of flexicurity.

As we shall see in the following, an important assumption in the EU's work to reduce youth unemployment is that a more flexible market, primarily with less stringent employment protection, will increase young people's opportunities for work. Opinion is divided as to whether flexibilization of working life really has led to more work opportunities for young people. Weakening employment protection probably makes it easier for new workers – primarily young people – to enter the labour market, but researchers in the field are not in agreement on this effect (Skedinger, 2011). At the same time, it is clear that flexibilization strategies have resulted in a greater number of jobs characterized by precarity and/or bad working conditions, and that young people are overrepresented among those performing such work.

While many young people in Europe have succeeded in finding work despite high youth unemployment, they work under significantly worse and less secure conditions than older workers, exacerbating the prosperity gap between generations. Therefore, in any discussion of the intergenerational prosperity gap, it is essential that the spotlight be put on the deregulation of labour legislation which has taken place in many EU member states. It is also important to note that this trend has accelerated during the economic crisis. In some countries, such as Greece and Portugal, the deregulation has been carried out to meet IMF requirements for emergency loans. It is against this background that efforts by the Union and the member states to reduce youth unemployment must be understood.

The following section describes how the high youth unemployment of the crisis years was handled at the EU level. I then discuss certain labour-law reforms at the national level, which seek to increase youth employment by limiting the rights of young employees.

THE EU: FROM YOUTH STRATEGIES TO STRATEGIES FOR YOUTH EMPLOYMENT

Just before the summit of the Council of Europe in June 2013, the Commission adopted a document entitled 'Working Together for Europe's Young People: A Call to Action on Youth Unemployment'. This document depicted overcoming youth unemployment as a top priority for the EU. The Commission's document is but one of many steps in a recent trend, whereby the status of young people in the labour market has drawn increased attention. This process began more than 20 years ago, when various proposals from the 1980s for initiatives and programmes for youth were replaced with a more unified approach to youth strategies within the EU. A new structure for cooperation was presented in 2001, in the Commission's white paper 'A New Impetus for European Youth'. The cooperative framework was based on the open method of coordination with respect to matters specifically for young people, and on the view that young people should be taken more into account in political programmes which are not necessarily directed specifically at youth. Where the latter was concerned, one of the most important measures was to unite the general strategies for integrating young people into society with the EU's general employment policy.

This ambition was followed up in connection with the attempt made by European leaders in 2005 to reinvigorate the Lisbon strategy. It was at this point that the Council adopted, among other measures, the 'European Youth Pact'. The Pact was designed to achieve the goals of the Lisbon strategy, which identified the potential of young people as one of the most important factors for ensuring that growth is maintained and is sustainable. The Pact dealt with youth issues such as employment, education, and the combination of work with family life. It stated that actions for these three areas should be taken within the framework for the European employment strategy, through its integrated guidelines for growth and employment and its strategy for social participation.

These days, the matter of youth employment has been distinguished from the broader range of young people's issues, and made the object of special attention. Now it mainly forms part of EU employment policy, where it holds a prominent position. The Youth Pact has been integrated into the Union's ten-year strategy for growth, known as Europe 2020. This integration has mainly been carried out through the 2020 strategy's two so-called flagship initiatives: 'Youth on the Move' and 'An Agenda for New Skills and Jobs'.

In late 2011, in an effort to implement these youth-oriented initiatives and to address the dramatically higher unemployment rates among young people, the Commission presented the 'Youth Opportunities Initiative'. This document proposed a number of actions at both national and EU levels to counteract the high levels of youth unemployment. The Commission made clear that, even if the ultimate responsibility for acting to reduce youth unemployment and for taking the most important measures in this area lies with the member states, the latter can nevertheless receive EU-level support – in two main ways. First, the growth, employment, and youth policies of the Europe 2020 strategy make it possible for the Commission to review, evaluate, and coordinate national measures and results, in accordance with the open method of coordination. The Commission can thus emphasize the issues that must be prioritized from an EU perspective, and propose actions in accordance with best practice. Second, the EU can provide economic support to national and cross-border efforts according to agreed-upon priorities. This can be arranged through the European Social Fund and a range of other programmes.

In view of the very serious situation, the initiative called upon the member states to act immediately in four main areas: to prevent students from leaving school early; to encourage youth to acquire skills relevant for the labour market; to support first-time job experience and training at the workplace; and to help young people obtain their first job. The foremost goal of the initiative, in addition to providing young people with relevant competence and work experience, was to increase young people's access to the labour market. In this connection, the initiative urged that member states take into account that excessively high non-wage labour costs – that is, social-security contributions and other salary-based costs – can make employers less willing to hire newcomers to the labour market. In particular, the Commission stressed, the member states must ensure that employment contracts are made more flexible, that persons who remain outside the labour market are protected, and that employment-protection legislation is reformed in accordance with existing recommendations.

Following on the 'Youth Opportunities Initiative', the Commission proposed a number of other measures as well. At the end of 2012, it introduced the 'EU Youth Employment Package', which expanded on the measures for young people that had been presented in a collection of political documents known as the 'Employment Package'. The Youth Employment Package called for action to increase the number and quality of apprentice and training programmes. It also introduced a youth guarantee, meaning that member states would commit themselves to helping each young person find employment or an apprenticeship/training position within four months. Soon after that, the 'Youth Employment Initiative' was adopted. It primarily addressed the predicament facing the vulnerable young people known as NEETs (not in education, employment, or training), and it was specifically aimed at regions where youth unemployment exceeded 25 per cent.

In June 2013, the Commission presented 'Working Together for Europe's Young People: A Call to Action on Youth Unemployment'. Reducing youth unemployment, this document declared, is a top priority for the EU. Taking a holistic approach to the problem rather than analysing the various measures separately, it treated all aspects of youth unemployment and the fight against it together: the youth guarantee; apprentice and training programmes; movement of the workforce within the EU; and – of greatest interest for our purposes here – measures to support job creation and to give employers incentives to hire young people. With regard to this particular area, the document repeated the calls to action made in the 2011 Youth Initiative, which had proclaimed the need for member states to reduce non-wage labour costs, and not least to reform legislation on job protection.

In 2016, the Commission presented the results of an investigation following up on the Youth Guarantee and the Youth Employment Initiative (European Commission, 2016a). It showed that around nine million young persons in the EU had at some point taken up the offer of a job or an apprenticeship/training position, and that the Youth Guarantee had been backed up by policy actions on education and apprenticeships. The very high levels of youth unemployment had slowly fallen in the Union and in most member states, and there was also a slight drop in the number of NEETs. The Commission recognized that the situation of young people is particularly sensitive to shifting macroeconomic conditions, and it found that the structural reforms supported by the Youth Guarantee had been a contributing factor to the fall in youth unemployment. The Commission therefore stressed the need for a continued political commitment to the Youth Guarantee, and it proposed to supplement the original appropriation with further financial support for the 2017–2020 period. It is clear that policies associated with the Youth Guarantee have had a visible impact in the member states, and that they have had some positive effects. On the other hand, social scientists have pointed to evidence from Spain that the Youth Guarantee does not in fact lead to the creation of new quality jobs. Instead it mainly redistributes existing employment, and so risks actually exacerbating precarity over the long run (Cabasés Piqué et al., 2016).

NATIONAL LABOUR-LAW REFORMS: REDUCING YOUNG WORKERS' SECURITY

Even if youth employment is an area where the EU carries out an active policy, the member states have the chief responsibility for determining the measures required to reduce youth unemployment, and for implementing EU employment policy at the national level. As we have seen, youth unemployment rates vary considerably among the member states. Differences can also be found in the causes of youth unemployment, and in how the individual countries deal with the problem.

Factors such as insufficient competence, precarious employment, early departure from school, and a limited availability of apprenticeships can probably be found in all member states. They are present, however, to varying degrees, depending on labour legislation, labour-market structure, educational systems, and opportunities for education in the workplace. The member states have implemented various measures to promote youth employment, in some cases through legislation, in others through collective regulation and labour-market programmes. In general, national measures have mainly had the goal of introducing workplace learning, developing educational systems, and making young people more attractive in the labour market. In a move to promote young people as good potential employees, many member states – among them Bulgaria, France, and Sweden – have introduced subsidies and tax relief for businesses that employ young people, for example in the form of subsidies that cover the social-security contributions required of employers. However, some countries have chosen another (or an additional) method: introducing special labour-law reforms which limit employee rights, especially for younger workers.

Once again it is important to emphasize just how much the member states differ in terms of the regulation of working life. The role of the social partners, the consequences of the financial crisis, and the importance of constitutional aspects such as the guarantee of basic rights are just a few of all the phenomena shaping national labour legislation. Even with this in mind, however, we can identify some general trends in national regulations which result in worse employment conditions for younger workers, and which have been adopted in an effort to promote youth employment. These labour-law reforms tend to reduce security for young people in two main areas: wages and employment protection.

Whereas the EU documents emphasize the importance of reducing *non-wage* labour costs in order to give youth access to the labour market, some national measures stress the importance of holding down youth wages as such. Wage levels for young people have fallen in some countries during the crisis, as a result of changes in regulations governing minimum wages. This has been the method of choice in, for example, Greece and the UK – countries which have reduced the minimum wage for younger workers to a level lower than that which applies for the rest of the working population. To comply with the EU's adjustment programme for Greece and to act quickly to counteract high unemployment, the Greek parliament enacted legislation (laws 3845/2010 and 4046/2012) reducing wage levels below what had been agreed upon previously in national collective agreements. The wage cut was comprehensive, but much more extensive for young employees. In the private sector, wages were cut by 22 per cent on average, while wages for employees under 25 were reduced by 32 per cent. This targeted wage cut for persons under the age of 25 – to a level known as the subminimum wage – has been declared to be in conflict with the Charter of Fundamental Rights of the European Union (more on this below). However, the national legislation remains in force. Of all EU countries, Greece has the highest number of workers receiving a minimum wage. It bears noting that the Greek wage cut also led to a reduction in benefits which are tied to national minimum-wage levels, such as apprentice wages and unemployment-insurance benefits. In the UK, too, gaps in this area have increased: the minimum wage for persons under 20 has remained unchanged through several years of the crisis, in contrast to that for adults, which has been raised (Low Pay Commission, 2013).

It is not unusual to see salary systems where principles such as seniority (often called LIFO – last in, first out) are recognized, or where a lack of work experience is reflected in salary levels. Nor does this have anything to do with the prevailing financial crisis. On the contrary, most countries in Europe with minimum wages have also introduced special wages for young people. However, the labour-law reforms discussed here are not about youth wages as such; they are about *cuts* in wages, imposed by various methods with one common denominator: they affect only or mostly younger workers. In an economic slump, these cuts hit harder in some member states than in others. Without a doubt, each new reduction of youth wages in countries where the general wage level has already been frozen or reduced – such as Greece, Spain, Cyprus, or Portugal – means that young people are working for very low pay.

In an effort to stimulate youth employment during the crisis, new forms of employment have been introduced, designed especially for young people. Many of these entail lower wages, and some also involve weaker job protection. The normal arrangement here is for a fixed-term employment agreement, which can often be extended and which tends to include long periods of probationary employment. In cases where the position is supposed to include training, the mechanisms for monitoring are at times plainly deficient, and clear legal requirements are lacking. This trend towards new forms of employment is a distinct indicator that a new class of workers is emerging in the European labour market – a group in a very vulnerable situation, made up of younger workers who to varying degrees have been deprived of their basic security in the employment relationship.

Examples of these fixed-term and poorly paid new jobs, designed to be filled by persons below a certain age, can be found in countries such as Spain. Persons under 30 can be employed through a *Contrato de Trabajo en Prácticas*, with a salary 40 per cent below the minimum wage for the first year, and 25 per cent below the minimum wage for the second year. A *Contrato Emprendedores*, for persons between 16 and 30, provides probationary employment for one year. Among Organisation for Economic Co-operation and Development (OECD) countries with continental European legal systems, no other country stipulates such a long probationary period. In the Netherlands, fixed-term contracts were previously allowed for longer periods in the case of workers under 27 years of age. This was a time-limited regulation, and it could have been extended in 2012. It was not extended, however, because it was assumed to come into conflict with the prohibition against age discrimination.

Some of the new employment forms which have arisen during the crisis years are intended to be different from other time-limited types, in that they include some kind of training. Apprentice or trainee positions have become a common way to promote youth employment in Europe. The apprentice system has been very successful in some countries. The German system is the best known, and it has been used as a model by many strategists, including at the EU level (Bosch, 2011; European Commission, 2012a and 2013; Brenke et al., 2013; Garz, 2013). Nevertheless, apprentice or trainee programmes should be designed with care, as such systems in some other countries have been shown to have serious negative effects for young employees, primarily because the training component of the programme has been badly underdeveloped in practice, or even essentially non-existent. Young people risk being exploited in such cases, because 'apprenticeship' can serve as window dressing for what really is cheap labour (European Commission, 2012b).

In 2010, Greece passed legislation on a one-year apprenticeship agreement, as a way of combatting youth unemployment during the crisis. This so-called youth agreement allowed employment at 80 per cent of the minimum wage, without employer social-security contributions and without the right to unemployment benefits at the conclusion of the period. However, the law completely lacked regulations for the training that is supposed to take place during the apprenticeship; for example, there were no demands on the trainer, no quality controls on the training provided, and no requirements as to the share of time spent on theoretical versus practical instruction. The Greek example is perhaps the most discouraging. As we shall see below, the law has been found to violate basic social rights; yet the legislation is still in force.

The misuse of apprenticeships and training programmes to acquire cheap labour has been criticized in many other member states, such as France, Great Britain, Italy, and Austria. In Sweden, a government inquiry in 2012 proposed that an *utbildningsanställning* (literally, a training employment or educational employment) be introduced for persons under the age of 23. A probationary period of 18 months would apply instead of the normal six, and during that time the employer would have the right to receive economic assistance from the state. According to the proposal, the training component would be designed by the employer, in consultation with the young person in question. No exact requirements would be made as to the scope or design of the training component; nor would this training be subject to review or inspection by public authorities. The proposal met with heavy criticism from the unions and others, and did not result in legislation.

It bears noting that none of the EU documents on youth employment that call for making job-protection legislation more flexible – such as the 'Youth Opportunities Initiative' or 'Working Together for Europe's Young People: A Call to Action on Youth Unemployment' – deals with employment protection for young people specifically. Rather, these documents give clear expression to the idea that flexible job-protection legislation leads in general to greater employment opportunities, by encouraging economic growth and contributing to increased mobility in the labour market. As we have seen, however, many national reforms introduced during the crisis years are based on the notion that youth employment can be furthered by limiting job protection for young people in particular.

ARE FUNDAMENTAL SOCIAL RIGHTS BEING PUT AT RISK?

In the past ten years, an increasingly rights-oriented view has gained ground in the Union and its member states. Some researchers call this a rights revolution (e.g., Lasser, 2009; Dawson et al., 2012). Not all scholars go this far, but it is clear that the legal discourse in Europe and the EU has come to focus strongly on rights.

One aspect of this trend is the increasing recognition of fundamental social rights (for more on the role of these rights in European integration, see Chapter 2 by Anna-Sara Lind in this book). In light of the ongoing crisis, the increasing influence of fundamental social rights is particularly interesting from a labour-law perspective. On a general level, this trend raises the question of whether a legal order based on fundamental social rights can withstand a dismantling of the social systems which have traditionally ensured a certain level of security in the employment relationship. Another question of particular interest for the discussion in this chapter is whether protection for fundamental social rights has the potential to slow down the expansion of the prosperity gap between generations in the EU.

Reforms involving the weakening of labour-law protections have been introduced in many European countries during the financial crisis, and they have been criticized for violating fundamental social rights. Cases arguing this point have been brought in national courts, as well as before the legal bodies of the International Labour Organization (ILO) and the Council of Europe. Statements from the ILO's Committee of Experts and recommendations from the Council of Europe's Social Committee are not binding, but they are usually adhered to by the member states. In a landmark decision from 2012, the Council of Europe's Social Committee found that the Greek apprentice agreements for persons aged 15–18 violated the European Social Charter, among other things in connection with the right to three weeks' paid holiday per year for persons under 18, and in regard to the effective exercise of the right to vocational training and social security (European Committee of Social Rights, Decision 66/2012 (23 May 2012) on the merits of collective Complaint No. 66/2011). Greece's sweeping cuts, especially in young people's minimum wage – resulting in subminimum pay for young workers – were found to be in breach of the right to a fair remuneration, as set out in Article 4.1 of the Social Charter, as well as in violation of the prohibition against discrimination enunciated in the Charter's preamble. The Committee declared that, while lower minimum wages for young people constituted special treatment on grounds of age, they could be justified if found to be proportional in relation to the legitimate purpose of promoting employment. But the wage cut in Greece could not be considered proportional. It was too extensive, and it applied to all workers under the age of 25. The Committee therefore found the measure to be discriminatory.

Notwithstanding the finding of the Social Committee, the subminimum wage for young workers still applies in Greece. The lack of action on the part of the Greek government is explained by reference to the commitments made in connection with Greece's bailout. It bears noting in this context that, on the basis of the Memorandum of Understanding annexed to the third bailout agreement, adopted in July 2015, a Committee of Independent Experts was established to review a number of labour-market practices in Greece – in connection with collective dismissal, industrial action, and collective bargaining – with the ultimate aim of bringing them into line with best practice in the EU. The Committee of Independent Experts published its report in September 2016. Regarding subminimum wages for young workers, the members of the Committee disagreed among themselves. One group on the Committee recommended that youth minimum wages be retained, and with the present age thresholds. The other group recommended that youth minimum wages be replaced by experience-based subminimum wages for a maximum of two years, followed by an evaluation. Negotiations between the Greek government and its creditors are still ongoing.

Labour-law reforms of this particular pattern – which seek to promote the employment of younger persons by restricting young workers' rights – are open to question in connection with many different fundamental social rights. In the case mentioned above, the issue was fair remuneration. Another and equally relevant matter is the right to protection against dismissal without just cause. Of particular importance here, however, is the fundamental right not to be discriminated against on grounds of age. In contrast with other rights, the right to protection against age discrimination is codified in the EU's secondary legislation – in Council Directive 2000/78/EC establishing a General Framework for Equal Treatment in Employment and Occupation (hereafter: the Framework Directive) – and it has been tested in several judgments by the EU Court. The right to protection against age discrimination has great significance for assessing labour-law reforms intended to combat youth unemployment, because it can be invoked in relation to all measures which limit the rights of younger employees.

The protection against age discrimination means that, in principle, inferior working and employment conditions cannot be assigned to anyone on the basis of age. Moreover, since the prohibition also encompasses indirect discrimination, divergent conditions cannot be assigned to different persons on the basis of classically age-related characteristics, such as life experience or maturity. It follows from the *Mangold* case, for which the EU Court handed down its judgment in 2005, that the prohibition against age discrimination is a basic principle of EU law, and that national legislation which conflicts with the prohibition must be set aside (case C 144/04 *Werner Mangold v Rudiger Helm* [2005] ECR 9981; see also the *Kücükdeveci* case discussed below).

At the same time, the Framework Directive offers a considerable scope for exceptions to the prohibition against age discrimination. Special treatment on grounds of age can thus be permitted, if just cause can be shown especially with respect to employment policy, the labour market, and vocational training; and if the special treatment is necessary and fit for purpose. The Directive states that the following kinds of special treatment are permitted for the purpose of protecting or promoting the employability of younger and older workers: special rates of remuneration; special provisions for dismissal; special conditions for access to employment; and special working conditions and terms of employment. In addition, age, work experience, and duration of employment may be used as a basis for imposing minimum requirements for access to a certain job, or to certain benefits associated therewith.

The EU Court has decided two important cases with respect to young workers. Both concern the recognition of merits acquired before a person has reached a certain age. The *Hütter* case (C-88/08 *Hütter v Technische Universität Graz* [2009] ECR I-5325), decided in 2009, involved an Austrian regulation which meant that, when an apprentice-trained worker was to be placed in the correct wage category, the employer was to disregard any apprentice training that the employee had completed prior to having reached 18 years of age. Two persons in the case who had completed the same apprentice training had been placed in different wage categories, based only on the fact that one of them had been under 18 upon starting the training. The purpose of the national regulation was to ensure that the wage system would not disadvantage those who had chosen to attend a general upper secondary school vis-à-vis those who attended vocational training. In the absence of such a regulation, it was feared that young people might choose vocational instead of general education. The rule was also designed to limit the public sector's costs for vocational training, and to facilitate entry into the labour market for young people who had undergone vocational training. The EU Court found these purposes to be legitimate; thus the special treatment was justified. However, the Court found the age limit to be neither suitable nor necessary for achieving said purposes. The interests of those who had chosen the general upper secondary alternative would have been more appropriately served by connecting the wage categories to workers' educational level, instead of to their age. As for the aim of promoting the recruitment of young people, the Court pointed out that the rule of not taking into account experience acquired before 18 years of age was not specific to young persons; instead it applied to all persons, irrespective of their age at the time of employment. The rule was therefore deemed unsuitable for the purpose of promoting young persons' entry into the labour market. The Court thus found the rule to be in breach of the prohibition against age discrimination.

In *Kücükdeveci*, a case decided in 2010, the EU Court examined a national regulation governing how a worker's notice period is to be calculated (case C-555/07 *Kücükdeveci v Swedex GmbH & Co KG* [2010] ECR I-365). The length of said period was to be determined based on the duration of a worker's employment; however, employment held before said worker had reached 25 years of age was not to be counted in his or her total duration of employment. The regulation was defended on the grounds that young workers may be assumed to possess greater flexibility in working and private life, in view of their age and their relatively limited social, family, and private obligations. For this reason, the employer's interest in personal flexibility should have priority over the employee's interest in protection. The Court did not discuss the substance of this argument; however, it pointed out that the national regulation did not just affect younger workers. Instead it was applied – as in *Hütter* – irrespective of an employee's age at the time of dismissal. The Court deemed the regulation to be discriminatory, and thus in breach of EU law.

An important reason why the Court rejected the national, age-discriminatory, rules in both these cases was that the rules were not exclusive to younger workers; instead they applied to all employees of all ages. Thus, the rules were not fit for achieving the purpose in question: creating different (and inferior) rules for young employees, with an eye to achieving certain goals of social and labour-market policy. This implies, indirectly, that the EU Court would have considered the rules suitable, should they have applied solely to persons below a certain age. In light of the current state of research, I find reason to criticize the position of the Court. Even if labour-law reforms which limit younger workers' rights do have the legitimate purpose of promoting youth employment, there is little evidence that such reforms are suited to achieving this objective. Research in the fields of economics and political science indicates that, in reality, reducing the job security of young people is not the right way to combat youth unemployment. There is simply not enough scientific evidence that this method really does work (Gautiér, 2009; Eldring and Alsos, 2012).

EMPLOYMENT POLICY FOR YOUNG PEOPLE MUST PROTECT FUNDAMENTAL RIGHTS

The many EU-level initiatives taken in 2012–2013 to combat youth unemployment are being implemented in the member states. The Youth Guarantee, proposed in the 2012 Employment Package for Youth, has involved around nine million young people. The EU Commission has also launched the 'European Alliance for Apprenticeships', in which actors from training institutes and labour-market organizations in various member states work together with representatives from state agencies, youth movements, and other organizations to exchange experiences and to improve the quality and availability of apprenticeships and training positions. Another area of importance in the effort to reduce youth unemployment is the cross-border movement of labour within the Union, which is supported by the 'Youth on the Move' document and the 'Youth Opportunities Initiative'. Youth unemployment is falling at a moderate rate; however, the high numbers of unemployed young persons is still identified at the EU level as a crucial problem that needs to be addressed actively. In the fall of 2016, the Youth Guarantee was prolonged to cover the 2017–2020 period, and its funding was extended. Shortly thereafter, in December 2016, the Commission presented 'Investing in Europe's Youth', in which it proposed three areas for action: access to employment; reform of education and training systems (with a special focus on quality in apprenticeships); and activities to promote mobility, as well as engagement in societal and solidarity work.

The actions being taken at the EU level reflect an insight into the special situation in which young people find themselves in the labour market in Europe today. They also represent an adaptation to this situation. The same is true for the many other activities taking place at the EU level and around Europe in order to overcome youth unemployment. But there is a clear difference between these measures and the broad deregulatory labour-law reforms targeting young people which have been proposed and introduced in a number of member states during the crisis – changes which have encroached primarily upon younger workers' wage levels and employment protection, by means of pay cuts, probationary employment, and extended periods on fixed-term contracts.

Advocates of these deregulatory reforms argue that they will help reduce high levels of youth unemployment, especially for young people who have left school early. However, research in the fields of economics and political science finds no evidence that restrictions on young workers' rights serve to enhance their prospects in the labour market. Against this background, there seems good reason to question the arguments used to justify unilateral restrictions on young workers' fundamental social rights.

The use of legal arguments that cite fundamental social rights is not unproblematic. Fundamental rights are often set out in more than one source of law (e.g., in both national legislation and EU legislation), so they can be interpreted in different ways by courts with different competences. Moreover, their interpretation may be influenced by the structure of the legal system in which they are to be applied. Yet, notwithstanding the practical difficulties that can arise in applying instruments that offer protection for fundamental social rights, it is important to emphasize the role and function of these rights from an overall perspective. Fundamental social rights have the potential to function as a protective barrier against legal reforms that weaken employees' security. In this context, fundamental social rights can have an impact – in two ways. First of all, due to their superior status, fundamental rights can be used to evaluate (and to call into question) labour-law reforms which have been introduced in order to promote flexibility in employment. Second, fundamental social rights have considerable potential to influence the design of future reforms in labour-market regulation, because an increased awareness of fundamental rights will unavoidably have consequences for both legislative activity and collective bargaining.

For younger workers, the fundamental right to freedom from discrimination on grounds of age provides general protection for their legal status in the labour market – the interest being protected being that of young persons in their capacity as young persons. Other fundamental rights, such as those relating to fair wages, freedom from economic exploitation, or protection against dismissal without just cause, apply instead to specific situations in the employment relationship where strong protection has been considered necessary. In relation to young workers, therefore, fundamental social rights have the potential to function in two dimensions. They can work as a barrier against the deterioration of specific working conditions, and they can counteract the general vulnerability that characterizes young people's position in the labour market.

To confront and remedy the prosperity gap that is growing between different generations in Europe's labour market, it is essential that fundamental social rights be observed and fully respected in relation to all citizens, including young persons who are – or who want to be – part of the workforce in the EU.

NOTE

* This chapter draws upon earlier research in the fields of age discrimination and young employees, see especially J. Julén Votinius, 'Young Employees: Securities, Risk Distribution and Fundamental Social Rights', *European Labour Law Journal*, **4** (3–4) (2014), 387–410, and J. Julén Votinius, 'Age Discrimination and Labour Law in Sweden', in A. Numhauser-Henning and M. Rönnmar (eds), *Age Discrimination and Labour Law: Comparative and Conceptual Perspectives in the EU and Beyond* (Kluwer Law International, Alphen aan den Rijn 2015).

REFERENCES

Armstrong, K. (2010), *Governing Social Inclusion: Europeanization through Policy Coordination*, Oxford: Oxford University Press.

Ashiagbor, D. (2005), *The European Employment Strategy: Labour Market Regulation and New Governance*, Oxford: Oxford University Press.

Auer, P. (2010), 'What's in a Name? The Rise (and Fall?) of Flexicurity', *Journal of Industrial Relations*, **52** (3) 371–386.
Barnard, C. (2012), 'The Financial Crisis and the Euro Plus Pact: A Labour Lawyer's Perspective', *Industrial Law Journal*, **41** (1) 98–114.
Biagi, M. (2000), 'The Impact of European Employment Strategy on the Role of Labour Law and Industrial Relations', *International Journal of Comparative Labour Law and Industrial Relations*, **16** (2) 155–173.
Bosch, G. (2011), 'The German Labour Market after the Financial Crisis: A Miracle or Just a Good Policy Mix?', in D. Vaughan-Whitehead (ed.), *Work Inequalities in the Crisis: Evidence from Europe*, Cheltenham, UK and Northampton, MA, USA: Edward Elgar Publishing.
Brenke, K., U. Rinne, and K.F. Zimmermann (2013), 'Short-Time Work: The German Answer to the Great Recession', *International Labour Review*, **152** (2) 287–305.
Cabasés Piqué, M.A., A. Pardell Veàb, and T. Streckerc (2016), 'The EU Youth Guarantee – A Critical Analysis of Its Implementation in Spain', *Journal of Youth Studies*, **19** (5) 684–704.
Capaldo, J. and A. Izurieta (2013), 'The Imprudence of Labour Market Flexibilization in a Fiscally Austere World', *International Labour Review*, **152** (1) 1–26.
Caspar, S., I. Hartwig, and B. Moench (2012), 'European Labor Market in Critical Times: The Importance of Flexicurity Confirmed', *Journal of Policy Analysis and Management*, **31** (1) 154–160.
Chenic, A.Ş. (2012), 'An Analysis of Current Labor Market Developments and Structures in European Union – in Correlation with Labor Market Flexicurity Requirements', *Theoretical and Applied Economics*, **19** (3) 91–108.
Clauwaert, S. and I. Schömann (2013), *The Crisis and National Labour Law Reforms: A Mapping Exercise. Country Report: Greece*, Brussels: ETUI.
Dawson, M., E. Muir, and M. Claes (2012), 'Enforcing the EU's Rights Revolution: The Case of Equality', *European Human Rights Law Review*, (3) 276–291.
Eldring, L. and K. Alsos (2012), *European Minimum Wage: A Nordic Outlook*, Fafo-report 2012:16, Norway: Allkopi AS.
European Commission (2006), *Employment in Europe 2006*.
European Commission (2007), *Towards Common Principles of Flexicurity: More and Better Jobs through Flexibility and Security*, COM (2007) 359.
European Commission (2012a), *Moving Youth into Employment*, COM (2012) 727.
European Commission (2012b), *Apprenticeship Supply in the Member States of the European Union*, Directorate-General for Employment, Social Affairs and Inclusion, Unit C3, January 2012.
European Commission (2013), *Work-Based Learning in Europe: Practices and Policy Pointers*.
European Commission (2016a), *The Youth Guarantee and Youth Employment Initiative Three Years On*, COM (2016) 646.
European Commission (2016b), *European Semester Thematic Fiche, Youth Unemployment*.
Eurostat (2016), *Early Leavers from Education and Training*.
Garz, M. (2013), 'Employment and Wages in Germany since the 2004 Deregulation of the Temporary Agency Industry', *International Labour Review*, **152** (2) 307–326.
Gautiér, J. (2009), *Le chômage*, Paris: La Découverte.
Goetschy, J. (2001), 'The European Employment Strategy from Amsterdam to

Stockholm: Has It Reached Its Cruising Speed?', *Industrial Relations Journal*, **32** (5) 401–404.

Heyes, J. (2011) 'Flexicurity, Employment Protection and the Jobs Crisis', *Work, Employment and Society*, **25** (4) 642–657.

Julén Votinius, J. (2012), 'Having the Right Attitude', *International Journal of Comparative Labour Law and Industrial Relations*, **28** (2) 223–248.

Julén Votinius, J. (2014), 'Young Employees: Securities, Risk Distribution and Fundamental Social Rights', *European Labour Law Journal*, **5** (3) 366–389.

Knijn, T. (ed.) (2012), *Work, Family Policies and Transitions to Adulthood in Europe*, Basingstoke: Palgrave Macmillan.

Koukiadaki, A. and L. Kresos (2012), 'Opening Pandora's Box: The Sovereign Debt Crisis and Labour Market Regulation in Greece', *Industrial Law Journal*, **41** (3) 276–304.

Lasser, M. (2009), *Judicial Transformations: The Rights Revolution in the Courts of Europe*, Oxford: Oxford University Press.

Laulom, S., E. Mazuyer, and M-C. Escande Varniol (2012), *Quel droit social dans une Europe en crise?*, Brussels: Larcier.

López, J., A. de le Court, and S. Canalda (2014), 'Breaking the Equilibrium between Flexibility and Security: Flexiprecarity as the Spanish Version of the Model', *European Labour Law Journal*, **5** (1) 18–42.

Loretto, W., D. Colin, and P.J. White (2000), 'Ageism and Employment: Controversies, Ambiguities and Younger People's Perceptions', *Ageing and Society*, **20** 279–302.

Low Pay Commission (2013), *National Minimum Wage*, Report Cm 8565, The Stationery Office Limited.

Moreira, A., Á. Alonso Domínguez, C. Antunes, M. Karamessini, M. Raitano, and M. Glatzer (2015), 'Austerity-Driven Labour Market Reforms in Southern Europe', *European Journal of Social Security*, **17** (2) 202–225.

OECD (2017), *Understanding the Socio-economic Divide in Europe, Background Report, 26 January 2017*. Paris: OECD.

Skedinger, P. (2011), 'Employment Consequences of Employment Protection Legislation', *Nordic Economic Policy Review*, **2** (1) 45–83.

Snape, E. and T. Redman (2003), 'Too Old or Too Young? The Impact of Perceived Age Discrimination', *Human Resource Management Journal*, **13** 78–89.

Suárez Corujo, B. (2014), 'Crisis and Labour Market in Spain', *European Labour Law Journal*, **5** (1) 43–62.

Tangian, A. (2010a), 'Not for Bad Weather – Flexicurity Challenged by the Crisis', *ETUI Policy Brief*, Issue 3/2010.

Tangian, A. (2010b), 'Not for Bad Weather – Macroeconomic Analysis of Flexicurity with Regard to the Crisis', *ETUI Policy Brief*, Issue 5/2010.

Wilthagen, T. (2002), 'The Flexibility–Security Nexus: New Approaches to Regulating Employment and Labour Markets', OSA-Working paper WP2002-18, Tilburg, the Netherlands, OSA/Institute for Labour Studies, Tilburg University.

8. The future of national systems of social security in the EU

Jaan Paju

INTRODUCTION

A national welfare model is created through the political positions that different parties actively take with regard to the scope, financing, and redistribution of welfare, as well as to the ways of organizing it. Ideas and perceptions with regard to welfare models are numerous and politically sensitive. Furthermore, welfare financing is increasingly a key issue (Crawford and Johnson 2011). The coming British exit from the European Union (EU) certainly brings the question to the fore. At the same time, we cannot disregard the fact that, over the course of the 2000s, the population pyramid has grown more and more inverted, with fewer and fewer economically active persons supporting a growing number of economically inactive ones. Migration flows, therefore, may offer a way to sustain the welfare state over the long term (European Commission 2015).

Social security is an important part of a welfare state. It has been a national affair in Europe ever since the 1870s, when Prussia adopted the first law on insurance against industrial accidents (cf. Pennings 2015, pp. 4 f.; Roberts 2010, pp. 8 ff.). Almost 150 years later, we have a Europe where social security continues to be a national concern, but where the EU has acquired parallel legislative competence in the area. The Union's growing competence in this regard has started to challenge conventional notions about the level on which such matters are to be handled.

Regulation 883/2004, on the coordination of social security systems in Europe, is of interest in this regard. It connects the independent systems with one another in such a way that people can be assured that they are covered by a national social security system, and that they will not lose such periods and rights as they already have earned upon moving to another member state. However, EU coordination functions within the context of the Union's Internal Market. As a result, it has developed in a more far-reaching manner than the member states initially intended. Since the end of the 1990s, moreover, the European Court of Justice (ECJ) has elaborated the concept of Union citizenship. The very idea of Union citizenship, alongside and in addition to national citizenship, has called into question the notion of nationally delimited solidarity. The ECJ has recently been trying to achieve a new balance in the Union's case law in this area, raising the question of how social security systems in the member states are to be organized in future (see Chapter 2 by Anna-Sara Lind in this book for a more in-depth discussion of the different social rights that arise from Union citizenship).

In this chapter, after reviewing some of the background in this area, I discuss the tension that has arisen between national social security models and the dynamically developing body of EU law. The focus of attention in the British referendum was largely on migration and its perceived impact on the British welfare state (for a more nuanced view, see Chapter 4 by Joakim Ruist in this book; cf. Soroka et al. 2016, p. 173). Conflicting interests are clearly in play. The domestic social security systems of the member states have been built on nationally and territorially delimited solidarity. The EU system, by contrast, is founded on the idea of economic integration through Union citizenship and the free movement of labour (cf. Schiek 2015, pp. 20 f.; de Witte 2015, pp. 52 ff.).

The Union has yet to recover from the deep economic crisis into which it was plunged during the global economic turmoil and the Euro crisis that resulted from it. In the wake of the crisis, and in connection with the politically significant enlargement of the EU to the east, growing gaps have emerged within the Union in terms of economic and social prosperity. This has led to substantial migration from less prosperous parts of the Union to regions with better employment opportunities. As a result, the solidarity embodied in the welfare systems of the receiving member states has come under increasing strain. At the same time, the EU describes itself as a social market economy (Article 3.3 in the Treaty on European Union, or TEU). In this chapter, therefore, I focus on whether EU coordination of the different national systems for social security has a role to play in managing the growing differences among member states in terms of economic and social prosperity – the prosperity gap which is the focus of this book – or whether such coordination serves in fact to counteract the Union's social dimension.

Following this introductory section, the chapter consists of six sections and a conclusion. In the first section, 'An Introduction to Social Security', I present the theoretical framework for my discussion. I describe how social security systems evolved along national and territorial lines, and I discuss how they can hinder the free movement of persons between states.

In the next three sections I present the EU legal setting and Regulation 883/2004, which coordinates and thereby connects the social security systems of the member states. Its purpose is to strengthen the free movement of persons within the EU, while at the same time respecting the independent systems of the member states. The last of the three sections sets Regulation 883/2004 in a wider EU legal context.

In the subsequent section, under the heading of 'Union Citizenship', I describe the development of a system for the free movement of persons within the EU which no longer necessitates connection to a job or a business activity. The development of a more general right to reside freely within the Union presents a particular challenge to social security systems based on residence. In this section, I look at some of the ways in which the ECJ has responded to the question of where the outer limits of social rights go.

The challenges and possible solutions are presented in the final section, 'Time for the Union to Decide'. Here I recommend a balance between the demands of market integration and the desire of member states to ensure the sustainability of their independent social security systems. Legal developments in this area have gone so far that the clock cannot be turned back. Moreover, member states are facing new challenges such as increasing globalization, an aging population, and growing social differences within the EU. When discussing how to deal with these matters in future, we can no longer confine ourselves within national borders. The chapter ends with a concluding section where I call for member state action.

AN INTRODUCTION TO SOCIAL SECURITY

If we are to understand the challenges faced by member states within the EU legal context, we must understand the concept of social security in a national setting. In what follows, therefore, I describe the basic ideas underlying social security, and I review how the solutions devised in this area have come about. As we shall see, moreover, the territorial limits of such solutions are relevant in a Union that aims to ensure the free movement of persons.

Generally speaking, social security comprises insurance programmes that support individuals during different stages of life. This includes sickness insurance, rehabilitation insurance, pension systems, insurance for people with disabilities, parental-insurance schemes like child benefit and parental leave, and insurance against loss of income in the event of industrial injury or occupational disease (Pieters 2006, pp. 2 ff.). Social security, one might say, follows a person from the cradle to the grave. The purpose of insurance is to protect people against risks like fire, burglary, or automobile damage. Social insurance differs from other kinds of insurance in that it is connected to a person's lifecycle, and the benefits it provides are paid out at different times over the course of that person's life.

Human beings have always faced the same basic challenge: how will they manage economically when they grow old, or when they have young children to take care of, or if they get sick for a long period of time, or if for some other reason they can no longer support themselves in the same way as before? These are 'risks' that can occasion lost income, due to decreased working capacity (Barr 2001, p. 18). All people run the same risk of being exposed to such challenges at some point in their lives. What they do not know is *when* they will contract an illness, or *if* and *when* they will have a child, or the like.

People have devised different ways over the centuries of protecting themselves from such risks. These ways have varied, according to historical and cultural background. In many earlier societies, individuals would 'insure' themselves against the risks of life through membership in groups, tribes, or small communities, wherein the strong would lead the group and take care of the weak, to the extent that resources allowed.

Closed communities of this kind no longer exist in modern society. We must therefore secure ourselves against life's unpredictable turns in some other fashion. One way an individual can do this is by accumulating money in a bank. An economic buffer of this kind, however, is far from being the best solution, because one cannot know if the buffer will be used, or when. A more rational approach is to combine the resources of many people into a joint economic buffer, from which one can draw assistance if and when it is needed. This collective solution was the basis for the creation of insurance systems (Barr 2001, pp. 1 f.).

At first glance, private insurance companies would seem to want to insure anything and everything: cars, boats, houses, children, even trips into outer space. But a private company will only offer insurance under certain conditions (Barr 2001, pp. 83 ff.). The event in question – of which there is a risk – cannot occur all the time; conversely, it cannot be something that never occurs. In the first case, no insurance company will have any economic incentive to offer insurance, because it will have to pay out compensation all the time and will never be able to turn a profit. In the latter case, no person or company will sign up for insurance, because there is no risk to insure against. Insurance premiums are thus based on the assumption that they will more than cover expected payouts. It is a matter, therefore, of finding the right balance between premiums and expected payouts.

With this type of weighting it is difficult, however, to find the right balance in areas like health insurance. In such areas, the same insurance covers both low-risk groups (who 'never' become ill) and high-risk groups (who are 'always' ill). If both groups pay the same premium, low-risk persons will end up paying sums far in excess of their expected payouts, while high-risk persons will end up doing the opposite. The result will likely be an insurance pool consisting only of high-risk individuals, where payouts are made more frequently than they would have been if the group had embraced both low-risk and high-risk persons. In these situations there is market failure: everyone wants insurance, but not on the conditions offered by the market (Barr 2001, pp. 26 ff.). The state in such a case will ultimately foot the bill, in the form of more expensive healthcare, for its efforts will be focused on acute care rather than on cheaper preventive care. (No one will take sick leave, for example, on account of the lack of insurance.) At the beginning of the twentieth century in Sweden, for example, health-insurance funds competed for policy-holders by (at first) insuring people with long compensation periods and without checking their medical history when they signed up. This approach was not sustainable in the long run: the funds attracted a greater number of sick clients than they could cover with their insurance. They therefore raised their premiums, which reduced the number of clients, leading to yet higher premiums – and so on in a vicious circle (Ståhlberg 2004, p. 16). Cases of this kind also figured in the debate over the health-insurance reform introduced in the United States by the Obama administration (Wilper et al. 2009).

The solution, as many economists among others advocate, is to make health insurance obligatory – or at least to have it regulated by the state, thereby ensuring that *all* groups are covered. It is this all-inclusive quality that marks such insurance as *social* insurance. This is a matter, after all, of the common welfare: society as a whole gains from having a system of compulsory national insurance (Roemer 1998, p. 115). Moreover, many states in modern times, especially in Western Europe, have been animated by a belief in social engineering and redistribution through social insurance (cf. Jackson 1994). The welfare state is thus most comprehensive in cases where the role of insurance has been not just to cover loss of income, but to achieve other social objectives as well (Rothstein and Kumlin 2005; Rothstein and Uslaner 2005), and hence one talks nowadays about social security. It is against this background of market failure and redistributive purpose that social security has become, at least in the Western world, a policy area that constitutes the very core of the nation. The EU's member states are highly reluctant, therefore, to expose their systems of social security to the Union's market-oriented policies (cf. Erhag 2016).

It was under the aegis of the nation-state, then, that social security systems initially developed. Accordingly, the geographical scope of such systems was usually limited to the territory of the state in question, with a focus on the state's residents (Pennings 2015, pp. 8 ff.). Furthermore, in addition to being territorially delimited, social security systems have developed in different directions in different European countries, according to the cultural and socioeconomic conditions at hand (Bonoli 2006). These systems reflect the economic, political, geographical, and cultural history of each nation.

Three welfare models are often mentioned in this connection. The first is *the Bismarckian model*, which developed in Prussia from the 1870s onward. In this model, employment is the basis for coverage by the social security system. Benefit levels reflect the income of the persons covered and the contributions they have made (Palier 2010; Scheubel 2013). *The Beveridge model*, found in Great Britain, differs from the Bismarckian model in covering all of the residents of a country. The system is funded out of general taxes and not by contributions, and benefit levels are low (Abel-Smith 1992, p. 5; see also Hennock 1987). The *Nordic model*, finally, is also residence based, and to a large extent funded out of taxes. Benefit levels, however, are higher than in the Beveridge model. An important aim of the Nordic model is to strive for redistribution and thus to achieve greater social equality (Esping-Andersen 1990). The three models all have one thing in common, however: they are territorially restricted to a given state.

Due to this territorial delimitation, and the associated differences between national systems of social security, individuals feel uncertain about taking up employment in other countries, and so are often reluctant to pursue such opportunities (Wyatt 1977, p. 411). This is beneficial neither for the individual nor for the state. If companies try to expand their operations beyond the borders of their home country, they run the risk that their staff will not be willing to work abroad. Business development is accordingly hindered. These consequences became apparent at an early stage – as soon as companies tried to induce some of their employees to work in another country (cf. Yoffe 1973).

Several intergovernmental agreements have been concluded since the early twentieth century to address this question, but they have largely been based on solving such problems as already have appeared, rather than preventing new ones from arising. The different states do not wish to prevent such problems at the cost of harmonizing their different national systems of social security; but they do seek, by means of coordinative agreements, to clear away a number of obstacles to cross-border employment.

The bilateral agreement that Sweden is negotiating with Japan illustrates the function of coordination nicely. Sweden's aim in these negotiations is to ensure that Swedes who have worked in Japan for 5–10 years will have contributions they have paid into the Japanese pension system refunded to them if they move back to Sweden. Such reimbursement, according to Japanese law, is only possible if a person has contributed to the Japanese system for at least 25 years. The Swedish government hopes, through negotiations, to induce its Japanese counterpart to relax this requirement in the case of Swedish employees who have worked in Japan for 5–10 years. Rather than requiring Japan to alter its national legislation, then, such a solution simply introduces a special case, through a convention.

In exactly the same way, the territoriality of different national systems of social security creates obstacles to the free movement of workers across borders within the EU. It is the aim of EU coordination to clear these obstacles away.

THE EU'S COMPETENCE AND THE LEGAL BASIS

For the EU to be able to legislate within a certain area, said area must fall within the Union's competence. In other words, there has to be a legal basis for EU action in the Treaties.

Social security does not figure in the Treaties as an independent area of competence wherein the member states have empowered the Union to legislate on a supranational level. Instead, the EU has competence in this area partly through the common social policy, and partly (but indirectly) through the free movement of labour. The ability of the Union to act within the framework of the common social policy is very restricted. EU social policy was introduced by the Treaty of Rome, in Articles 117–122. These were and continue to be imprecise (cf. current Articles 151 and 153 TFEU), as well as non-binding for the member states (Watson 2014, p. 38). The Union can only take action in this area to support and complement policies promulgated by the member states. Moreover, legislation in this field must be enacted through a specific legislative procedure, in which each of the member states has a veto. Furthermore, Article 153(4) of the TFEU specifically states that the member states continue to control their social security systems, without any restrictions.

However, the sovereignty of the member states with regard to their own social security systems can have an impact on the free movement of labour within the EU. As we saw above, this can mean that persons employed outside their home country are unable to obtain compensation for periods they have previously earned, or that payouts from their previous state of residence are withheld. Consequences of this kind can affect people's willingness to move to another member state for work. National systems of social security can thus limit the free movement of workers and other groups within the EU. The Union's competence in the field of social security, then, is based on the free movement of workers, Article 45 TFEU. Article 48 TFEU foresees special rules in this respect in the area of social security. These have found expression in the coordination of the member states' systems through EU regulations on social security since 1958.

The Treaty of Rome entered into force on 1 January 1958, and included rules on the coordination of the member states' systems for social security. A couple of weeks prior to this, within the framework of the European Coal and Steel Community (ECSC), the same states had signed a multilateral coordinative convention with the same objective. Instead of waiting for the ratification process for the ECSC Social Security Convention to run its course, while at the same time negotiating a similar regulation within the European Economic Community (EEC, the EU's predecessor), the member states took a pragmatic approach. They simply fashioned the adopted Convention into a regulation, EC Regulation 3/58, which entered into force on 1 January 1959. The ECSC Social Security Convention was thereby transformed into an EC regulation, notwithstanding differences in wording at the time between ECSC Treaty Article 69(4) and Treaty of Rome Article 51. The former article's wording left it open to the signatories to adopt a multilateral convention that would apply alongside the ECSC Treaty; the latter envisioned legislation in a whole new intergovernmental legal environment within the framework of the Treaty of Rome (cf. Pennings 2015, p. 117).

The EEC incorporated the multilateral Convention into evolving EC legislation, as a result of which the Convention went through a metamorphosis. It became an instrument by which, as we will see, the signatories 'lost control' to a strong and independent ECJ. The latter started to promote integration (Watson 2014, p. 75) and to reduce the independence of the member states' social security systems.

The relevant question here, however, is whether the signatory parties had wanted to do things differently in 1958. During those negotiations, France had in fact proposed that social security systems be harmonized (Watson 1980, pp. 33 ff.). Furthermore, neo-functionalism was the leading ideology at the time of the Treaty of Rome. (David Mitrany, one of the leading functionalists, summarizes the theory in his classic work *A Working Peace System – An Argument for the Functional Development of International Organization* (1943). For an EU law context, see Barnard 2016, p. 13.) This school of thought can best be described with a snowball metaphor: when a snowball starts rolling down a hill, it grows bigger and bigger and soon takes everything with it. The masters of the Treaties saw nothing harmful in an organic path of development for the Community, where the solution to a problem in one area would produce problems in another area, necessitating a solution which would spill into a third area, and so on. A common Internal Market could thus be developed on the foundation of necessities, rather than through lengthy political negotiations (Burgess 2000, pp. 32 ff.).

At the same time, it must be stressed that the signatory states were neither naive nor unaware of the 'risks'. They were of the opinion, however, that the advantages of European cooperation outweighed the disadvantages. They believed a state becomes stronger by cooperating with its neighbours than by carrying its burdens on its own. It is simply most cost-effective to cooperate with other countries (Moravcsik 1993, p. 473).

The snowball has had a striking effect: the Internal Market has grown more encompassing than the Treaty itself envisioned, and likely more far-reaching than the signatory states could have foreseen (Burgess 2000, p. 35). One question worth asking here is how the postwar states would have fared on their own in the face of economic challenges. Perhaps we would have had a Europe where everyone signed agreements with everyone else on a bilateral basis, but at a higher cost than if all the states had done so jointly. A Europe where possibly – in the worst-case scenario – mistrust of one state for another would have emerged once again. Would such a scenario have been desirable? The signatory parties, who had the Second World War fresh in their memory, preferred undertaking a joint project to embarking on separate parallel development tracks. And coordination of the social security systems of the member states forms an important part of this joint project.

MAIN FEATURES OF REGULATION 883/2004

The objective of EU regulation in this area is relatively simple and straightforward: to coordinate the social security systems of the member states without harmonizing or unifying them. The basic idea is to reduce the territoriality of the systems through coordination. If social security is strictly limited to the territory of a given member state, people who have worked in more than one country can fall between two stools, losing their rights when they move across borders. From the perspective of the state, however, it is important to avoid a situation where a person is 'double insured' and receives benefits from both states. In other words, the member states need to be able to decide on their respective social security arrangements with regard to form, benefit levels, and eligibility periods. At the same time, the territoriality of the systems should not serve to hinder the free movement of persons.

Regulation 883/2004 provides answers to the question of *where*, *when*, and *how* the systems of the member states are to be coordinated. It specifies which member state is to be responsible for insuring a person who moves from one state to another (i.e., which is the competent state), and it explains how the coordination of social security is to take place.

Let us begin with the question of *when*, and with a legal assessment of how the Regulation is to be applied in a given situation. Four questions need to be asked here. They make up a sort of checklist that must be complete for the Regulation to apply:

- Has a cross-border movement taken place between two member states?
- Is the benefit in question a social security benefit according to the Regulation?
- If the benefit is a social security benefit, does it fall within the material scope of the Regulation?
- Does the person in question fall within the personal scope of the Regulation: that is, is he/she a member of one of the target groups to which the Regulation refers?

Regulation 883/2004 is only applicable if a person moves between two states. This point would appear to be obvious, since the purpose of the Regulation is to facilitate free movement between the member states. In a purely national situation, by contrast, there is no need for any coordination between the social security systems of two or more member states.

So, before analysing the consequences of the Regulation for the social security systems of the member states, we must first ask ourselves, can the benefit in question be seen as a social security benefit according to the Regulation? In order for a benefit to be covered by the Regulation, it must be regulated by the national social security system of a member state, in line with Article 1(1). The relevant case law makes clear that the focus of the ECJ here is on a system which is built on solidarity (read: obligatory insurance), and which is at least supervised by the state. Furthermore, the system cannot be aimed at making a profit (see the joined cases C-159–160/91, *Poucet*; case C-244/94, *Paternelle*). If the system does not display these characteristics, it may instead be a commercial system and therefore subject to other Union legislation, particularly EU competition law (cf. Winterstein 1999).

This means that social security benefits based on collective agreements or the like are not covered by the Regulation's rules of coordination. The same goes for insurance benefits (whether optional or compulsory) within a specific profession. The next step, after we have concluded that the benefit is de facto regulated by the social security system of a member state, is to determine whether the benefit can be seen as a social security benefit under the terms of the Regulation. The material scope of the Regulation is comprehensive. The majority of social security benefits – for example, pensions, healthcare, sickness benefits, unemployment benefits, child and parental benefits – are covered. According to Article 9 of the Regulation, member states must report, in an annex to the Regulation, all benefits which they consider to fall within the material scope of the Regulation. (If a benefit is included in the annex, it is no longer possible for a member state to reverse its inclusion there; case 35/77, *Beerens*; case 12/14, *COM v. Malta*.)

However, this does not stop the ECJ from seeing national benefits as social security benefits which fall under the Regulation's provisions for coordination. When analysing whether a benefit falls within the material scope of the Regulation, a natural starting point is to check for what absolutely does not fall within that scope, and thereafter to move towards the borderline area. It is in the borderline area that the ECJ makes its general position most evident.

When reviewing the ECJ's case law in this area, we need to differentiate between two types of benefit:

- Benefits that are social security benefits, but which the member states do not wish to classify as falling within the material scope of the Regulation. Here the ECJ analyses the objectives of the programme and the criteria for granting a benefit, rather than whether or not the benefit was classified as a social security benefit by the national legislator. According to the rulings of the Court in this area (which are extensive), the concept of a benefit in the sense of the Regulation should be understood broadly (see, for example, case 39/74, *Costa*; case 139/82, *Piscitello*; and case C-45/90, *Paletta*).
- Benefits for which there is a consensus that they clearly fall within the material scope of the Regulation, but where the prevailing view is that they ought not to be exported, because they are closely connected to the specific living conditions in a member state. These benefits – so-called Hybrid Benefits – fall on the borderline between classic social security benefits and redistribution benefits. They are social security benefits, inasmuch as they involve a legally defined right to a social security benefit. But they also show traits of a redistribution benefit, since they do not depend on employment-based contributions. Instead they are residence-based benefits or support measures, the objective of which is to furnish certain vulnerable groups with financial assistance: for example, pensioners who receive only the basic national pension, or disabled individuals that need special support in their daily lives (Pennings 2015, pp. 65 ff.).

It can be said in general that the Court's case law in this area is far-reaching, and that the Regulation's scope has thereby expanded over time. In the case of special schemes, the idea is to show solidarity with vulnerable groups of citizens. Subjecting programmes of this kind to EU coordination is an extra sensitive matter, since they are focused on a given country even more than social security benefits are. Recent preliminary rulings here – case C-140/12, *Brey*; case C-333/13, *Dano*; case C-67/14, *Alimanović*; and case C-299/14, *García-Nieto* – illustrate the balancing act which the Court had to perform in this sensitive area. I describe this balancing act below, in the section dealing with Union citizenship.

As regards the fourth and final checkpoint, it follows from Article 2 that the Regulation covers a broad personal scope. This personal scope applies to all citizens of the member states as a whole, as well as to refugees and stateless persons residing in the member states. The focus of this personal scope is not, unlike the case with previous regulations, on the free movement of labour, but instead more broadly on the free movement of Union citizens (who need not be economically active).

The last question to be answered is *how* coordination between the member states is to take place. The Regulation is based on the following principles:

- A person covered by the Regulation is only covered by the legislation of one nation. This is stated in the Regulation's rules on applicable legislation.
- One of the cornerstones of EU law is that all discrimination on the basis of nationality is prohibited (Article 18 TFEU). This general prohibition is specified in Articles 4 and 5 of the Regulation, which deal with rights and obligations in connection with social security. Thus, a person covered by the Regulation will be treated in the same way as a citizen of the competent state (*the principle of equal treatment*).
- One of the main objectives of coordination in this context is to ensure that an earned benefit does not evaporate when the person who has earned it moves from one country to another. A person covered by the Regulation has the right to obtain/retain earned rights from the competent state, even if he/she is not a resident of that state (*the principle of exportability*).

The fundamental question that needs to be resolved, once it has been ascertained that the Regulation is applicable, is which national legislation applies in the case of a person in a cross-border situation – that is, *where* should the person be insured? This is determined through a coordination procedure that establishes which state is competent (i.e., which state the person is to turn to). Since the Regulation is not based on a person's citizenship or residence, the fact that someone is, say, a Greek citizen does not in itself mean that said person falls under the Greek social security system. Instead, the person is to turn to the member state which the Regulation establishes as the competent state.

The Regulation's rules on applicable legislation are exclusive. According to its rules on conflicts of law, persons who are covered by social security in one member state cannot be covered at the same time by the social security system of another member state.

Article 11.3 a of the Regulation states that economically active persons, whether employees or self-employed, are to be insured in the state where they work. If a person lives in state A but works in state B, that person will be covered by the social security rules of state B.

There are no rules without exceptions, however. The cross-border migration of economically active persons requires a different solution. The categories listed in Article 11.3 b–d are regulated differently. In their case, applying the general rule in 11.3 a could lead to obstacles to the free movement of persons. Accordingly, public servants stationed abroad remain within the employment system of the country they serve; unemployed persons can be covered by the system of their country of residence, even if their unemployment insurance derives from another member state; and persons on military duty are covered by the social security system of the country in whose defence they are engaged.

As mentioned above, the Regulation pertains to all EU citizens who are or have been covered by the social security system of a member state. Those who are not economically active are a mixed category. Pensioners make up the largest group of economically inactive persons. Students are another group. There are also EU citizens who cannot work, or who choose not to work for various reasons. The Regulation lays down that economically inactive persons are covered by the social security system of the member state in which they reside (Article 11.3 e).

The principle of aggregation comes into play when a person cannot add his or her vesting periods from previous states of employment when applying for a benefit or a pension in his/her new working state. The idea behind the Regulation is that people who move to another member state should not lose their previously earned rights. Thus, the Regulation guarantees not just that the rights which people have earned in other member states will be retained, but also that they can be aggregated so as to form the basis for claiming rights in the new competent state.

The Regulation provides, furthermore, that when a person is entitled to a benefit on the basis of a vesting period in another member state, he/she has the right to receive the amount corresponding to that vesting period (the *pro rata temporis* principle). A fictitious example may serve to illustrate how these principles interact:

> Kalle, a citizen of state A, works in state A for 23 years. He then moves to state B, where he works until he retires 17 years later. Kalle chooses to remain in state B after retirement. The national legislation of state A does not allow export of pensions abroad. The pension system of state B provides that a person must work in state B for at least 20 years in order to be eligible for a national pension. Furthermore, state B distinguishes between foreigners and its own citizens, by granting the latter a special supplementary pension in order to compensate for increases in healthcare taxes.

From a purely national perspective, states are free to fashion their own social security systems. In the case of Kalle, however, the outcome of these national systems is not particularly appealing: Kalle will not get a pension from state A, since he now lives in another state; nor will he receive a pension from state B, since 20 years of employment in that country are needed before the pension can be paid out. Regulation 883/2004 removes the line separating these national systems. Now Kalle will get a pension from both states, and under the same conditions as apply to the residents of said states: state A has to pay out the earned pension (the principle of exportability is applied), and state B must pay out a pension as well, because Kalle can include his 23 years of employment in state A when he applies for a pension in state B (the principle of aggregation is applied). Furthermore, state B has to pay out the pension to Kalle despite him not being a citizen, in line with the principle of equal treatment. States A and B will split the pension between them: state A will pay 23/40 and state B 17/40 of their respective pension levels (the *pro rata temporis* principle is applied).

To sum up, people need to be assured that they will receive healthcare, regardless of national rules based on citizenship. An injury at work in another member state should not prevent a person from returning to his/her home state. Child benefits should be paid by the state in which children are resident when one or both of their parents are working in another member state. When national rules pose an obstacle to the free movement of persons, Regulation 883/2004 is triggered. The member states have thus agreed to reduce the territoriality of their social security systems.

THE EU'S LEGAL DIMENSION

The above example is a typical case of the Regulation working for the best of both worlds. In these situations, the Regulation functions like any other agreement between two states that wish to encourage mobility for the sake of economic development.

Regulation 883/2004 is designed as an intergovernmental solution. When it is incorporated into EU law, however, a new dimension appears: the member states lose control and their independent authority is restricted.

The legal setting, in terms of EU law, can be summarized briefly as follows:

- Regulation 883/2004 is EU legislation. In this area, the Commission has the right of initiative and the Council (the member states' governments) is empowered to legislate, together with the European Parliament.
- The Commission oversees compliance with Regulation 883/2004, in the ultimate instance by bringing member states before the ECJ over cases of infringement.
- Regulation 883/2004 is directly applicable in the member states. It can therefore be invoked by individuals in national courts, just as national law can.
- The Court interprets the Regulation both when the Commission brings a member state before it (through infringement proceedings) and in the case of preliminary rulings, when national courts refer to the ECJ for guidance.
- ECJ case law is binding not only on the parties but also on all national courts, as well as on all Union agencies.
- Other EU legislation, such as Directives, can have an impact on the interpretation of the Regulation. EU treaties (primary law) and their general principles can have an impact as well.
- Other EU legislation can be applied in parallel with the Regulation.

This evolving legal landscape has had a strong impact on the social security systems of the member states. As shown by the extensive case law in this field (almost 600 rulings by the ECJ since the Treaty of Rome entered into force: Watson 2014, p. 75), developments in this area have gone much further than they would have done had the coordination taken place outside the EU. At the same time, we must bear in mind that the member states do in fact support the free movement of persons within the Union. Or perhaps we should say that they have a love–hate relationship with the free movement of persons, since the member states are only able to benefit from the Internal Market if they sacrifice certain sacred national cows.

Extensive and proactive interpretation by the ECJ has resulted in the enlargement of both the material and the personal scope of the Regulation. More people are covered by more issues, strengthening personal mobility at the expense of the prerogatives of the member states. This enlargement has also entailed further preliminary rulings, bringing an increasing number of issues and limitations to the fore. The free movement of persons in the field of social security has thus continued to develop at a faster pace than it would have done had the Court applied a more restrictive interpretation of the material and personal scope of the Regulation.

A review of the previous case law in this area merits the conclusion that the Court, as much as possible, confines itself to interpreting the text of the Regulation (i.e., it engages in textual interpretation), and that it refrains from applying primary law or general principles in order to reach its decisions. It seeks solutions within this small context – the legal framework itself. The ECJ thus respects the independent social security systems of the member states, and defers to their consensus on the basic organization of social security. However, the Court acts differently in cases where the free movement of persons is restricted by conditions not foreseen in the Regulation.

Looking back, we can say that Regulation 883/2004 and its predecessors have not progressed at the same pace as the movement of persons between the member states, which has developed far faster.

The EU's infrastructure has developed radically since 1958, with better roads, faster railways, low-cost flights, and Skype. Many people now commute long distances daily, or do their work online for an employer based in another member state. Prevailing legislation, however, is still based on notions from 1958, according to which migration from one member state to another follows a fairly static pattern. Meanwhile, the social security systems of the member states have evolved into highly complex structures, where the interaction with EU law is getting harder and harder to predict – as is the outcome.

In line with new patterns of migration and other unforeseen situations, questions have arisen which the Regulation cannot answer, but which require an answer all the same. It is at these crossroads that the Court has to choose between 'more' and 'less' Europe.

When the ECJ makes and repairs the Union's legal patchwork, it relies on the EU's primary law: the idea of an Internal Market. In other words, while there is certainly coordination between the member states in the area of social security, this does not mean the legal framework is an exclusive one.

The ECJ's mindset in case C-165/91, *van Munster* provides a nice illustration of its teleological method of interpretation (Moore 1998, pp. 410 ff.). The *van Munster* case concerned the payment of a pension from both Belgium and the Netherlands to a Mr van Munster. The pension was divided between the two states in line with the Regulation's rules on payment and years of employment. The level of the pension was calculated in line with national rules, since the Regulation only *coordinates* the social security systems of the member states.

The Dutch legal framework sought a solution where everyone, economically active or not, would be entitled to an individual pension. (The change in Dutch pension calculations was a step towards complying with the Directive on gender-neutral legislation with regard to social security: Council Directive 79/7/EEC.) If a pensioner's spouse had not been economically active, and was not yet of retirement age either, the household in question would receive an additional payment. This supplement would be withdrawn when said spouse retired and started receiving his/her own pension. The total amount accruing to the household would thus stay at the same level as when just one person was receiving a pension. The Dutch design thus prevented a situation from arising where a household's income falls substantially when its economically active member retires and his/her stay-at-home spouse has not reached retirement age yet.

The Belgian system, on the other hand, distinguished between household pensions and individual pensions. The amount was larger when only a single pension based on the household was paid out. When the Belgian authorities realized that the members of the household in question – the van Munster couple – had kept their individual pensions after Ms van Munster had reached retirement age, they reduced Mr van Munster's Belgian pension to the level of an individual pension. They did so despite the fact that the total amount of the Dutch pension remained the same.

When considered as isolated cases, the different national systems appear quite logical. When their operations within the Union need to be coordinated, however, they seem distinctly less so. In the case reviewed just above, the national rules led – together with a literal interpretation of the Regulation's rules – to a loss of income which would not have been suffered if Mr van Munster had worked only in Belgium throughout his life. This prompted the following observation by the Court:

> . . . it is not, however, in dispute that the aim of Articles 48 and 51 of the treaty would not be met if, through exercising their right to freedom of movement, migrant workers were to lose social security advantages guaranteed to them by the laws of a member state. Such a consequence might discourage Community workers from exercising their right to freedom of movement and would therefore constitute an obstacle to that freedom. (*van Munster*, p. 27)

In its preliminary ruling, therefore, the ECJ declared that the Belgian court would need to review its national legislation, in order to prevent, 'as far as is at all possible, . . . its interpretation from being such as to discourage a migrant worker from actually exercising his right to freedom of movement' (*van Munster*, p. 35). Belgium was thus ordered by the ECJ to alter its national legislation so as to ensure that its rules would henceforth be interpreted in such a way as to support the free movement of persons.

In other rulings too, like case C-443/93, *Vougioukas*; case C-137/04, *Rockler*; and case C-185/04, *Öberg*, the ECJ has ordered member states to disregard their national legislation if its effect would be to pose an obstacle to the free movement of persons.

The Court has not hesitated, then, to intervene in situations that the EU legislator failed to foresee, and which therefore are not covered by Regulation 883/2004. It has particularly emphasized in these rulings that unpredictable situations can arise. Such uncertainty can affect people's willingness to move and to take a job in another member state. The Court's rulings show as well how the principle of free movement for persons is posing an ever more serious challenge to the desire of the member states to set the conditions for coverage by their social security systems. The inherent dynamic of the internal market is thus leading to a situation where an increasing number of social security benefits are subject to EU coordination. In other words, coordination is no longer being conducted on the terms of the member states.

UNION CITIZENSHIP

The free movement of persons subjects the view of welfare and solidarity entertained by the member states to an entirely different and more profound challenge than the free movement of goods and capital does. The latter, after all, are purely factors of production. They certainly have an impact on national finances, and an indirect impact on welfare thereby. But they have no direct effect on the organization of social security systems. The free movement of persons, on the other hand, cuts right to the core of a nation's understanding of what solidarity is, whom it is intended for, and how one contributes to it.

With the free movement of workers, there is full focus on the Internal Market, and migrating workers often do everything to contribute to it (see Chapter 4 by Joakim Ruist in this book). Since 1993, however, there has been a parallel track – unrelated to the Internal Market – by which the right to move freely is granted to all citizens of the Union. That track is Union citizenship.

Ever since the Maastricht Treaty introduced the concept of 'Union Citizenship', debate has raged among academics and politicians over Union citizenship and its implications for access to the welfare system of one's country of residence (cf. Hailbronner 2005; Kochenov and Plender 2012). The concept was introduced on an initiative from Spain during the negotiations leading up to the Maastricht Treaty. It formed part of an attempt to promote the positive aspects of the EU by strengthening the political rights of the individual in an EU context. (Kochenov is of the view that the introduction of Union citizenship brought nothing new, since quasi-citizenship already existed through the relevant case law: Kochenov and Plender 2012, pp. 373 f.) The politicians had no intention, however, of introducing far-reaching changes. Such changes as they brought about in this area were modest, and did not challenge the prerogatives of the member states in any significant way. (Weiler describes the introduction of Union citizenship as 'little more than a cynical exercise in public relations on the part of the High Contracting Parties': Weiler 1996, p. 68.) The new arrangements incorporated a limited set of political rights, and simply confirmed citizens in their possession of rights that already stemmed from the Treaty. Yet, notwithstanding this, legal developments in the field have been intensive. They were codified in Directive 2004/38 (the Citizens Rights Directive), which the member states incorporated into their national legislation on 1 May 2006.

Economically inactive Union citizens who reside in another member state do not pay taxes or social contributions to that state. With Union citizenship, then, we have started to move away from purely economic reasons for free movement and towards an EU where Union citizenship is 'the fundamental status of the nationals of the member states', as the ECJ put it in case C-34/09, *Zambrano*.

The Citizens Rights Directive interacts with Regulation 883/2004 in a complex way. The Directive builds on the idea that Union citizens who are not economically active have the right to reside in another member state as long as they do not burden the social-assistance system of that state (Article 7.1 b Citizens Rights Directive).

The *Beveridge* and *Nordic* models are both based on residence. A certain idea of solidarity is embedded in these models, whereby the working community provides for other groups of residents. Welfare models of a residence-based kind are inevitably put at risk in an arrangement of the sort established by Regulation 883/2004, because said Regulation makes the social security system of the state of residence the competent one for Union citizens who are not economically active.

An understanding of solidarity based on residence made sense when the member states decided whom could reside within their bounds. Under that arrangement, countries took care of 'their own'. With Union citizenship the situation is reversed: now it is individuals who decide where they reside. The states no longer issue residence *permits* to citizens of other states; instead, EU citizens have a *right* to reside where they will. They can reside in another member state as long as they do not burden the social-assistance system of that state. (As I explain below, however, social assistance is one thing; social benefits is another.) It could be that they only take up residence in another member state for a brief time, and that they do not become resident in a literal sense. But the fact that they are explicitly covered by the Regulation means that they are able to take advantage of the right of residence. This calls conventional conceptions of a welfare state into question.

Here the Regulation paradoxically supports the right of residence, in that its rule on applicable legislation in Article 11.3 e points out the state of residence as the competent state. If said state offers social security benefits based on residence, then economically inactive EU citizens within its bounds are guaranteed access to those benefits (child benefits, for example). These persons will thereby burden the social finances of that state, even if they do not burden its social-assistance system in particular.

A ruling by the Swedish Migration Court of Gothenburg points up this paradox (UM 2516-09, *Lewandowska*). In the judgement of the Migration Court, the fact that the Swedish Social Insurance Agency was paying out both housing allowance and maintenance support to eligible pensioners could not influence a decision on whether or not the Union citizen Lewandowska had the right to reside in Sweden. In the Court's view it was clear, from the preparatory work which had led to the Swedish Aliens Act, that the concept of 'burdening the social benefit system' only referred to social assistance in the meaning of the Social Services Act. The fact that Lewandowska received benefits from the Social Insurance Agency did not mean, therefore, that she had forfeited her right to reside in Sweden. The Migration Board appealed the ruling, but the Migration Court of Appeal confirmed it (UM 10307-09).

In response to this paradox, more recent case law in the area of Union citizenship has broadened the concept of social assistance, and limited the right to social security benefits for economically inactive Union citizens.

From the perspective of an individual, it may be said that the ECJ – after its rulings in *Brey*, *Dano*, *Alimanović*, *García-Nieto*, and most recently case C-308/14, *Commission v. United Kingdom* – has de facto limited the right to free movement for economically inactive Union citizens. It has done so in three ways:

1. There is, the Court has found, no explicit right to social assistance in the state of residence. The Citizens Rights Directive fully regulates the terms and conditions for gaining the right to such assistance.
2. Hybrid benefits under the Regulation are also to be seen as social assistance, making them subject to the Directive's conditions for a right to reside.
3. Since the Regulation's rules on applicable legislation are only coordinative in nature, access to the social security benefits of a given

member state may depend on national eligibility criteria, including the requirement that recipients have the right to reside in said state.

At this point, therefore, the Citizens Rights Directive is increasingly the central piece of legislation when it comes to ascertaining the rights of Union citizens to social benefits in a broad sense. However, the legal arguments presented by the ECJ have serious shortcomings.

The ECJ created a bridge between Regulation 883/2004 and the Citizens Rights Directive in its preliminary ruling in *Brey*, in which it found that certain social security benefits resembling social assistance can be regarded as social assistance in the meaning of the Directive. This enabled the Court to find that the requirement of a right to reside in connection with a certain Austrian social security benefit – which had some characteristics of social assistance – was in line with EU law. This bridge was then used in *Dano*, and consolidated in *Alimanović* and *García-Nieto.* These cases disregard, however, the fundamental difference between social security benefits on the one hand and social assistance on the other. Social security benefits are based on the idea of insurance; social assistance, by contrast, is essentially temporary assistance tendered to people who would otherwise fall below subsistence level. It is true that social security benefits may incorporate an element of redistribution, whereby the contributions paid in are not the same as the amount received back. This does not automatically mean, however, that social security benefits of this type can be seen as social assistance (cf. Verschueren 2014, pp. 165 ff.). This is the underlying reason why benefits of the two types are regulated in two separate EU legal frameworks. This makes for two different perspectives on the free movement of persons. As a result, different welfare systems are permitted to produce different outcomes, even if these might be considered 'unjustified'.

When it comes to social security benefits that can be seen as 'classic' – meaning that they bear no resemblance to social assistance – the situation is different. Such benefits do not fall under the Citizens Rights Directive and its rules for a right to reside. The ECJ nonetheless found, in *Commission v. United Kingdom*, that member states can differentiate between migrant workers and economically inactive EU citizens when it comes to social security benefits. The Court presumed such a differentiation when it concluded that the rule on applicable legislation in Article 11.3 e can lead to a situation where family benefits are sought 'by persons other than those to whom Article 11.3 a–d applies, that is to say, in particular, economically inactive persons' (*Commission v. United Kingdom*, p. 63). In light of this, it is not surprising that the Court applied a narrow textual interpretation of the Regulation's rules on applicable legislation. The Court concluded on the basis of this narrow understanding that it is legally possible to supplement Article 11.3 e of the Regulation with national material eligibility criteria, such as a right to reside.

The Court disregards some fundamental factors in this ruling, however. When it was adopted in May 2004, Regulation 883/2004 broadened the personal scope to include practically all economically inactive Union citizens. Coordination through the Regulation would then apply to this broadened personal scope. When economically inactive persons move to another member state, they are normally not covered any longer by the social security system of their previous state of residence. In such circumstances, Article 11.3 e of the Regulation points to residence as the criterion for determining the competent state. In this way, the Regulation ensures that persons encompassed by its personal scope do not fall between two stools. In *Commission v. United Kingdom*, however, those who are economically inactive do indeed fall de facto between two stools, since they enjoy no substantive right to social security. The aim of the Regulation – to support the free movement of persons falling within its personal scope – becomes a chimera.

The Court has not succeeded in building a sustainable legal bridge between Regulation 883/2004 and Directive 2004/38. It is also difficult to disregard the fact that it issued its ruling in *Commission v. United Kingdom* only days before the British referendum in June 2016. Its ruling gave the green light – but not on the basis of any proper legal argumentation – to national legislation that puts limits on the free movement of persons. There is a risk here, therefore, that its ruling will be seen as having been an interjection in the run-up to the referendum.

Recent case law in the area of Union citizenship will inevitably call the personal scope of the Regulation into question. Should it be restricted by the EU legislator to just migrating workers, so as better to reflect the member states' current understanding of the outer limits to transnational solidarity?

TIME FOR THE UNION TO DECIDE: ERODED WELFARE OR ACCELERATED COORDINATION?

On paper, the Union guarantees that the social security systems of the member states will remain independent. As we have seen, however, these systems are nonetheless influenced by the mechanisms of the Internal Market and by the development of Union citizenship.

It has also become clear that a residence-based model of welfare, and even of social security more narrowly, is subject to greater strain under such conditions than a non-residence-based model would be. As a result, national legislators feel tempted to change their social security arrangements so as to make them more resistant to this strain.

When Sweden joined the EU in 1995, its policy-makers were aware that residence-based benefits are more exposed than employment-based ones under the conditions in question. They therefore divided the country's social security programmes into two sections: employment-based social security, with payment levels calculated on the basis on income; and residence-based social security, with benefits for all residents of Sweden. In addition, the previous national pension was replaced with one based on qualifying periods. The previous national pension had offered a fixed sum without consideration of qualifying periods: accordingly, a short period of residence could furnish the basis for claiming a pension. This, in combination with the requirement laid down by Regulation 883/2004 that social security benefits must be made available to Union citizens who reside in another member state (the principle of exportability), entailed a certain kind of risk, namely that persons from other EU member states would move to Sweden, qualify themselves quickly for the Swedish national pension, and then move back home – and receive the full Swedish national pension for the remainder of their days.

If a member state chooses to keep its national policy of redistribution without restriction, it faces the risk that costs will rise due to an influx of Union citizens intent on exploiting the benefits which it provides. If, as a result, the cost of providing such benefits rises sharply, the welfare system of the country may eventually become unsustainable. *Commission v. United Kingdom* shows, however, that a member state may require a right to reside, so that economically inactive citizens of the Union cannot receive residence-based social security benefits.

A member state can also defend itself against the consequences of Union citizenship and its requirement of equal treatment by converting residence-based benefits into employment-based ones. Doing this, however, is tantamount to abandoning the objective of redistribution in large part – an objective which may have been central in the welfare policy of the country in question.

Finally, a state can choose to cancel certain social security benefits altogether. In the 1990s, for example, Germany chose to bury a legislative initiative to establish a supplementary national pension scheme (the *Fink* model) for low-income people. Otherwise, policy-makers feared, the country might suffer an export of its social security monies in future. They deemed this move necessary, notwithstanding the political consensus in Germany on the need for such a programme (Conant 2002, p. 194).

Regardless of which path is taken, it is clear that EU law influences the social security benefits and national welfare models of the member states.

In view of this influence, the member states could easily turn their efforts inward, rather than striving in concert to address the growing gaps in economic and social prosperity which have resulted from the economic crisis. They may elect to focus on achieving domestic stability, while at the same time turning a blind eye to the need for stability at the level of the Union.

It is not that the member states fail to appreciate the desirability of coordinating social security benefits in the case of migrant workers who contribute through taxes and social security contributions to the national system of the competent state. It is more that they feel uncomfortable with the EU dictating how national law is to be understood in situations for which Regulation 883/2004 has no answer. EU law, after all, takes precedence over national law, and the Regulation requires that persons be covered who are not considered under national law to be entitled to coverage. As we saw in the *van Munster* ruling above, EU law cuts deeps into the national structure of authority in these situations, obliging the competent authorities to act outside national rules and administrative systems.

In the same way, the development of Union citizenship has led to the inclusion of economically inactive people as well within social security programmes which are animated by national aims of redistribution. The benefits provided by such programmes are based on residence within a given state – a state within which citizens show solidarity with one another. In situations of this kind, Union citizenship – and its associated right to move freely within the Union – calls conventional conceptions of territorially based welfare and solidarity into question (cf. Schiek 2015 and de Witte 2015, pp. 70 ff.). EU law cannot reasonably be seen as applicable to national policies of redistribution. Such policies represent the core of a welfare state, and the aim of the benefits they offer is not to prevent the free movement of persons. Benefits of this kind lie on the border of social security; they do not require employment; and they are based on a sense of solidarity which so far has been found only at the national level. The ECJ showed an understanding of these facts in *Brey*, *Dano*, *Alimanović*, *García-Nieto*, and *Commission v. United Kingdom*.

In the year 2018, nationalist winds are still blowing. In the debate that followed the enlargement of the EU to the east and the Lehman Brothers crash in 2008, many have portrayed the free movement of persons as a problem: migrant workers, the suspicion goes, only come to the country to exploit its welfare system (cf. Chapter 3 by Ann-Cathrine Jungar in this book on right-wing populist parties). The British referendum basically focused on this issue; migrant workers were described as causing the shortcomings in British welfare provisions. No longer was the focus on the contributions that migrant workers make to British welfare, prosperity, and growth through the much-needed labour they provide; instead it was on the threat they presumably pose to the welfare state (research shows the opposite, however: cf. Chapter 4 by Joakim Ruist in this book, and also Soroka et al. 2016).

The states which remain members have nevertheless committed themselves, in the TEU, to working towards a 'new' Europe – a Europe that will not repeat its past recurrent mistakes and wars. For this reason, Article 3.3 TEU holds out an Internal Market that 'shall work for sustainable development of Europe based on balanced economic growth and price stability, a highly competitive social market economy, aiming at full employment and social progress . . .'. The Treaty's talk of a new social market economy, however, remains as yet to be specified (cf. Schiek 2015, pp. 1 f.). Can the member states continue to claim full independence for their national social security systems under such circumstances?

For a long time, the member states have tried to turn a blind eye to the inherent explosive force of the Internal Market. Now, however, they must ask themselves whether they want to stick to limited welfare programmes based on territoriality or whether they prefer to open the way to a welfare Europe – with Union citizenship, enhanced individual rights to social security, and dismantled borders between its member states.

There are actually two paths ahead when it comes to social security. The first entails no change of course from the present – the member states continue to show solidarity with migrant groups. This runs the risk of higher costs which may be unfunded in part, and of rising dissatisfaction among large parts of the population. The second path leads in the direction of federalism, where the Union takes responsibility for social-welfare provision. When it comes to welfare, after all, the solidarity already enjoined by EU law is no longer confined within national borders.

No matter how we twist and turn the question, the fact is that the member states and the EU have to act. As we have seen, the social security systems of the member states cannot remain unaffected by the larger EU legal context. The question to be answered, then, is whether the continued evolution in this area should be led by the EU legislator, or whether it ought instead to be dictated – as it mostly has been for the last fifty years – by the ECJ.

CONCLUSION: FROM CASE LAW TO DEMOCRATIC DECISION MAKING ON WELFARE?

It may appear that the member states have to choose between two bad things. Under such circumstances, it may be useful to look at the situation from an entirely new perspective.

The social security system and its interactions are so complex that no scheme for achieving distributive justice can ensure absolute fairness. Instead of trying, then, to construct a comprehensive system of compensations, perhaps we should ask ourselves a fundamental question: are we faced with a threat, or with a potential opportunity?

The fact is that a majority of the Union's member states have negative population growth. An ever larger population of retirees has to be supported by ever fewer economically active persons. On current demographic trends, the population in EU countries will soon be insufficient to support their social-welfare systems (on this topic, see Wadensjö 2012). The member states will accordingly be forced in future, regardless of how things look at present, to compete for workers by offering generous conditions for the migrating labour force – and this includes attractive social security benefits. If this tug of war is to be constructive and sustainable over the long term, current ideas about the role of the nation-state will have to be revised; and migrants will need to be appreciated for the potential which they offer for the development of sustainable welfare systems on a shared and collective basis. The member states should therefore take the initiative, and stop relinquishing these responsibilities to the ECJ.

We must not forget that the Court lacks the authority to develop sustainable social security systems. It can only find on separate cases in accordance with the rules of the Internal Market and the provisions for Union citizenship. Its case law cannot form the foundation for a new, more dynamic welfare system.

The starting point for the discussion ought to be how the member states want the Union to look 25 years from now, taking into account both present and future regional differences. Our models for the future should be aimed at overcoming the gaps in welfare and prosperity that exist today, but without completely eroding the differences between the member states in terms of domestic economic and social arrangements. In an increasingly globalized world, the future of the EU lies in (comm)unity, not in separation or particularity. Paradoxically, the development of ECJ case law can furnish a starting point for this discussion, inasmuch as the Court has started to dismantle territorial solidarity. And we must remember: 'Though one may be overpowered, two can defend themselves. A cord of three strands is not quickly broken' (Ecclesiastes 4:12 NIV).

REFERENCES

Abel-Smith, B. (1992), 'The Beveridge Report: Its Origins and Outcomes', *International Social Security Review*, vol. 45, no. 1–2, pp. 5–16.

Barnard, C. (2016), *The Substantive Law of the EU – The Four Freedoms*, 5th ed., Oxford University Press, Oxford.

Barr, N. (2001), *Economics of the Welfare State*, 4th ed., Oxford University Press, Oxford.

Bonoli, G. (2006), 'New Social Risks and the Politics of Post-Industrial Social Policies', in Armingeon, K. and Bonoli, G. (eds), *The Politics of Post-Industrial Welfare States*, Routledge, Abingdon, pp. 3–26.

Burgess, M. (2000), *Federalism and European Union: The Building of Europe, 1950–2000*, Routledge, Abingdon.

Conant, L. (2002), *Justice Contained: Law and Politics in the European Union*, Cornell University Press, Ithaca, New York.

Crawford, R. and Johnson, P. (2011), *The Changing Composition of Public Spending*, Institute for Fiscal Studies, www.ifs.org.uk/bns/bn119.pdf (accessed 30 October 2017).

Erhag, T. (ed.) (2016), 'EU Citizenship, Free Movement and Residence-Based Social Security Schemes' [Special Issue], *European Journal of Social Security*, vol. 18, no. 2, pp. 94–245.

Esping-Andersen, G. (1990), *The Three Worlds of Welfare Capitalism*, Polity Press, London.

European Commission (2015), *The 2015 Ageing Report Underlying Assumptions and Projection Methodologies*, http://ec.europa.eu/economy_finance/publications/european_economy/2014/pdf/ee8_en.pdf (accessed 30 October 2017).

Hailbronner, K. (2005), 'Union Citizenship and Access to Social Benefits', *Common Market Law Review*, vol. 42, no. 5, pp. 1245–1267.

Hennock, E. P. (1987), *British Social Reform and German Precedents: The Case of Social Insurance 1880–1914*, Clarendon, Oxford.

Jackson, W. (1994), *Gunnar Myrdal and America's Conscience: Social Engineering and Racial Liberalism, 1938–1987*, University of North Carolina Press, Chapel Hill.

Kochenov, D. and Plender, R. (2012), 'EU Citizenship: From an Incipient Form to an Incipient Substance?', *European Law Review*, vol. 37, no. 4, pp. 369–396.

Mitrany, D. (1943), *A Working Peace System – An Argument for the Functional Development of International Organization*, Royal Institute of International Affairs, Chatham House, London.

Moore, M. (1998), 'Freedom of Movement and Migrant Workers' Social Security: An Overview of the Court's Jurisprudence 1992–1997', *Common Market Law Review*, vol. 35, no. 2, pp. 409–457.

Moravcsik, A. (1993), 'Preferences and Power in the European Community: A Liberal Intergovernmentalist Approach', *Journal of Common Market Studies*, vol. 31, no. 4, pp. 473–524.

Palier, B. (ed.) (2010), *A Long Goodbye to Bismarck?*, Amsterdam University Press, Amsterdam.

Pennings, F. (2015), *European Social Security Law*, 6th ed., Intersentia, Antwerpen – Oxford – Portland.

Pieters, D. (2006), *Social Security: An Introduction to the Basic Principles*, Kluwer Law International, Alphen aan der Rijn.

Roberts, S. (2010), 'A Short History of Social Security Coordination', in Jorens, Y. (ed.), *50 Years of Social Security Coordination: Past, Present, Future*, European Union Publications Office, Luxembourg.

Roemer, J. E. (1998), *Theories of Distributive Justice*, Harvard University Press, Cambridge, MA.

Rothstein, B. and Kumlin, S. (2005), 'Making and Breaking Social Capital: The Impact of Welfare State Institutions', *Comparative Political Studies*, vol. 38, no. 4, pp. 339–365.
Rothstein, B. and Uslaner, E. (2005), 'All for All: Equality and Social Trust', *World Politics*, vol. 58, no. 1, pp. 41–72.
Scheubel, B. (2013), *Bismarck's Institutions: A Historical Perspective on the Social Security Hypothesis*, Mohr-Siebeck, Tübingen.
Schiek, D. (2015), 'Perspectives on Social Citizenship in the EU – from Status Positivus to status Socialis Activus via Two Forms of Transnational Solidarity', CETLS Paper Series, vol. 4.
Soroka, S. N., Johnston, R., Kevins, A., Banting, K. and Kymlicka, W. (2016), 'Migration and Public Spending', *European Political Science Review*, vol. 8, no. 2, pp. 173–194.
Ståhlberg, A.-C. (2004), *Socialförsäkringarna i Sverige*, SNS Förlag, Stockholm.
Verschueren, H. (2014), 'Free Movement or Benefit Tourism: The Unreasonable Burden of Brey', *European Journal of Migration and Law*, vol. 16, no. 2, pp. 147–179.
Wadensjö, E. (2012), 'Nationell migrations-, arbetsmarknas- och socialpolitik som utmaning för den europeiska sammanhållningen', in Bakardjieva Engelbrekt, A., Oxelheim, L. and Persson, T. (eds), *Arbetslöshet, migrationspolitik och nationalism – hot mot EU:s sammanhållning?*, Europaperspecktiv 2012, Santérus, Stockholm.
Watson, P. (1980), *Social Security Law of the European Communities*, Mansell Publishing, London.
Watson, P. (2014), *EU Social and Employment Law*, 2nd ed., Oxford University Press, Oxford.
Weiler, J. (1996), 'Citizenship and Human Rights', in Winter, J. A., Curtin, D. M., Kellerman, A. E. and de Witte, B. (eds), *Reforming the Treaty on European Union*, Kluwer, The Hague, pp. 57–86.
Wilper, A. P., et al. (2009), 'Health Insurance and Mortality in US Adults', *American Journal of Public Health*, vol. 99, no. 12, pp. 2289–2295.
Winterstein, A. (1999), 'Nailing the Jellyfish: Social Security and Competition Law', *European Competition Law Review*, vol. 20, pp. 324–333.
Witte, F. de (2015), *Justice in the EU: The Emergence of Transnational Solidarity*, Oxford Studies in European Law, Oxford University Press, Oxford.
Wyatt, D. (1977), 'The Social Security Rights of Migrant Workers and Their Families', *Common Market Law Review*, vol. 14, pp. 411–433.
Yoffe, W. M. (1973), *International Social Security Agreements*, Research Report No. 43, U.S. Department of Health, Education, and Welfare, Social Security Administration, Office of Research and Statistics, Washington.

Legal Acts

Regulation 3/58, OJ No 30, 16.12.1958.
Directive 79/7/EEC, OJ L 6, 10.1.1979.
Directive 2004/38/EC, OJ L 158, 30.4.2004.
Regulation 883/2004, OJ L 166, 30.4.2004.

Case Law (CJEU)

Case 39/74, Luciana Costa, spouse Mazzier v. Belgian State, EU:C:1974:122.

Case 35/77, Elisabeth Beerens v. Rijksdienst voor Arbeidsvoorziening, EU:C:1977:194.

Case 139/82, Paola Piscitello v. Istituto nazionale della previdenza sociale (INPS), EU:C:1983:126.

Case C-45/90, Alberto Paletta and others v. Brennet AG, EU:C:1992:236.

Joined cases C-159–160/91, Christian Poucet v. Assurances générales de France och Caisse mutuelle régionale du Languedoc-Roussillon and Daniel Pistre and Caisse autonome nationale de compensation de l'assurance vieillesse des artisans (Cancava), EU:C:1993:63.

Case C-165/91, Simon J. M. van Munster v. Rijksdienst voor Pensioenen, EU:C:1994:359.

Case C-443/93, Ioannis Vougioukas v. Idryma Koinonikon Asfalisseon (IKA), EU:C:1995:394.

Case C-244/94, Fédération française des sociétés d'assurance, Société Paternelle-Vie, Union des assurances de Paris-Vie and Caisse d'assurance et de prévoyance mutuelle des agriculteurs v. Ministère de l'Agriculture et de la Pêche, EU:C:1995:392.

Case C-137/04, Amy Rockler v. Försäkringskassan, EU:C:2006:106.

Case C-185/04, Ulf Öberg v. Försäkringskassan, länskontoret Stockholm, EU:C:2006:107.

Case C-34/09, Gerardo Ruiz Zambrano v. Office national de l'emploi (ONEm), EU:C:2011:124.

Case C-140/12, Pensionsversicherungsanstalt v. Peter Brey, EU:C:2013:565.

Case C-333/13, Elisabeta Dano and Florin Dano v. Jobcenter Leipzig, EU:C:2014:2358.

Case C-67/14, Jobcenter Berlin Neukölln v. Nazifa Alimanović and others, EU:C:2015:597.

Case C-12/14, European Commission v. Republic of Malta, EU:C:2016:135.

Case C-299/14, Vestische Arbeit Jobcenter Kreis Recklinghausen v. Jovanna García-Nieto m.fl., EU:C:2016:114.

Case C-308/14, European Commission v. United Kingdom of Great Britain and Northern Ireland, EU:C:2016:436.

Case Law (Sweden)

UM 2516-09, Lewandowska.

UM 10307-09, Lewandowska (appeal).

9. The role of trust in explaining health and wealth gaps in the EU

Martin Ljunge

INTRODUCTION

There are large differences in well-being and prosperity between countries in the European Union (EU) and within the Member States. Social capital, and trust in particular, has been highlighted as an important factor in social and economic development (see for example Knack and Keefer 1997; Zak and Knack 2001; La Porta et al. 1997, 1999). More recent papers make a stronger case that trust causes development (see Algan and Cahuc 2010; Tabellini 2008, 2010; and the overview by Algan and Cahuc 2014).

The differences that have come to light following the economic crisis can be seen as reminders of the structural differences between countries in the EU. It is possible that the fast development in the EU's periphery following the single currency's inception was a digression and that the underlying structural differences between countries are again shaping development. Social capital is such a deep underlying difference, and social trust differs markedly across the EU.

In this chapter I highlight how new research can provide answers to how gaps in health and wealth can be reduced. The focus is on an approach that can identify the causal direction of the connections between trust, health, and prosperity. I find clear evidence that trust promotes health and prosperity. The results point to the importance of promoting social trust among EU citizens to counter the effects of the economic crisis and the structural differences between the Member States.

The chapter is divided into a number of sections. First, I discuss what trust is and how it differs geographically in Europe and the world. The next section presents the approach of studying children of immigrants and how their trust, health, and prosperity are linked to factors in their country of ancestry. The following two sections present evidence of how trust among children is shaped depending on factors in the mother's and the father's country of birth. The next two sections study how trust affects health, and how migrants bring their health with them and in what way it influences their happiness. The subsequent section studies how trust affects labor supply. The last section summarizes the findings and discusses implications for policy in the EU and the Member States.

TRUST – WHAT IS IT?

Scandinavia is the world leader in trust. Sweden, Norway, Denmark, and Finland hold the four top spots among the countries of the world regarding their attitudes toward trusting people in general. This is one feature that distinguishes Scandinavia from the rest of the world. The Scandinavian countries are also socially and economically highly developed, in part as a result of the high social trust. The high level of development may also help maintain high trust; hence there is a beneficial self-reinforcing social equilibrium.

What do we mean by trust? There are many aspects to trust. The dimension that has garnered the most attention and has the strongest connection to a high level of development is generalized or social trust. This means trust in people in general, that is, individuals who we do not have any direct relation with. These weak ties prove important, and are distinct from the strong ties and particularized trust vis-à-vis, for example, the family, relatives, neighbors, or the police. I focus on social trust.

How do we measure trust? It is usually measured through a survey question that reads "Generally speaking, would you say that most people can be trusted or that you need to be very careful in dealing with people?" The answer that you in general can trust most people captures that an individual has high trust.

It may seem hard to compare such a question, trusting people in general, between different countries. Is the question perceived similarly in different cultures? It is of course impossible to know exactly how it is perceived around the globe, but the question does capture important differences. Countries where many say you can generally trust people are also places where a lost wallet with cash as well as the owner's address is returned to the owner, often with the cash. Countries with high trust also have low corruption and diplomats who pay their parking tickets.

Considering the Swedish population, two out of three express that you can trust people in general. In Italy, half as many express high trust. Northern Europe has higher trust than southern Europe but lower than Scandinavia. Eastern Europe is less trusting than southern Europe. Looking across the world, English-speaking countries are high trusting but a little less than Scandinavia. Africa and Latin America have the lowest levels of trust. In Brazil, one out of seventeen individuals express that most people can be trusted.

A NATURAL EXPERIMENT BASED ON FAMILY BACKGROUND

If you ask people about their trust, health, and prosperity, it is likely that those expressing high trust are also feeling healthy and doing fairly well in the labor market. Can we conclude that trust caused their well-being? It is of course possible, but it could also be that those who are in good health and have nice jobs express high trust because life has gone well for them. Similarly, those with poor health and less prosperity may express suspicion toward people in general. To understand if trust leads to well-being, we must go beyond studying correlations among individuals as they may measure causal effects in both directions.

How can the problem of determining the causal direction between trust and well-being be resolved? We need a measure of trust that cannot be influenced by the individual's well-being. Here the children of immigrants come to the rescue as they constitute one kind of "natural experiment." They all live in the same country and are influenced by the same institutions and the environment, but their parents have different backgrounds. If trust is transmitted within the family, from parent to child, then trust in the ancestral country can be used as a measure of the child's trust. Crucial for this approach is that the well-being of the child, living in a country other than where their parents were born, cannot affect trust in another country. If there is a link between trust in the ancestral country and the child's well-being, the causal direction can only be from trust to well-being. In my research I have used this approach that addresses reverse causality from well-being to trust.

The first step in the approach is to study if any factor in the ancestral country is affecting the trust expressed by the child. If so, the factor that affects the child's trust can be used as a measure of the child's trust, as it captures the persistent component of trust transmitted across generations. In the second stage the factor in the ancestral country is related to the child's health or prosperity. In the next section I study the ancestral factors that shape trust on the maternal side, and in the following section factors on the father's side. The method is based on the cultural transmission theory by Bisin and Verdier (2001, 2010) and discussed in further detail by Fernandez (2010).

The individual data I use is from the European Social Survey. The survey is conducted every two years, beginning in 2002. I study 30 countries including most EU countries plus a number of neighboring countries (e.g. Norway, Turkey, Ukraine).

One distinctive feature of this survey is that it includes questions about the respondent's country of birth and the parents' birth countries. This means that I can identify the children of immigrants and which countries they have ancestry from. The survey also contains information on social trust, health, education, labor supply, and occupational status, in addition to demographic information like age and gender.

The children of immigrants I study are adults, on average 43 years old. They are similar to the general population along observable dimensions. They have similar education and marital status. They have slightly higher unemployment but also slightly higher labor force participation than the general population. Therefore, it would not appear that the studied population, children of immigrants, differs from the general population. Notably, the children of immigrants express as high a level of trust as the general population, on average. However, this similarity on average conceals systematic differences based on ancestry, which I present below.

The data on the share of the population that express high trust in the ancestral country has been obtained by combining the European Values Study and World Values Survey (EVS/WVS). With the help of those surveys I can extend the originating countries beyond Europe to all parts of the world. I can match children of immigrants in the European Social Survey to some 90 ancestral countries in the worldwide survey.

TRUST TRANSMISSION WITHIN THE FAMILY – THE ROLE OF THE MOTHER

There is a strong positive relationship between the child's trust and the percentage that express high trust in the mother's country of birth. The connection is illustrated in Figure 9.1. The horizontal axis measures the proportion expressing high trust in the mother's country of birth. The vertical axis denotes the difference in trust between those with a certain ancestral country and the natives (it is an average across the 29 countries of birth in the study). For example, 0.5 means that children of immigrant mothers express a half point higher trust than natives (with native mothers). The trust measure on the vertical axis is from the European survey in which individuals may select their trust on a scale from 0 (lowest trust) to 10 (highest trust). On the horizontal axis is the data from the worldwide survey. Here trust is measured as the proportion expressing high trust, so 0.4 indicates that four out of ten in the country express high trust.

Figure 9.1 illustrates that those with a mother from a country with a high level of trust (e.g. Sweden, "SE" in the figure) have higher trust than those with a mother from a low trust country (e.g. Portugal, "PT" in the figure). The positive correlation indicates that the trust is transferred from the mother to the child even if the child is born and lives in a dif-

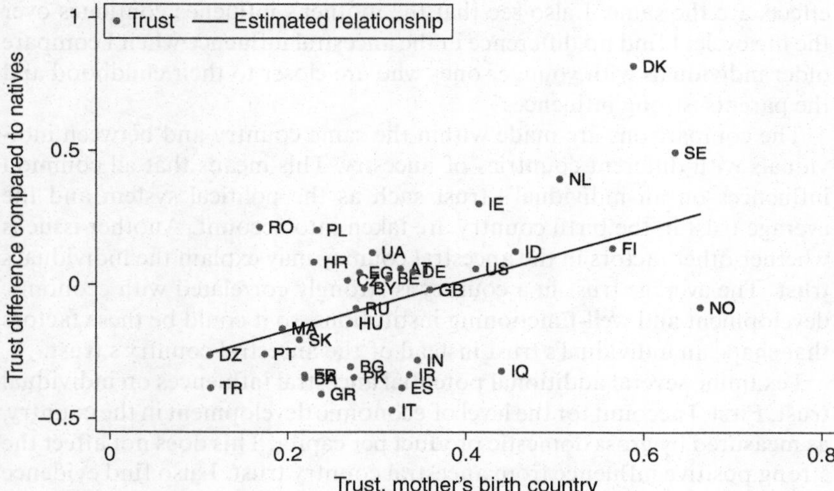

Source: Ljunge (2014a).

Figure 9.1 Differences in trust among children of immigrants and the share with high trust in the mother's birth country

ferent environment than where the mother was born. It thus shows that family is important for the formation of the child's trust. Part of the trust persists across generations even if the child lives in a completely different environment.

In Figure 9.1 we see the relationship without taking into account other factors. It is possible that children with ancestry from countries with high trust differ from others in various ways. In the analysis I have taken into account age, gender, education, labor market participation, marital status, and religion. It does not affect the strong correlation. It could also be that women who migrated are different from others and meet other spouses. In order to take into account differences among the parents, I have accounted for the mother's and father's education and whether they worked when the child was 14 years old. These factors do not affect the relationship between the individual's trust and the trust in the ancestral country. High parental education has a positive relationship with the child's trust. It indicates that increased education could have beneficial long-term effects because it could increase the trust in the next generation.

Do mothers have greater influence on daughters than sons? I find no evidence that this is the case. The estimated effect is a little higher for daughters than sons, but it cannot be ruled out with any certainty that the effects are the same. I also see that the mother's influence continues over the life cycle; I find no difference in the ancestral influence when I compare older individuals with younger ones who are closer to their childhood and the parents' strong influences.

The comparisons are made within the same country and between individuals with different countries of ancestry. This means that all common influences on an individual's trust such as the political system and the average trust in the birth country are taken into account. Another issue is whether other factors in the ancestral country may explain the individual's trust. The average trust in a country is strongly correlated with economic development and well-functioning institutions, so it could be these factors that shape an individual's trust instead of the ancestral country's trust.

I examine several additional potential ancestral influences on individual trust. First, I account for the level of economic development in the country, as measured by gross domestic product per capita. This does not affect the strong positive influence from ancestral country trust. I also find evidence that those with ancestry from a more developed country have higher trust. In the next step I account for how democratic the political institutions are (as measured by the polity2-variable). The political institutions in the mother's country of birth have no noticeable influence on the individual's trust. I also account for women's labor force participation as well as education in the ancestral country. Here, I find that ancestral countries where more women work have a strong positive predictive power over the individual's trust (but when this factor is included, economic development is no longer a significant predictor). The influence of trust in the ancestral country remains a strong positive predictor for the individual's trust, even when all other factors in the ancestral country are included in the model.

The estimated effect of ancestral country trust is quantitatively important. The increase in trust from the level of Portuguese ancestry to the Swedish equivalent corresponds to more than the effect of a high school education (compared with less training) and half the effect of a college education. Education is the factor that most powerfully predicts trust, and the estimated effect of ancestral country trust is on the same level as education, which indicates that the estimated influence of inherited trust is important in terms of effect size.

Another way to evaluate the role of trust is to compare it with the influence of other factors in the ancestral country. If we relate the average differences in trust across ancestral countries to the factors in each country we investigated above (in addition to trust, it was economic development, democracy, women's work, and education), we find that ancestral trust accounts for 65 percent of the explained variation in individual trust.

This comparison also indicates an important role for ancestral trust transmission.

Does it matter in which country the individual lives or which country the mother originates from? You can imagine that it does matter for the trust adaptation of the child whether their birth country trust is higher or lower compared to the trust in the mother's country of birth. For example, it could be that individuals are faster to adapt to lower trust levels. A person with high trust can quickly get burned by unreliable individuals in a country with low trust, and quickly learn not to trust people in general. On the other hand, wary individuals with low trust may resist engaging with individuals they do not know in high trust environments as well. They may thus get few lessons that it may be worthwhile to trust people when they stay inside their shell and it takes a long time to adjust the trust level upwards.

I have divided the sample into two groups. In the first group are those who were born in a country with lower average trust than in the mother's country of birth (i.e. adjusts to the lower levels). The second group consists of those born in a country with higher trust than in the mother's country of birth (i.e. adjusts to the higher levels). I estimate to what extent trust is transmitted in each group. I find a higher point estimate in the latter group, which could point to a slower adaptation to higher trust levels. This is in line with the argument above. The difference between the groups, however, is not so big that we can rule out the possibility that it is the same in both groups. The results provide an indication of differences depending on birth and ancestral countries.

We can learn more about how the transmission of the trust varies when we study four groups. The countries are divided based on whether they have high or low trust in both the individual's and the mother's birth country (creating four groups based on all high and low trust combinations of birth and ancestral countries). Then the extent of transmission of trust is estimated in each of the four groups. Birth countries with high trust can be found mainly in northern and western Europe, while southern and eastern Europe tend to have low trust. Ancestral countries where at least 30 percent of people have high trust are classified as high trust countries and those with a lower percentage than this low trust countries.

I estimate a strong transmission of trust for individuals born in high trust countries, regardless of ancestry. The point estimate is highest for those with ancestry from countries with low trust. For individuals born in countries with low trust, there is no clear effect of trust in the ancestral country, whether it was high or low. The pattern fits the description above. In low trust countries it seems that individuals adapted their trust to the local level by the second generation. The strong estimates in high trust countries shows that it takes a long time to build trust, at least two generations. The higher estimate for those with ancestry from low trust countries also indicates that it takes even longer to build trust in this group.

In the next step I change what is considered high trust ancestry. The new dividing line is that at least 40 percent express high trust. The estimates for the four groups are similar to the preceding paragraph, but with one fascinating exception. The highest estimate is now for the group with ancestry from very high trust countries that live in countries with low trust. It shows an exception to the idea that individuals quickly adjust to low trust.

If trust in the country is high enough, it is transmitted to the next generation even if they live in an environment that does not encourage high trust. This is done through transmission within the family, from parent to child. The result shows an extra advantage of having very high trust, such as in Scandinavia. Very high trust can survive dramatic changes in the environment, due to the important role of the family in shaping norms. It provides an explanation for why Scandinavia has sustained high trust; at very high levels trust may overcome environmental influences due to strong transmission in the family. This is a new result in the literature that only has had explanations for the persistence of low trust.

So far, only trust in the mother's birth country has been considered. What does the father's side look like? When I estimate the effect of trust in the birth country of the father, I find a positive estimate, but it is not strong enough to reasonably exclude that there is no effect. This means that there is no strong evidence that the trust in the father's birth country has a clear influence on the child's trust.

I have also studied a model where the trust in both the mother's and the father's countries of origin are included. I find a strong effect on the mother's side but no clear effect on the father's side, as in the previous separate models. In this joint model, I find that the difference between the mother's and the father's influence is significant. It shows that there are distinct differences between the role of the mother and the father for how norms like trust are formed in the family, in line with Dohmen et al. (2012) who study parental and child trust in Germany.

The result does not mean that fathers do not play a role in shaping norms like trust. It is possible that fathers have other influences not taken into account of in the analysis discussed above. The role of the father is explored in the next section.

TRUST TRANSMISSION WITHIN THE FAMILY – THE ROLE OF THE FATHER

On the father's side, I find that democratic institutions shape trust. Individuals with fathers from more democratic countries express greater trust than those with fathers from less democratic countries. As previously discussed this approach provides a clear causal direction from more democracy to higher trust.

The result provides ammunition to democracy promoters. Democracy can be seen as an end in itself. My analysis shows that greater democracy may promote trust – one factor that has been associated with better economic and social development (see for example Algan and Cahuc 2010 and Tabellini 2010). More democracy could therefore have a number of positive consequences such as increasing trust. Such effects provide additional arguments to the dissemination of democratic institutions in the world.

The analysis also provides direct support to one of the hypotheses in Putnam (1993), where he studies different regions of Italy. He finds well-functioning political institutions and high trust in northern Italy, while the southern part is characterized by low trust and poorly functioning public institutions. He interprets that the positive correlation between trust and political institutions reflects causality in both directions. I provide evidence for the hypothesis in the direction from more democratic institutions to higher trust (see Ljunge 2012).

I also find evidence that it is the population characteristics that matter and not necessarily the place where the institutions are located geographically, building on the work by Putterman and Weil (2010). The individuals I study, children of immigrants, live with different institutions than those where their ancestors were born. I do not estimate an effect of the political institutions where they exist. I estimate the effect of the political institutions on individuals' attitudes that are in turn transmitted within the family also when the parents have migrated. The results also give an indication of how persistent the impact of political institutions is; they survive at least two generations. It takes generations to shake off an undemocratic heritage. The result also points to the importance of a long-run perspective for experiencing the full effects of more democracy.

I take into account individual factors such as demographic characteristics, education, income, and religion in the analysis. These factors do not have any significant effect on the estimated effect of democracy on trust. The same applies to parents' education and labor force participation.

More developed countries tend to be more democratic. To distinguish the influences of ancestry from countries with higher development and more democracy, I have accounted for the gross domestic product per capita in the ancestral country. Economic development has no apparent influence on trust while democracy remains a strong predictor. I also account for the rule of law with the same result. Moreover, trust in the ancestral country does not have a clear effect on the father's side, unlike the maternal side as previously discussed.

An additional measure of political influences is how important politics is considered to be in the ancestral country. This measure turns out to have a strong positive influence on trust, along with the democratic institutions that continue to have a significant influence. The results provide further fuel for the finding that political factors are important for the formation of trust as only the two variables that measure politics have significant estimates when all the above-mentioned factors are included in the estimation.

As many European countries have the highest value of the democracy measure, one could imagine that these most democratic countries are behind the result. I study the relationship for all ancestral countries except the most democratic to investigate the concern. The model includes all the above-mentioned factors in the ancestral country. Only the democracy measure turns out to have a significant influence on trust in this case. It strengthens the analysis that it is the political institutions that constitute the significant factor even in the case when fully democratic ancestries are excluded.

TRUST PROMOTES HEALTH

Thus far the discussion has concerned how trust is shaped by various influences on the mother's and father's side. On the mother's side the strong factor is trust in the ancestral country while on the father's side it is the degree of democracy. Does trust have any impact on the choices people make and how they feel? I have studied several aspects of how people behave, their welfare, and how it is related to trust. In the following section I focus on the influences on the mother's side as this is where the strong trust transmission was found.

First, I study the individual's health. The primary measure is self-assessed health, which is measured by a question in the survey I use. The individual is asked how they feel about their health in general. The five response options are very good, good, fair, poor, or very poor. Most say their health is good (2 out of 5) or very good (1 out of 4).

Individuals with a parent born in a high trust country express better health than those with a parent born in a country with low trust. The method is the same as when studying how trust is transmitted across

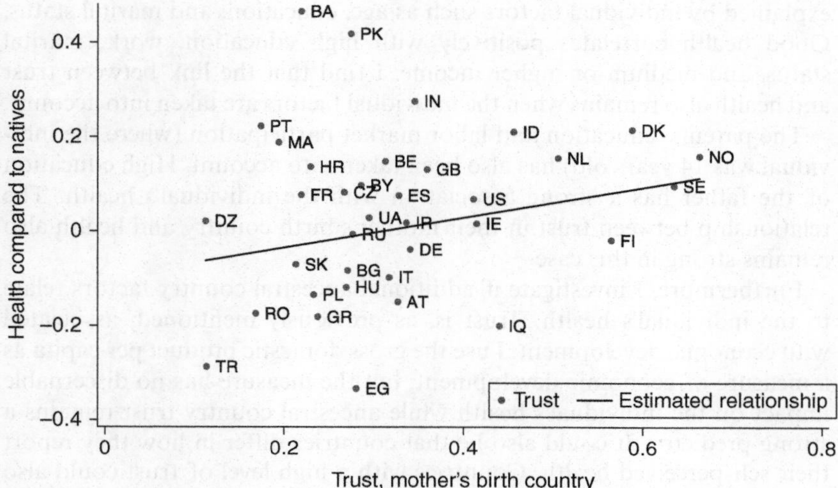

Source: Ljunge (2014b).

Figure 9.2 Differences in health among children of immigrants and the share with high trust in the mother's birth country

generations. I study children of immigrants and relate their self-assessed health to trust in the mother's birth country.

The positive association between trust and health is illustrated in Figure 9.2. The horizontal axis presents the share of the population that expresses high trust in the mother's country of birth (as in the previous figure). The vertical axis indicates the difference in self-assessed health among children of immigrants with a given ancestry and natives (the difference is an average over the 30 European countries where the children live).

The positive relationship in Figure 9.2 shows that those with ancestry from countries with high trust express better health than those who have ancestry from low trust countries. What does the relationship mean? As previously seen trust in the ancestral country is a measure of the individual's trust. This persistent part of an individual's trust, as measured by the ancestral country's trust, can thus be interpreted as a cause behind the individual's health. A major advantage of the approach to study children of immigrants, as previously discussed, is that it provides a clear causal direction from trust to health. It is not reasonable that an individual's health affects the average trust in another country.

I have also examined if the relationship between trust and health can be explained by individual factors such as age, education, and marital status. Good health correlates positively with high education, work, marital status, and medium or higher income. I find that the link between trust and health also remains when the individual factors are taken into account.

The parents' education and labor market participation (where the individual was 14 years old) has also been taken into account. High education of the father has a strong association with the individual's health. The relationship between trust in their mother's birth country and health also remains strong in this case.

Furthermore, I investigate if additional ancestral country factors relate to the individual's health. Trust is, as previously mentioned, associated with economic development. I use the gross domestic product per capita as a measure of economic development, but the measure has no discernable impact on the individual's health while ancestral country trust remains a strong predictor. It could also be that countries differ in how they report their self-perceived health. Countries with a high level of trust could also have a very high self-assessed health, and it could be the self-assessed health rather than trust that affects an individual's health. I find, however, that the average self-assessed health in the ancestral country has an insignificant influence on an individual's health but that trust continues to be a strong factor.

In addition to self-assessed health I also take into account objective health measures in the country of origin. I use three broad dimensions: average life expectancy, infant mortality, and the probability of a child dying before turning five years of age. None of these measures have a significant relationship to an individual's health when I take into account the country-of-origin trust, which has a strong influence on health.

I have also taken into account institutional factors in the ancestral country. High trust societies tend to be characterized by more equal income distribution, the rule of law, and democratic political institutions. These factors could have an impact on individuals' health. In particular, income inequality and health has been debated intensively after the book *The Spirit Level* by Wilkinson and Pickett (2009), who argue that more equality promotes health. I use two measures of income inequality, the Gini coefficient and the ratio of the incomes of the highest and lowest quintile of the population (the Gini coefficient is used more generally, while the ratio is preferred by Wilkinson and Pickett). I do not find any significant effect of inequality when using either of the measures, while trust is a strong influence as previously. The estimates indicate that if there is an effect of inequality on health then the effect is not persistent.

The other two institutional factors, the rule of law and the degree of democracy, have no clear associations with the individual's health. Trust continues to be a strong factor. A survey measure related to trust is happiness (see Uslaner 2002). I find no correlation between the level of happiness in the ancestral country and the individual's health, while the influence of trust remains strong.

Moreover, I study a more objective health measure. The survey asks whether the individual is hindered in their everyday life by any illness or disability. I find that fewer among those with high trust express that their daily lives are hindered by health problems, compared to those with low trust ancestry. This shows that the effect of trust not only predicts higher self-assessed health but also influences an objective manifestation of good health.

How could trust affect health? There are many possible channels. Trusting individuals could have a greater tendency to seek care from health-care professionals and they may be more likely to follow the doctor's prescriptions. Those with higher trust may also have larger social networks where they can access information about good health. Networks may also act by encouraging healthy living if it is cherished in the group. Trust may also influence the individual choices that are risk factors for health. Labor market status, for example, has a strong association with health. If the trust affects labor market status then the relationship can explain some of the positive relationship between trust and health. As discussed in a later section, I find that trust promotes a range of labor market factors that are positively associated with good health.

IMMIGRANTS' HEALTH AND HAPPINESS

There may be concerns that migrants differ from the general population. In particular, a healthy immigrant effect has been documented in the U.S. That is, immigrants are healthier than natives upon arrival, but become more like natives the longer they spend in the new country. Such effects caution against considering migrants as similar to natives in all dimensions. Are similar patterns observed in Europe?

Migrants to Europe have similar health to natives, on average. The self-assessed health level among migrants and natives in 30 European countries are very similar, contrasting with the U.S. experience. Moreover, the socioeconomic gradient of health, the predictive power of socioeconomic characteristics for health, is similar for natives and migrants in Europe, as found in Ljunge (2016). The only exception is Muslim migrants who appear to pay a health penalty, while there is no such effect for native Muslims.

The similarities of average health and the socioeconomic gradient across natives and migrants do mask some systematic differences across ancestral groups. Health is significantly higher for those born in countries with better health. This indicates that migrants bring their health with them, and that health is not solely determined by current contextual factors but also by persistent influences.

The persistence of health can be used to shed light on the issue of health and well-being. Individual data show a very strong correlation between health and well-being measures such as happiness and life satisfaction, but it is hard to understand the causal relationships in such data as it could run both ways.

By studying migrants and using birth country health as a measure of individual health, it is possible to study one direction of the relationship. Since the well-being of a person in one country cannot plausibly determine the average health in another country, there cannot be reverse causality from well-being to health.

The results show that those with better health, where variation in birth country health is used as an instrument for individual health, express substantially higher happiness and life satisfaction. The results are robust to accounting for a range of other birth country characteristics. A one standard deviation improvement in health predicts higher happiness by more than four times the happiness difference of changing employment status from unemployed to employed.

TRUST PROMOTES LABOR SUPPLY, OCCUPATIONAL STATUS, AND LESS UNEMPLOYMENT

The previous literature has found evidence that trust raises the level of economic development (see for example Algan and Cahuc 2010 and Tabellini 2008, 2010). These studies have been based on comparisons of European regions or countries. The literature has mainly argued that high trust promotes growth through an effect on society as a whole. It is beneficial for economic development if cooperation can work through shaking hands rather than through long and detailed contracts which are enforced by the legal system. Everyone in a high trust society benefits from the fact that all others have high trust.

I, however, have a striking finding beyond the social externality of high trust. I find that your trust affects your choices and ultimately your economic prosperity. Thus, there is an impact on the individual outcomes of their own trust. I have analyzed a number of individual choices in a similar way to the study of how health is affected by ancestral trust. I relate the individual's choice to trust in the ancestral country.

How could trust affect the individual's decision? Individuals with a high level of trust have been found to be more likely to take risks and to think it is less bad if one fails compared to those with low trust (see Fehr 2009). These attitudes toward risk indicate an optimistic character trait. Individuals with high trust are more likely to take risks, and if it does not go their way, it is not so bad. This means that the threshold to make various investments is lower among those with higher trust compared to those with lower trust. Investments with uncertain outcomes include taking a new job and starting a business. People with high trust may more often make these leaps of faith and try something unknown.

Does it pay to be an optimist with high trust? It need not if the starry-eyed optimists make choices that usually fail. The high level of trust, however, does not seem to be so naive. In my research I find that those with high trust have higher economic status than those with low trust. The result suggests that, on average, it pays to make these leaps of faith.

A series of important decisions are studied using the same approach as above. I compare the actions taken by children of immigrants in a country and relate them to trust in their mother's country of birth. By comparing individuals within the same country, I account for all the factors that affect everyone in the country, such as the education system and labor market rules. Individuals vary by ancestry from countries with different levels of trust. It provides a clear causal direction from trust to individual choices, as the individual choice cannot plausibly affect the average trust in the country where the mother was born.

Individuals with high trust are more likely to report work as their main activity in a given week. They also have a lower probability of being unemployed or retired. This means that those with higher trust work more and are retired for a shorter period of time than those with low trust. With regard to unemployment, I find that it is lower in a given week for those with high trust. Moreover, longer periods of unemployment are less common among individuals with higher trust. This applies to periods of unemployment of both at least three and at least twelve months. If we consider an increase in trust by a standard deviation, it corresponds to a reduction in the risk for a one-year or longer period of unemployment by a quarter. It is a substantial effect size.

Moreover, high trusting individuals work in occupations where the employee has more influence over how the work is organized. It suggests that workers with high trust are given more autonomy that allows for individual creativity in performing the tasks, which could lead to higher productivity. Autonomy enables the employee to use their specific knowledge about the work situation to carry out the work in the best way. The study complements the work by Bloom et al. (2012) and Rose (2011).

I have taken into account a wide range of additional factors in the country of origin that could explain individuals' economic choices. The ancestral country's level of economic development or its economic and political institutions cannot explain individuals' choices, while trust continues to be a strong predictor, even when these aspects are taken into account. Also, less formal influences have been studied. I have accounted for the average level of happiness, work norms, family ties, personality traits, human capital, and individualism in the country of origin. These do not affect the strong impact that trust has on income and choice. In most cases, these additional influences have no clear link to the individual's choices. Trust is particular. It has a strong impact on a number of important choices, and prosperity, and as we saw in the previous section, trust also has a positive influence on health.

PROMOTE TRUST – AN IMPORTANT PUBLIC POLICY OBJECTIVE FOR CLOSING THE PROSPERITY GAP

My research has shown how trust is an important factor behind individuals' health and prosperity. Those with higher trust have more autonomous and more skilled jobs, higher labor supply, and better health. The results indicate that health and prosperity gaps in the EU can be reduced if trust increases.

There is an important role for the EU and the Member States. They can actively work to increase trust among citizens. I have already discussed some factors that can increase trust. Political institutions constitute one factor. I have found that greater democracy promotes trust. To democratize the EU is an issue that is discussed extensively. My research points to a reason in favor of further democratizing the EU. Such a development could increase the trust of the citizens, which in turn has good implications for labor supply and well-being.

The second factor I discussed is education, which has a strong positive correlation with trust. Both the individual's own and their parents' level of education predict higher trust, as we have seen. Promoting education has many positive aspects, one of which is that it could increase trust. Both democratization and increased education points to the long horizon required to increase trust in society. We see trust being transmitted across generations when children are affected by their parents' experiences. It takes a long time for the full effects of changes to materialize.

Research has also shown other factors that promote trust. In general, the pattern emerges that trust is promoted by more social interactions on equal terms and fewer hierarchical institutions. One example is teaching methods. Algan, Cahuc, and Shleifer (2013) find that students taught with more hierarchical methods express lower trust. Those who learn through less hierarchical methods, such as more group work and discussions, express higher trust.

A very interesting experiment has been conducted in Montreal in Canada. One hundred disadvantaged boys, at risk of falling behind in school as well as socially, were offered a program with training in social skills during the first years of school. The program involved a series of tutorials explaining how to act in groups, how to interpreting others' intentions, and how to handle frustration. Parents participated at different stages as well. Importantly, there was also a control group of similar boys that received no additional support beyond what normally is offered. Both boys who got additional aid and those who did not get it have been followed through their schooling and the beginning of adult life. The groups have dramatically different outcomes as reported by Algan et al. (2013). Those who received the social training have higher education, work more, and are much less likely to be incarcerated. Interestingly, the authors attribute a large part of the better outcomes to higher trust. This applies in particular to the economic outcomes. The results of the experiment with social skills training is highly interesting, and similar social training could be implemented in the EU Member States, preferably also with a control group to facilitate evaluation of the training program.

This is perhaps the single most important action that Member States can implement to reduce gaps in prosperity and health within countries. The focus is on children at risk with different types of behavioral tendencies. Many have challenging family circumstances. The children are at high risk of lacking essential skills in a more demanding job market and instead could end up involved in crime. If these children could learn crucial life skills, such as how to handle social dynamics in groups and how to manage frustration, it would increase their chances to educate themselves, to establish themselves in the labor market, and to have well-functioning relationships. This is fully in line with the new research, which studies how interventions in childhood affect non-cognitive skills such as perseverance and conscientiousness, and how those skills in turn affect individuals' choices (see for example Almlund et al. 2011 for an overview).

Regarding additional factors that influence trust, Aghion et al. (2010) studied economic regulations. They argue that more regulation is an expression of disbelief, since the regulations are demanded in order to protect the individual against being exploited by entrepreneurs. There is a strong empirical correlation between low trust and demand for government intervention in the economy. For example, it is more difficult to start a business in countries with low trust. Aghion et al. (2010) has also argued for, and showed evidence that, more economic regulations damage social trust. Berggren and Jordahl (2006) provide related evidence that economic freedom promotes trust.

To reduce gaps in health and wealth, both as a result of the economic crisis but also due to the underlying structural factors, it is important to increase trust among the more suspicious. Increasing the trust of those where it is lowest can improve their health and prosperity in accordance with the research discussed in this chapter. To increase the trust of the distrustful may also have additional effects as it might increase the average trust level in society, which could benefit everyone.

The importance of increasing trust, particularly among those with low trust, applies both within Member States and across countries. There are groups with low trust in all countries, and it is an important task to increase trust in these groups in each country. There are also large differences between the Member States: both southern and eastern Europe have lower trust than in the northern and western parts. The economic crisis has impacted southern and eastern Europe harder. Thus, it is especially important for these countries to increase trust as a way to counteract the effects of the crisis on prosperity and well-being.

One might think that it would be easy to increase trust in countries with low trust since the initial level is low. However, it is important to remember that low trust in a society is often a self-reinforcing equilibrium. The whole society may be built around the notion that people in general are not to be trusted. Parents teach their children to be leery. Public institutions can be designed with the premise that people are not reliable. Citizens do not believe that public money is put to good use. There may be corruption. It takes a holistic approach to transform such societies. The efforts to increase trust require a long-term approach and perseverance.

Yet, targeted reforms, such as social training in the early school years, are not without effect. They can have big effects on the individual's well-being. But there may be huge synergies for the community if several reforms work in tandem. Implementing reforms to increase trust in different domains might lead to a self-reinforcing feedback loop where trust is increasing in society as a whole, which in turn may fuel further increases in trust. Greater democracy can increase trust as discussed in Ljunge (2014c). At the same time, public institutions could increase their transparency and further emphasis could be put on using tax funds effectively. The effective management of public resources leads to higher trust among citizens as Charron and Rothstein (Chapter 10 in this volume) discuss in another chapter of this book. At the same time, teaching methods could be reformed to include more horizontal learning in the form of discussions and group work if this is not already the case, as Algan et al. (2013) find higher trust when such methods are used. Economic regulations can be made less hierarchical, as Aghion et al. (2010) argues this may promote trust.

The point is that if one reform to increase trust succeeds, it increases the likelihood that trust increasing reforms in other domains are successfully. It would be very beneficial if such trust-promoting processes could start in countries with low trust. One must remember, however, that there are significant challenges in starting and maintaining an increasing trust dynamic. At the same time, the gains are substantial as greater trust contributes to economic and social development. I have found that individuals with high trust work more, have more independent and qualified occupations, are less unemployed, and experience better health.

Moreover, Ljunge (2014a) has shown that there are mechanisms that protect the high trust from the influences of low trust, as families with high trust retain it even in low trust environments. This points to another advantage of achieving high trust in society: it is not only low trust that is self-reinforcing, but high trust as well.

ACKNOWLEDGMENTS

My research discussed in this chapter has been funded by the Swedish Council for Working Life and Social Research grant number 2012:1261, the Swedish Research Council grant numbers 2012-643 and P2007-0468:1-E, and the Torsten Söderberg Foundation grant number E1-14.

REFERENCES

Aghion, Philippe, Yann Algan, Pierre Cahuc, and Andrei Shleifer (2010), "Regulation and Distrust." *Quarterly Journal of Economics*, **125** (3), 1015–1049.

Algan, Yann, and Pierre Cahuc (2010), "Inherited Trust and Growth." *American Economic Review*, **100** (5), 2060–2092.

Algan, Yann, and Pierre Cahuc (2014), "Trust, Growth and Well-Being: New Evidence and Policy Implications." In Philippe Aghion and Steven N. Durlauf (eds.), *Handbook of Economic Growth*, vol. 2. Amsterdam: Elsevier, 49–120.

Algan, Yann, Pierre Cahuc, and Andrei Shleifer (2013), "Teaching Practices and Social Capital." *American Economic Journal: Applied Economics*, **5** (3), 189–210.

Algan, Yann, Elisabeth Beasley, Frank Vitaro, and Richard E. Tremblay (2013), "The Long-Term Impact of Social Skills Training at School Entry: A Randomized Controlled Trial." Working paper.

Almlund, M., A. Duckworth, J. J. Heckman, and T. Kautz (2011), "Personality Psychology and Economics." In E. A. Hanushek, S. Machin, and L. Wößmann (eds.), *Handbook of the Economics of Education*, vol. 4. Amsterdam: Elsevier, 1–181.

Berggren, Niclas, and Henrik Jordahl (2006), "Free to Trust: Economic Freedom and Social Capital." *Kyklos*, **59** (2), 141–169.

Bisin, Alberto, and Thierry Verdier (2001), "The Economics of Cultural Transmission and the Dynamics of Preferences." *Journal of Economic Theory*, **97**, 298–319.

Bisin, Alberto, and Thierry Verdier (2010), "The Economics of Cultural Transmission and Socialization." In Jess Benhabib, Alberto Bisin, and Matt Jackson (eds.), *Handbook of Social Economics*. Amsterdam: North-Holland, 339–416.

Bloom, Nicholas, Raffaella Sadun, and John Van Reenen (2012), "The Organization of Firms across Countries." *Quarterly Journal of Economics*, **127** (4), 1663–1705.

Dohmen, Thomas, Armin Falk, David Huffman, and Uwe Sunde (2012), "The Intergenerational Transmission of Risk and Trust Attitudes." *Review of Economic Studies*, **79** (2), 645–677.

Fehr, Ernst (2009), "On the Economics and Biology of Trust." *Journal of the European Economic Association*, **7** (2–3), 235–266.

Fernandez, Raquel (2010), "Does Culture Matter?" In Jess Benhabib, Alberto Bisin, and Matt Jackson (eds.), *Handbook of Social Economics*. Amsterdam: North-Holland, 481–510.

Knack, Stephen, and Philip Keefer (1997), "Does Social Capital Have an Economic Pay-Off? A Cross Country Investigation." *Quarterly Journal of Economics*, **112** (4), 1251–1288.

La Porta, Rafael, Florencio Lopez-de-Silanes, Andrei Shleifer, and Robert W. Vishny (1997), "Trust in Large Organizations." *American Economic Review*, **87** (2), 333–338.

La Porta, R., F. Lopez-de-Silanes, A. Shleifer, and R. Vishny (1999), "The Quality of Government." *Journal of Law, Economics and Organization*, **15**, 222–279.

Ljunge, Martin (2012), "Cultural Transmission of Civicness." *Economics Letters*, **117**, 291–294.

Ljunge, Martin (2014a), "Trust Issues: Evidence on the Intergenerational Trust Transmission from Children of Immigrants." *Journal of Economic Behavior and Organization*, **106**, 175–196.

Ljunge, Martin (2014b), "Social Capital and Health: Evidence that Ancestral Trust Promotes Health among Children of Immigrants." *Economics and Human Biology*, **15**, 165–186.

Ljunge, Martin (2014c), "Social Capital and Political Institutions: Evidence that Democracy Fosters Trust." *Economics Letters*, **122**, 44–49. DOI: 10.1016/j.econlet.2013.10.031.

Ljunge, Martin (2016), "Migrants, Health, and Happiness: Evidence that Health Assessments Travel with Migrants and Predict Well-Being." *Economics and Human Biology*, **22**, 35–46.

Putnam, R. D. (1993), *Making Democracy Work: Civic Traditions in Modern Italy*. Princeton, NJ: Princeton University Press.

Putterman, Louis, and David N. Weil (2010), "Post-1500 Population Flows and the Long-Run Determinants of Economic Growth and Inequality." *Quarterly Journal of Economics*, **125** (4), 1627–1682.

Rose, David (2011), *The Moral Foundation of Economic Behavior*, Oxford: Oxford University Press.

Tabellini, Guido (2008), "Institutions and Culture." *Journal of the European Economic Association Papers and Proceedings*, **6** (2–3), 255–294.

Tabellini, Guido (2010), "Culture and Institutions: Economic Development in the Regions of Europe." *Journal of the European Economic Association*, **8** (4), 677–716.

Uslaner, Eric M. (2002), *The Moral Foundations of Trust*. Cambridge: Cambridge University Press.

Wilkinson, Richard G., and Kate Pickett (2009), *The Spirit Level: Why More Equal Societies Almost Always Do Better*. London: Allen Lane.

Zak, Paul J., and Stephen Knack (2001), "Trust and Growth." *Economic Journal*, **111** (470), 295–321.

10. Regions of trust and distrust: how good institutions can foster social cohesion

Nicholas Charron and Bo Rothstein

INTRODUCTION

Since the 1993 publication of Robert Putnam's modern classic *Making Democracy Work*, which analyzed the politics of regions in Italy, issues of social capital and social trust have become the object of a huge research industry. Defined as a combination of interpersonal, generalized (that is, social) trust and networks based on reciprocity, social capital is now generally recognized as a major asset for groups and societies (Castiglione et al. 2008; Svendsen and Svendsen 2009). The reason for the strong interest is that a high level of social trust in a society indicates a high level of social cohesion and correlates with a number of other variables that for most people are highly desirable. At the individual level, people who believe that most other people in their society can be trusted are also more inclined to have a positive view of their democratic institutions, participate more in politics, are more active in civic organizations, and are more tolerant towards minorities and to people who are not like themselves. People who are trusting also have a more optimistic view of their possibilities to influence their own life chances and, not least important, tend to be even more happy with how their life is going (Uslaner 2002; Delhey and Newton 2005; Helliwell 2006; Freitag and Traunmuller 2009; Leung et al. 2011; Dinesen 2013).

The same positive pattern exists at the societal level. Countries with more trusting people are likely to have more functional democratic institutions, more open economies, greater economic growth, and less crime and corruption (Keefer and Knack 2005; Uslaner 2008; Bjørnskov 2009; Richey 2010). Thus, at both the individual and the societal levels, many things that are normatively desirable seem connected to social trust and social capital.

With regard to the interpretation of what the standard survey question about social trust actually measures, we support the idea offered by

Uslaner (2002), who argues that when people answer whether they think that "most other people can be trusted," their response can be understood as their evaluation of the moral standard of the society in which they live. This implies that trust can be seen as an informal institution, as argued by North (1998), and therefore as a source of social cohesion, creating a system of beliefs that the various groups in society have both a shared responsibility and an ability to provide public and merit goods (Rothstein 2005).

Our understanding of this research is that there is a nearly general agreement that social trust is beneficial for a society and its individuals.[1] This book examines the great social challenge the European Union (EU) currently faces and asks how the Union can secure social cohesion in the aftermath of the economic crisis and large immigration. In this context, there are lessons to be learned from research on social trust. Yet what factors create or erode social trust and social cohesion remains debated. At the aggregate level, a high level of *civic participation* has been identified as a source of social trust. However, this explanation has been questioned by another group of scholars who have instead pointed to the importance of the *quality of government institutions* in building social trust. Yet others have pointed to a negative effect of *ethnic diversity* on social trust and hence on social cohesion. It has also been proposed that *social and economic inequality* may have a negative effect on social trust.

Building on these previous analyses, this study makes several noteworthy contributions to our understanding of the formation of social trust and social cohesion. First, while comparative empirical research on trust has blossomed in recent years, it has been confined to the country level, which implies that little is known about how much trust varies within countries, at the regional level. While several analyses investigate trust patterns at the regional or municipal level in a single country (Putnam 1993, 2007; Alesina and La Ferrara 2005; Letki 2008), the question has not been investigated in a multi-country context. We address this gap using original data collected by the authors to explore both generalized trust and institutional quality based on two almost identical large-scale surveys.[2] The first survey, which was carried out in 2010, included about 34,000 respondents in 172 regions in 24 EU member states (Charron et al. 2013). The second survey was carried out in 2013 and consists of data from some 85,000 respondents in 189 regions in 25 European countries. In total, more than 120,000 respondents have been interviewed, making this the largest empirical investigation on this topic conducted so far.[3] Combining our survey data with register data for the various regions in the European countries gives us unique opportunities to analyze the effects of several competing explanations of social trust. Moreover, Europe offers an excellent test case due to its remarkable variation in trust at the national level (Hooghe et al. 2009); with our new combination of survey and register data, we show significant variations in trust at the sub-national level as well, particularly in Italy, Germany, Belgium, Spain, and France. We can demonstrate that inferences about trust at the regional level are more precise than national-level comparisons. Moreover, sub-national, between-country comparisons provide many advantages, as they increase the number of observations, provide inherent natural controls, and strengthen causal inferences (Snyder 2001).

Before proceeding with our analyses, we present the relevant literature on factors said to increase social trust and strengthen social cohesion. After outlining our specific contribution to this debate, we present our novel data, which constitute to our knowledge the most comprehensive survey to date on social trust and quality of government (QoG). Our results indicate that QoG is far and away the strongest predictor of regional variations in social trust that we have found. We also find that experiences with corruption erode trust much more in high-QoG regions than in those with lower QoG. We conclude with a discussion and suggestions for future research.

WHAT CREATES OR DESTROYS SOCIAL TRUST?

While the positive effects of high levels of social trust have become generally accepted, several factors relating to how trust is generated have been much debated and become quite controversial. The first, and to a large extent still dominating, view is that social trust is generated by civic participation. Putnam's studies emphasized that citizens learn to develop social trust and understand the importance of positive reciprocity by participating in voluntary associations (Putnam 1993, 2000). According to this society-centered, Tocquevillian approach, the capacity of a society to produce social capital and social trust is determined by citizens' activity in voluntary associations.

However, a large number of studies over the last decades have called into question the effect of civic participation and voluntary associations on social trust. While it is true that people who are joiners also generally trust others more, this seems to be an effect of self-selection; people who score high on the social ability to trust and cooperate with others join voluntary associations disproportionately, but activity in such organizations does not increase the individuals' social trust. Rather, association members become more trusting only of their fellow members, and they cooperate more only for group purposes (Uslaner 2002; Stolle 2003). Thus, the notion that associational membership creates social capital has not survived empirical testing (Claiborn and Martin 2000; Delhey and Newton 2003; Wollebæck and Selle 2003; Armony 2004; Herreros 2004; Robbins 2011; Dinesen 2013). To take one example, researchers conducting a large-scale empirical study drawing on World Values Study survey data from no less than sixty countries to explain variations in social trust concluded that "perhaps most important and most surprising, none of the four measures of voluntary activity stood up to statistical tests, in spite of the importance attached to them in a large body of writing, from de Tocqueville onwards" (Delhey and Newton 2004, 27).

As an alternative to the society-centered approach, the institution-centered accounts of social capital theory claim that if it is to flourish, social trust must be embedded in and linked to the political context as well as to formal political and legal institutions (Berman 1997; Encarnación 2003; Rothstein and Uslaner 2005; Rothstein and Eek 2009; Kumlin and Rothstein 2010; Richey 2010; Robbins 2011; You 2012; Villoria et al. 2013). According to this line of thinking, it is trustworthy, uncorrupt, honest, and impartial government institutions that exercise public power and implement public policies fairly that create social trust and increase social cohesion. For example, Delhey and Newton found that "government, especially corruption free and democratic government, seems to set a structure in which individuals are able to act in a trustworthy manner and not suffer, and in which they can reasonably expect that most others will generally do the same" (2004, 28). Using survey data from European countries, Serritzlew et al. (2014) concluded that a low level of corruption is strongly correlated with a high level of social trust. Analysing conclusions from their study, also based on comparative survey data, Freitag and Buhlmann (2005) concluded that political institutions that support norms of fairness, universality, and the division of power contribute to the formation of interpersonal trust.

Using scenario experiments in low-trust, high-corruption Romania and in high-trust, low-corruption Sweden, Rothstein and Eek (2009) found that persons from both countries who experience corruption among public healthcare workers or the local police when traveling in an "unknown city and unfamiliar country" lose trust not only in these authorities but also in people in the unknown society in general. Rothstein and Eek's theory for the causal mechanism between corruption and social trust is that since people cannot really know if "most people" in an unknown society can be trusted, they have to use some kind of shortcut or heuristic to determine how much to trust. Thus, people make inferences from the behavior of public officials when forming beliefs about to what extent people in a society can be trusted. Moreover, if local public officials are known to be dishonest, corrupt, discriminatory, or unfair, many people will make a second inference – namely, that in order to get by in a society with dishonest public officials, ordinary people also have to engage in various forms of dishonest behavior (corruption, nepotism, favoritism) and because of this they cannot be trusted.

A major issue in the social trust, social cohesion, and social capital literature has to do with ethnic diversity. The initial positive view of the many good effects of social trust has been challenged by findings showing that societies with a high level of ethnic diversity tend to have lower social trust and that diversity may erode social cohesion (Alesina and La Ferrara 2005; Putnam 2007; Schaeffer 2013). The logic behind this argument is fairly straightforward. People trust other people whom they perceive as ethnically similar to themselves but they distrust people whom they perceive as ethnically different. Some economic studies claim that ethnic diversity, through its negative effects on social trust and social cohesion, explains why many poor countries fail to produce the public goods necessary for social and economic development (Easterly and Levine 1997; Habyarimana et al. 2007). Putnam (2007) and Alesina and La Ferrara (2002) have also reported evidence of this relationship at the sub-national level for the United States. Others have claimed that the increasing ethnic diversity in western Europe will diminish social cohesion, making redistribution to various welfare state programs more difficult (Alesina et al. 2001; Eger 2010). This argument has not gone without criticism and several studies have pointed out that ethnic diversity does not necessarily destroy social trust, or only does so under specific conditions (Freitag and Traunmuller 2009; Gesthuizen et al. 2009; Banting 2010; Kumlin and Rothstein 2010; Uslaner 2012; Dinesen 2013; Banting and Kymlicka 2017). Economic inequality and residential segregation have been offered by Uslaner (2012) as alternative explanations for the deterioration of social trust.

In a recent meta-analysis of the research about ethnic diversity and social cohesion that looked at no less than 480 empirical findings from 172 studies, Schaeffer (2013) showed that many studies about this controversial issue come to different conclusions. This inconclusiveness, according to him, arises from variations in research design, such as which region of the world is examined, what type of ethnic diversity is scrutinized, and what indicators are used to measure social cohesion. Schaeffer points out that while there is a slight overweight for confirmatory studies, discipline matters a lot. Many more studies published in economics journals confirm the negative effect of ethnic diversity on social cohesion than studies published in political science or sociology journals. However, Schaeffer also shows that for the 58 studies that have social trust as the dependent variable in the analysis, the results are close to a draw: 30 empirical results refute and 28 corroborate the hypothesis that ethnic diversity is a negative indicator for social trust (Schaeffer 2013, 27–31). Thus, it seems fair to say that the verdict is still out.

MEASURING SOCIAL TRUST BY COUNTRY AND REGION AND EXPLORING VARIATION AT BOTH LEVELS

To capture social trust, we take advantage of a regional QoG survey carried out in 2013 (see Charron et al. 2015).[4] The survey samples at what is known in the vocabulary of the EU as NUTS 1 and NUTS 2 levels. We looked at NUTS regions in 22 European states,[5] including between 400 and 450 respondents for each such region. The trust question was asked in the standard format used in previous studies, such as the World Values Survey: "Generally speaking, would you say that most people can be trusted or that you can't be too careful in dealing with people in your area?"[6]

Figure 10.1 highlights the distribution of social trust by country level[7] and shows regional variation around each country estimate. Our first result is that social trust varies remarkably across, as well as within, European states. Moreover, while national contexts do matter a great deal, as shown by the consistent clustering of regions around countries, the differences between regions within many EU countries are noteworthy and clearly demonstrate the limits of previous national-level analyses.

While the grand sample mean score for trust is 0.425, we also find noteworthy national-level variation, as many earlier studies have shown. While Scandinavian states display very high levels of social trust, several EU member countries, like France and Poland, display surprisingly low levels. To some degree, social trust appears to be determined by geography or history (that is, western vs. eastern Europe), yet we observe that some of the "old" western EU countries such as France, Greece, Portugal, and Belgium have no regions where more than half of the respondents state they are "trusters" (with a trust score above 0.5, as shown by the dashed line in Figure 10.1). At the country level, the vast majority of respondents in Sweden and Denmark, as well as in the United Kingdom, Finland, Austria, Ireland, and the Netherlands, say that they trust others, yet social trust is extremely low in several other European states. For example, in Hungary, Greece, Bulgaria, and most regions in France, less than 30 percent of respondents say that they feel they can trust others. In the Czech Republic, Slovakia, and Serbia, this number drops below 20 percent. When we compare these data with other recent empirical analyses, we find our country-level estimates to be highly consistent with those from alternative data sources.[8]

The regional-level variation across Europe is striking, with trust scores ranging from 0.08 (for the *Východné Slovensko* region in Slovakia) to a stunning 0.80 (the Copenhagen region in Denmark). This means that, at the extreme, the difference in social trust between regions in Europe is tenfold. Moreover, several countries, such as Italy, Spain, Germany, Austria, France, and Belgium, have noteworthy regional variation in social trust within the country, while others, such as Slovakia, Denmark, and Poland, do not.

In Germany, the region with the highest level of social trust, Schleswig-Holstein, is among the top 10 percent in our full sample of regions, with a vast majority of respondents claiming that they can trust others. But in Saarland, a German region close to France, the trust score is far below the sample average, with less than 34 percent of respondents feeling that they can trust others. We find a similarly large gap in Italy, with Friuli Venezia-Guilia and Bolzano in the north showing quite high levels of social trust while Campania in the *mezzogiorno* south stands out as relatively low. Germany and Italy both have regions that have the same levels of social trust or higher as those found in Finland, Austria, or the United Kingdom, while several regions in these countries have lower social trust indicators than regions in Portugal, Romania, Spain, Belgium, or Poland – all countries with noticeably lower levels of trust at the national level. Spain and Belgium also have noteworthy variation, with social trust in Flanders almost twice as high as it is in Wallonia. For Spain, the majority of respondents in the País Vasco region trust others (54 percent), while less than 38 percent do in the Canarias or Murcia regions.

While regional-level comparisons are more scarce, these findings are generally consistent with previous studies that have explored social trust at the regional level in Europe (Beugelsdijk and Van Schaik 2005; Tabellini 2010) and correlate rather strongly with the most recent round of the European Values Survey (EVS) at the regional level. To provide a further test of external validity, we gathered trust data from the latest round of the EVS (2008), which is available at the same regional level we used and which uses the exact same trust question we have. We find that among the 182 regions our data and the EVS have in common, the Spearman rank coefficient is 0.58. However, many regions in the EVS data have insufficient observations (less than 100); when comparing only regions that have at least 100 observations in the EVS (117 total), the Spearman rank coefficient increases to 0.70. When comparing the 68 regions that have at least 200 observations in the EVS, the Spearman rank increases to 0.79, demonstrating that the estimates begin to converge as the sample size increases, which provides evidence of external validity for our measure. However, we would argue that the data we have collected are more

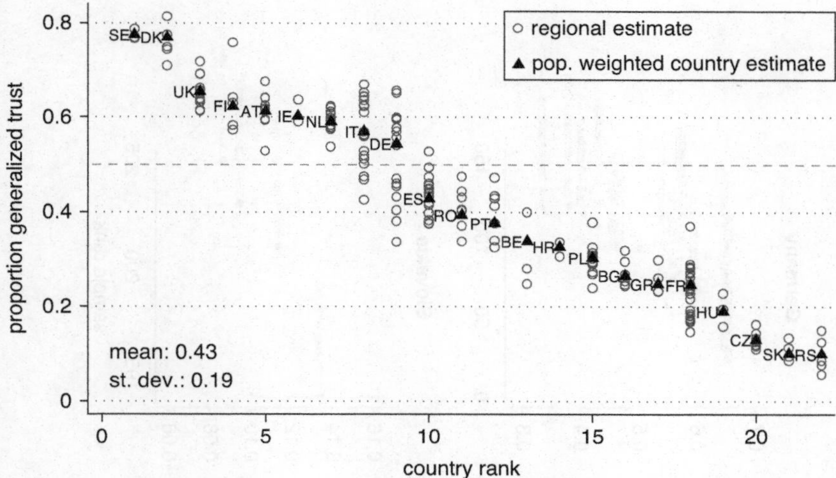

Figure 10.1 Generalized trust in 22 European countries and regional variation

representative and thus more reliable than regional data used in previous studies, as the sample size per region we have is more than twice that of the EVS or the World Values Survey.[9] Our survey also has the advantage of having data points from the same year, as opposed to the other surveys, which have data merged in rounds of two- to three-year periods.

To test whether any pairwise within-country regional differences are significant, we constructed confidence intervals (95 percent) around each region's estimate.[10] In 13 of the 22 countries we examined, there is at least one pairwise distinction, while in 9 of the countries, there is no pairwise significant difference between any of the regions. In Figure 10.2, we highlight the three countries with the most and the three with the least regional variation in generalized trust, showing highly significant variation in Belgium, Italy, and Germany, and none in Sweden, the Netherlands, and Slovakia.

How much of the total variation in generalized trust is explained at the regional and country levels? To calculate this, we ran an empty ("intercept only") hierarchical model with the regional level of trust as the dependent variable, accounting for country-level random intercepts. The results demonstrate that the regional level accounts for 22 percent and the country level accounts for 78 percent of the geographical variation in generalized trust in Europe. Thus, although the country context is highly relevant, a sizeable portion of the variation is left unexplained if one ignores the regional level,

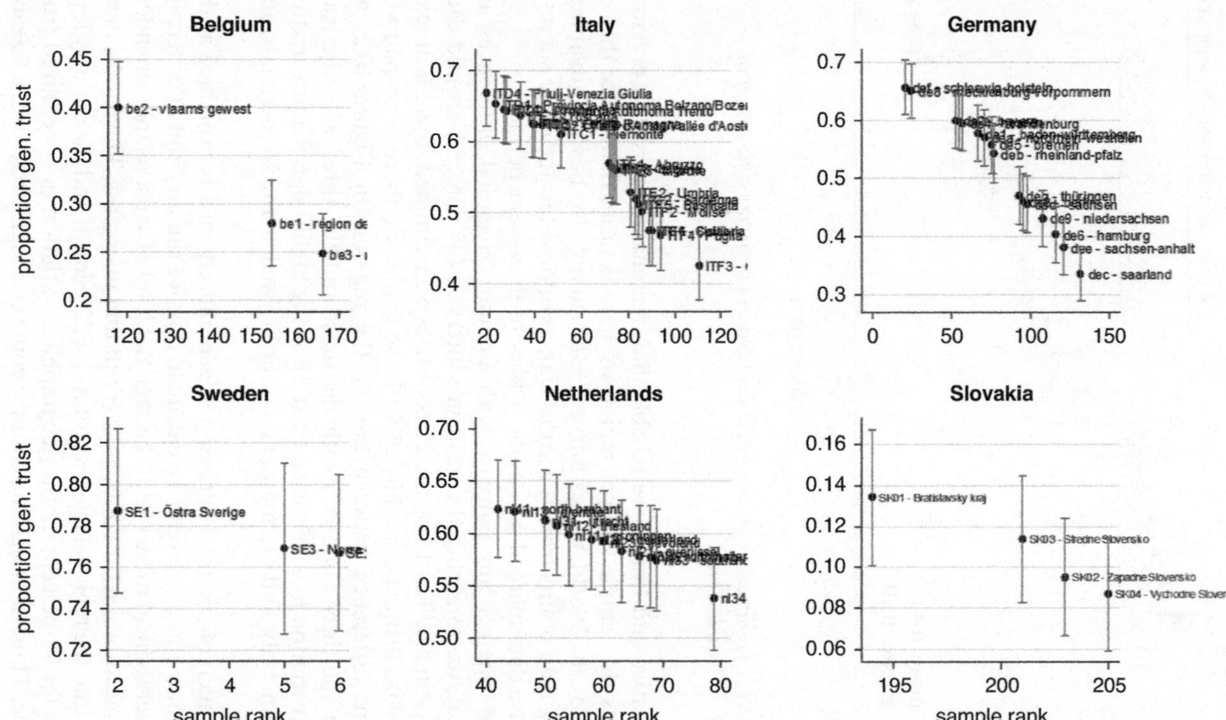

Figure 10.2 Regional variation in generalized trust in six countries

particularly in those states with high levels of within-country variation, such as Germany, Italy, and Belgium.

REGIONAL-LEVEL DIFFERENCES IN SOCIAL TRUST: EXPLANATORY VARIABLES AND METHODS

In this section, we model statistically several leading explanations of social trust. While register and survey data at the sub-national level is growing in relevance, it still cannot compare in terms of scope and availability to national-level register and survey data; thus, we are somewhat limited in our selection of indicators. Below we describe how our key concepts are operationalized.

a. *Quality of public-sector institutions.* For this variable (QoG), we use the survey we carried out in 2010, from which we calculated a regional score labeled the European Quality of Government Index (EQI; Charron et al. 2014). Using the earlier data set ensures that the data on social trust and the data on experiences and perceptions of institutional quality are not from the same respondents, avoiding the problem of simultaneity. It is also an advantage that the measure of this independent variable precedes the measure of the dependent variable (social trust). The EQI measure captures the extent to which regional public services are impartial, of high quality, and free from corruption, based on the experiences and perceptions of our citizen-respondents. To maximize the importance of the regional level, the data focus on services primarily administered or financed by sub-national actors, such as public education, public health services, and law enforcement. The survey also included questions about the extent to which regional elections were perceived as being free from corruption and the level of perceived political impartiality in the regional mass media. From this, we created a regional index for the survey as a whole as well as for several sub-components, such as impartiality and corruption.[11]
b. *Economic inequality*. While inequality measures such as the Gini index, the Theil index, 90/10 or 80/20 ratios of income earners, or median-to-mean income are now widely available at the national level, such measures are unfortunately scarcer at the sub-national level for the wide sample of countries. Fortunately, one valid measure is available for all regions in our sample – the percentage of the population at risk of poverty (after social transfers) from Eurostat. This at-risk-of-poverty measure is calculated as having "equivalised

disposable income (i.e. adjusted for household size and composition) of less than 60% of national median" (EU Commission 2010).[12] While this does not show the extent to which the very rich are wealthier than the middle class, it represents a clear and comparable measure of the extent to which economic inequality affects those at the bottom of the income ladder across regions.

c. *Voluntary civic participation and social networks*. We capture civic participation and social networks with two measures. First, taking survey data from the latest round of the EVS (2008), we combined six relevant questions about voluntary civic participation into one index.[13] For each of the six items, we took the aggregate proportion of "yes" responses and, after obtaining weights from a principle component factor analysis (PCFA), we combined the six items into a single index (the *civic index*) for each region.[14] The index ranges from 0 (no participation) to 1 (full participation in all activities).

   Second, we use the voter turnout in regional parliamentary elections, averaged for all available electoral data from 1990 to 2010. Since these are not national elections, they give an even better sense of how much civic engagement can vary from region to region as well as how engaged citizens are in local politics.

d. *Ethnic diversity*. While most data on population heterogeneity is available only at the national level, the extent to which regions are ethnically homogenous or heterogeneous is captured with two measures. First, we employ a measure from Eurostat, the percentage of each region's population born outside of the EU. This measure is constructed by adding together all residents of each included region who were born in Africa, Asia, the Americas, and Oceana and dividing them over the region's total resident population. To capture the degree to which ethnic heterogeneity varies by region, we take the measure of regional ethnic diversity from Alesina and Zhuravskaya (2011), calculating the percentage of the population that belongs to the main ethnic group for each region. While the first measure is comprehensive, the second is limited to roughly 90 regions in the sample.

We also include in our analysis several other structural factors elucidated by the literature, including a measure of the extent to which politics in a region is polarized or competitive. From regional elections data,[15] we calculated several measures of elite, political competition. First, we capture the extent to which regional parliamentary elections are competitive, based on a common measure from the literature on party competition, the vote percentage difference between the two largest parties in a given election (Jackman 1987).[16] Second, we created a regional measure of party fractionalization. This is calculated using a Herfindal index, which essentially elucidates the likelihood of randomly drawing out two members of parliament (MPs) of the same political party, with scores ranging from 0 to 1. A score of 0 indicates that all MPs are of different parties, while a score of 1 indicates that all MPs belong to the same party. On this scale, we take "1-Herfindal" to render higher numbers equaling more fractionalization.

Finally, in keeping our model as parsimonious as possible, we control for the level of economic development, captured by taking the average logged GDP (PPP), per capita income (averaged) for 2007–2009 (Eurostat). We also control for region size, in terms of both population and area, using a measure of population density (Eurostat) from 2010, logged. We expect from previous research that higher development is associated with higher trust, while more-urban areas will have lower levels of trust on average. Further, we check whether a region being a capital or whether it is autonomous or not (0/1) plays a role in determining variation in levels of regional trust.[17]

Our trust variable is available for 25 European countries, however, Ukraine, Turkey, Kosovo and Serbia are dropped from most models due to the limitations of register data at the regional level. For models testing QoG, inequality, and diversity, we have between 181 and 189 regions in 21 countries. Data on civic engagement are more limited, and several countries drop out, reducing the number of regions in these models.

Moreover, the political and administrative relevance of the NUTS regions varies by country. In some cases, such as Spain, Belgium, Denmark, Poland, and Germany, the regional level in the data corresponds directly with politically meaningful units that have elected parliaments and exercise policy control over several areas, such as healthcare and education. Others, however, such as the NUTS units in Sweden, Bulgaria, Romania, and Portugal, are simply statistical units whose borders are drawn by the EU Commission. We check the results via limited samples that include only politically relevant regions (*prr*), which are coded as all regions in Italy, Germany, Spain, Denmark, Belgium, Poland, France, and Austria; three regions from the United Kingdom (Scotland, Wales, and Northern Ireland); and two from Portugal (Açores and Madeira). When testing the variables of political fractionalization and competitiveness along with civic engagement, we have data only for politically relevant regions, which reduces the number of participating regions to 125.

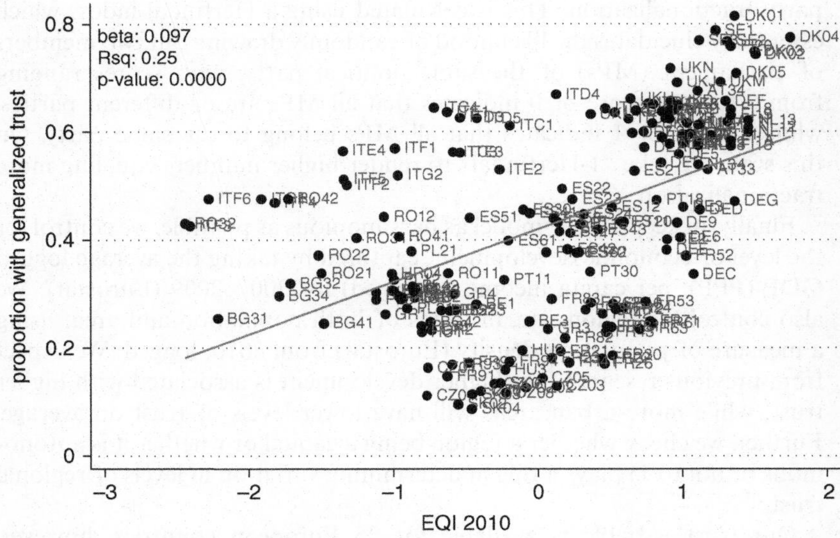

Figure 10.3 Institutional quality and generalized trust in European regions

RESULTS

Figure 10.3 shows the scatterplot and a fitted linear relationship between the two variables. The scatterplot confirms the general expectation of a positive and significant relationship between these two factors, with the bivariate regression accounting for 25 percent of the variation in regional trust. We notice, however, that the relationship is not consistent across all values of our EQI, largely due to country effects. Slovak and Czech regions for example, which have EQI scores at or slightly below the mean, have much lower trust scores than the bivariate model would predict. At the other end, several regions in southern Italy have much higher levels of generalized trust than would be predicted by the EQI.

Issues of endogeneity or reverse causality are ever-present in cross-sectional studies, and our study is no exception. Although it is not a perfect remedy, we address this by taking all independent variables temporally prior to our measurement of TRUST. In addition, as Figure 10.3 shows, the data are heterogeneous and diagnostic checks confirm this – in particular for several of the key variables, such as QoG and inequality – with much more variation in the dependent variable at low levels of the key explanatory factors than at high levels. That the observations are not independent can of course be driven by sub-population differences (for example, countries) and can result in biased estimates. We account for this in the models, electing to model the data in two ways – hierarchically as well as with country-fixed effects in OLS estimation, both reported in Table 10.1.

Overall, our main finding is that there is strong and consistent support for the hypothesized relationship between institutional quality and social trust. Controlling for the region's level of economic development and population size (density, logged), we find that the marginal effect of a one standard deviation increase in the EQI results in an expected increase in regional social trust of 4 percent, holding all other variables constant. Economic development and population density are significant positive and negative predictors, respectively, of regional variation in trust.

In our study, we also examine if other factors are systematically related with levels of trust at the regional level in Europe. While diversity's effect is in the negative direction, that effect becomes negligible when controlling for economic development, population size, and QoG. We do find however that the measure of economic inequality is a significant predictor of levels of trust. For example, an increase of 10 percent in the regional poverty risk results in an expected decrease in social trust of 2.3 percent. Our measure of civic participation also has a slight positive effect on trust levels. We find that even when re-estimating the results with country-fixed effects, the findings are mostly indistinguishable from the results reported above, with the exception of the coefficient estimate of civic participation, which becomes insignificant. In addition, we run a number of robustness checks whereby we use alternative measures of our concepts, use various weights for the observations, remove outliers, and estimate only regions in countries that have sizeable trust gaps (see the Appendix, Table 10.A2). The effect of QoG on social trust, however, is significant at the 99 percent level of confidence throughout all the models.

THE QUALITY OF PUBLIC INSTITUTIONS MATTERS FOR SOCIAL COHESION

Social trust has been shown to be a highly relevant and beneficial societal characteristic. In this study, we make two significant contributions to the literature explaining variations in social trust and social cohesion. First, we present the most comprehensive data on social trust available to date for European countries and regions. When mapping generalized trust at and below the country level, we find significant variation that has been overlooked by previous data limitations that have driven country-level analyses. While we find the country-level analyses remain highly relevant, regional

Table 10.1 The effect of institutions on trust in EU regions

	Hierarchical estimation w/ random country slopes				OLS estimation w/ country fixed effects			
	1	2	3	4	5	6	7	8
EQI (2010)	0.04***	0.04***	0.03***	0.05***	0.04***	0.04***	0.02***	0.05***
	(4.93)	(4.44)	(2.96)	(3.67)	(5.25)	(4.84)	(2.77)	(4.53)
Diversity (nonEUbrn)		−0.006				−0.007		
		(−0.95)				(−1.12)		
Econ. Inequality			−0.002***				−0.003***	
			(−2.91)				(−3.88)	
Civic participation				0.31*				0.28
				(1.75)				(0.97)
PPP per capita(log)	0.08***	0.09***	0.05***	0.10***	0.09***	0.08***	0.03*	0.10***
	(5.63)	(5.26)	(2.77)	(3.53)	(4.56)	(4.63)	(1.74)	(3.62)
Pop. Density (log)	−0.01**	−0.01**	−0.01**	−0.04	−0.01**	−0.01**	−0.01**	−0.04
	(−2.64)	(−2.34)	−2.49)	(−1.21)	(−2.65)	(−2.25)	(−2.31)	(−1.26)
Constant	−0.37**	−0.41**	0.01	−0.47*	−0.27**	−0.31**	0.13	−0.47**
	(−2.52)	(−2.48)	(0.06)	(−1.86)	(−2.02)	(−2.25)	(0.78)	(−2.01)
Obs	189	183	181	111	189	182	181	111
Countries	21	20	20	9	21	20	20	9
Rsq.					0.94	0.94	0.95	0.91
Root MSE					0.046	0.047	0.044	0.051
Log likelihood	269.6	257.8	261.7	156.1				
Sigma	0.14	0.15	0.16	0.13				
Residual	0.05	0.05	0.05	0.05				
Interclass correlation (IC)	0.89	0.90	0.91	0.87				

Note: Dependent variable is generalized trust from 2013 (0–1). Z-scores and t-scores in parentheses. For models 1–4, IC is calculated as the squared standard deviation of the random country intercepts over the squared regional residual + the squared standard deviation of the random country intercepts, and ranges from 0–1, with low scores indicating little relevance for the 2nd level (country) random effects. ***p<0.01, **p<0.05, *p<0.10.

variation represents a significant minority of the overall spatial variation in trust across Europe – in particular in several (mostly federal) countries, such as Belgium, Germany, Italy, and Spain. Moreover, we find significant regional differences even in non-federal countries, such as France, Poland, and even Romania and Portugal, suggesting that sub-national patterns of social trust are not determined exclusively by the boundaries of sub-national political units.

Second, using our novel data, we test several of the main theoretical propositions regarding what explains variations in social trust. Our argument is that testing even established theories at multiple levels is salient for developing stronger empirical relationships and ruling out potential issues of spuriousness. We tested the theory of the relation between the QoG and social trust against several other theoretical propositions (such as the effects of economic inequality, civic participation, ethnic diversity, and political environment). Our central finding is that QoG is a highly robust predictor of aggregate levels of social trust at the regional level, both within and across countries. We show that the results are highly robust to multiple model specifications, alternative measures of the concepts, observation weights, and various sample specifications.

Previous research at the national level has found support for the theory that low-corruption, high-QoG institutions are associated with higher levels of social trust across countries; that argument is strengthened by these findings at the sub-national level. We would argue that the regional lens we have used is the preferred test for several reasons, most significantly that cultural and institutional differences that are difficult to capture in cross-country tests are naturally controlled for when comparing regions within countries.

We also confirm results from several other studies showing that activity and membership in voluntary associations have negligible effects on the propensity for individuals to trust other people. More surprising is that the effects of ethnic diversity on social trust turns out to be negligible when controlling for QoG. Since all the studies we have seen that have shown a negative effect of ethnic diversity on social trust have left out variables measuring institutional quality, our finding is of some importance. This study has thus taken an additional step in furthering our understanding of spatial variations in generalized trust across and within countries.

However, our measure of economic inequality remained a robust indicator of generalized trust along with QoG, suggesting that the two factors are relevant at the country as well as sub-national levels. As for shedding light on future theory, based on experimental research about the importance of reciprocity for social solidarity and social cohesion (Henrich 2004; Gintis et al. 2005; Svallfors 2013), we would suggest an explanation for the importance of QoG for social trust in regions along the following lines. If a person living in an EU region with low QoG experiences an influx of immigrants from either inside or outside Europe, this person may come to think that because QoG is low, the new residents will get away with various types of opportunistic behavior, such as tax avoidance and overuse or abuse of social services. Thus, people in general cannot be seen as worthy of trust. However, if QoG in the region is high, the same person may think that although the newcomers are "different," because of high institutional quality they are likely to follow the rules; thus, most people in these high-QoG regions are more likely to think that most people in general, including the newcomers, can be trusted.

To conclude, we suggest that the EU and its member countries need to focus on improving the quality of public-sector institutions and fighting corruption if social cohesion is to be enhanced. Although this is not an easy fix, according to our results it is the best way to bridge the growing prosperity gap and handle the increased socio-economic inequality in Europe.

NOTES

1. But see Berman (1997) and Satyanath et al. (2013).
2. The data are in the public domain and can be found at the homepage of the Quality of Government Institute at University of Gothenburg (www.qog.pol.gu.se).
3. Funding for this research comes in part from the European Commission's Seventh Annual Framework Programme.
4. For a description of the survey, codebook, and access to the data, please see http://qog.pol.gu.se/QoG-institutet/data/nedladdningsbaradatamängder/qogeuregionaldata.
5. NUTS stands for "nomenclature of territorial units for statistics"; more can be read about them at http://epp.eurostat.ec.europa.eu/portal/page/portal/nuts_nomenclature/introduction.
6. At the individual level, the response "Most people can be trusted" is coded as 1 and "Can't be too careful" is coded as 0. At the regional level, we take the proportion of respondents who answered, "Most people can be trusted" over those who answered, "Can't be too careful," such that aggregate responses over 0.5 indicate that the majority of people in a region believe that most people can be trusted, while a result less than 0.5 indicates that a majority believes that one "can't be too careful." The measure is continuous and bound between 0 and 1.
7. Country levels are calculated as a population-weighted average of the regional-level scores for each country. Population data by region taken from Eurostat.
8. For example, two recent studies employ a European, or largely European sample (Freitag and Buhlmann 2009; Hooghe et al. 2009). The Spearman rank coefficients between our common countries and theirs are 0.85 and 0.86, respectively.
9. Using EVS data instead of ours for the 189 regions in common with our study would result in about 40,000 fewer individual observations (31,368 compared with 72,800) or an average regional N of 175 compared with 410 for our study.
10. Our estimate is a proportion (p) of trust per region; thus, the formula to construct the standard error is se = $\sqrt{\frac{(p(1-p)}{n}}$. In most cases, n is roughly 400. The standard error

is then added to 1.96 and added/subtracted from each region's estimate of trust to calculate the 95 percent confidence interval.

11. For purposes of robustness, we employ an alternative "hard measure" that captures public-sector institutional quality more broadly. While there is no perfect measure available to capture this concept, as a proxy for the quality and effectiveness of regional public-sector institutions, we take a measure of health outcomes that is commonly associated with quality health services, namely the average life expectancy from less than one year old, averaged for the five-year period 2008–2012. The measure is then standardized (as is the EQI). The correlation between the EQI measure and life expectancy is 0.48 (p=0.0000, n=206). A possible alternative might have been aggregate student scores on math, reading, and science in the international PISA tests, but these are not available at the regional level in most countries.
12. Comparing this measure to a recent study that constructed several measures of inequality for regions within four countries – France, the Czech Republic, Italy, and Spain – we find that the measure of the population in poverty correlates very highly with the median/mean income measure (between 0.81 and 0.94 in the four countries).
13. The six participation items were captured in the EVS in a single question: "Which, if any, do you belong to? A) Political parties or groups B) Religious or church organizations C) Education, arts, music or cultural activities D) Sports or recreation E) Local community action on issues like poverty, employment, housing, racial equality F) Other groups."
14. The PCFA showed all six components clustered strongly onto one factor (according to the Kaiser criteria), as there was only one factor with an Eigenvalue over 1 and it explained over 60 percent of the total variation.
15. Data taken from http://www.parties-and-elections.eu/.
16. In the case of some regions, primarily in Italy where parties announce other parties with whom they will form a coalition before Election Day, we take the difference between the two largest pre-election coalition blocs.
17. We find, however, that the latter two variables are mostly insignificant factors and fail to improve model strength in a post regression comparison (LR test); thus, they are not reported in the main tables.

REFERENCES

Alesina, Alberto, and Eliana La Ferrara (2002), "Who Trusts Others?", *Journal of Public Economics* **85** (2), 207–234.

Alesina, Alberto, and Eliana La Ferrara (2005), "Ethnic Diversity and Economic Performance", *Journal of Economic Literature* **43** (3), 762–800.

Alesina, Alberto, and Ekaterina Zhuravskaya (2011), "Segregation and the Quality of Government in a Cross Section of Countries", *American Economic Review* **101** (5), 1872–1911.

Alesina, Alberto, Edward L. Glaeser, and Bruce Sacerdote (2001), "Why Doesn't the United States Have a European-Style Welfare State?", Harvard Insitute of Economic Research, Discussion paper 1933.

Armony, Ariel C. (2004), *The Dubious Link: Civic Engagement and Democratization*. Stanford, CA: Stanford University Press.

Banting, Keith G. (2010), "Is There a Progressive's Dilemma in Canada? Immigration, Multiculturalism and the Welfare State", *Canadian Journal of Political Science – Revue Canadienne De Science Politique* **43** (4), 797–820.

Banting, Keith G., and Will Kymlicka (2017), *The Strains of Commitment: The Political Sources of Solidarity in Diverse Societies*. Oxford: Oxford University Press.

Beugelsdijk, S., and T. Van Schaik (2005), "Differences in Social Capital between 54 Western European Regions", *Regional Studies* **39** (8), 1053–1064.

Berman, Sheri (1997), "Civil Society and the Collapse of the Weimar Republic", *World Politics* **49** (3), 401–429.

Bjørnskov, Christian (2009), "Economic Growth", in G. T. Svendsen and G. L. H. Svendsen (eds.), *Handbook of Social Capital*. Cheltenham, UK and Northampton, MA, USA: Edward Elgar Publishing, pp. 337–353.

Castiglione, Dario, Jan van Deth, and Guglielmo Wolleb (eds.) (2008), *Handbook of Social Capital*. Oxford: Oxford University Press.

Charron, Nicholas, Lewis Dijkstra, and Victor Lapuente (2014), "Regional Governance Matters: Quality of Government within European Union Member States", *Regional Studies* **48** (1), 68–90.

Charron, Nicholas, Lewis Dijkstra, and Victor Lapuente (2015), "Mapping the Regional Divide in Europe: A Measure for Assessing Quality of Government in 206 European Regions", *Social Indicators Research* **122** (2), 315–346.

Charron, Nicholas, Victor Lapuente, and Bo Rothstein (2013), *Quality of Government and Corruption from a European Perspective: A Comparative Study of Good Government in EU Regions*. Cheltenham, UK and Northampton, MA, USA: Edward Elgar Publishing.

Claiborn, Michele P., and Paul S. Martin (2000), "Trusting and Joining? An Empirical Test of the Reciprocal Nature of Social Capital", *Political Behavior* **22** (4), 267–291.

Delhey, Jan, and Kenneth Newton (2003), "Who Trusts? The Origins of Social Trust in Seven Societies", *European Societies* **5** (2), 93–137.

Delhey, Jan, and Kenneth Newton (2004), "Social Trust: Global Pattern or Nordic Exceptionalism", Berlin: Wissenschaftszentrum Berlin für Socialforschung.

Delhey, Jan, and Kenneth Newton (2005), "Predicting Cross-National Levels of Social Trust: Global Pattern or Nordic Exceptionalism?", *European Sociological Review* **21** (4), 311–327.

Dinesen, Peter Thisted (2013), "Where You Come From or Where You Live? Examining the Cultural and Institutional Explanation of Generalized Trust Using Migration as a Natural Experiment", *European Sociological Review* **29** (1), 114–128.

Easterly, William, and Ross Levine (1997), "Africa's Growth Tragedy: Policies and Ethnic Divisions", *Quarterly Journal of Economics* **112** (4), 1203–1250.

Eger, Maureen A. (2010), "Even in Sweden: The Effect of Immigration on Support for Welfare State Spending", *European Sociological Review* **26** (2), 203–217.

Encarnación, Omar G. (2003), *The Myth of Civil Society: Social Capital and Democratic Consolidation in Spain and Brazil*. New York: Palgrave Macmillan.

European Commission (2010), *Fifth Report on Economic, Social and Territorial Cohesion – Investing in Europe's Future*. Luxembourg: EU Commission publication.

EVS (2008), *European Values Study 1981–2008, Longitudinal Data File*. GESIS Data Archive, Cologne, ZA4804 Data File Version 2.0.0, doi:10.4232/1.11005.

Freitag, Markus, and Marc Buhlmann (2005), "Political Institutions and the Formation of Social Trust: An International Comparison", *Politische Vierteljahresschrift* **46** (4), 575–586.

Freitag, Markus, and Marc Buhlmann (2009), "Crafting Trust: The Role of Political Institutions in a Comparative Perspective", *Comparative Political Studies* **42** (12), 1537–1566.

Freitag, M., and R. Traunmuller (2009), "Spheres of Trust: An Empirical Analysis of the Foundations of Particularised and Generalised Trust", *European Journal of Political Research* **48** (6), 782–803.

Gesthuizen, Maurice, Tom van der Meer, and Peer Scheepers (2009), "Ethnic Diversity and Social Capital in Europe: Tests of Putnam's Thesis in European Countries", *Scandinavian Political Studies* **32** (2), 121–142.

Gintis, Herbert, Samuel Bowles, Robert Boyd, and Ernst Fehr (eds.) (2005), *Moral Sentiments and Material Interests: The Foundations for Cooperation in Economic Life*. Cambridge, MA: The MIT Press.

Habyarimana, James, Macartan Humphreys, David N. Posner, and Jeremy M. Weinstein (2007), "Why Does Ethnic Diversity Undermine Public Goods Provision?" *American Political Science Review* **101** (4), 709–725.

Helliwell, John F. (2006), "Well-Being, Social Capital and Public Policy: What's New?", *Economic Journal* **116**, C34–C45.

Henrich, Joseph Patrick (2004), *Foundations of Human Sociality: Economic Experiments and Ethnographic Evidence from Fifteen Small-Scale Societies*. Oxford, New York: Oxford University Press.

Herreros, Francisco (2004), *The Problem of Forming Social Capital: Why Trust?* New York: Palgrave Macmillan.

Hooghe, Marc, Tim Reeskens, Dietlind Stolle, and Ann Trappers (2009), "Ethnic Diversity and Generalized Trust in Europe: A Cross-National Multilevel Study", *Comparative Political Studies* **42** (2), 198–223.

Jackman, R. W. (1987), "Political Institutions and Voter Turnout in the Industrial Democracies", *American Political Science Review* **81** (2), 405–423.

Keefer, Philip, and Stephen Knack (2005), "Social Capital, Social Norms and the New Instituitonal Economics", in C. Menard and M. M. Shirley (eds.), *Handbook of New Institutional Economics*. Amsterdam: Springer, pp. 701–725.

Kumlin, Staffan, and Bo Rothstein (2010), "Questioning the New Liberal Dilemma: Immigrants, Social Networks and Institutional Fairness", *Comparative Politics* **41** (1), 63–87.

Letki, Natalia (2008), "Does Diversity Erode Social Cohesion? Social Capital and Race in British Neighbourhoods", *Political Studies* **56** (1), 99–126.

Leung, Ambrose, Cheryl Kier, Tak Fung, Linda Fung, and Robert Sproule (2011), "Searching for Happiness: The Importance of Social Capital", *Journal of Happiness Studies* **12** (3), 443–462.

North, Douglass C. (1998), "Economic Performance through Time", in M. C. Brinton and V. Nee (eds.), *The New Institutionalism in Sociology*. New York: Russell Sage Foundation, pp. 247–257.

Putnam, Robert D. (1993), *Making Democracy Work: Civic Traditions in Modern Italy*. Princeton, NJ: Princeton University Press.

Putnam, Robert D. (2000), *Bowling Alone: The Collapse and Revival of American Community*. New York: Simon and Schuster.

Putnam, Robert D. (2007), "E Pluribus Unum: Diversity and Community in the Twenty-First Century: The 2006 Johan Skytte Prize Lecture", *Scandinavian Political Studies* **30** (2), 137–174.

Richey, Sean (2010), "The Impact of Corruption on Social Trust", *American Politics Research* **38** (4), 676–690.

Robbins, Blaine G. (2011), "Neither Government nor Community Alone: A Test of State-Centered Models of Generalized Trust", *Rationality and Society* **23** (3), 304–346.

Rothstein, Bo (2005), *Social Traps and the Problem of Trust*. Cambridge: Cambridge University Press.

Rothstein, Bo, and Daniel Eek (2009), "Political Corruption and Social Trust: An Experimental Approach", *Rationality and Society* **21** (1), 81–112.

Rothstein, Bo, and Eric M. Uslaner (2005), "All for All: Equality, Corruption and Social Trust", *World Politics* **58** (3), 41–73.

Satyanath, S., N. Voigtlaender and H. J. Voth (2013), "Bowling for Fascism: Social Capital and the Rise of the Nazi Party", NBER Working Paper No. 19201, National Bureau of Economic Research.

Schaeffer, Merlin (2013), "Ethnic Diversity, Public Goods Provision And Social Cohesion: Lessons from an Inconclusive Literature", Berlin: WZB Social Research Center, Discussion paper SP V 2013-103.

Serritzlew, Sören, Kim M. Sonderskov, and Gert T. Svendsen (2014), "Do Corruption and Social Trust Affect Economic Growth? A Review", *Journal of Comparative Policy Analysis* **16** (2), 121–139.

Snyder, R. (2001), "Scaling Down: The Subnational Comparative Method", *Studies in Comparative International Development (SCID)* **36** (1), 93–110.

Stolle, Dietlind (2003), "The Sources of Social Capital", in M. Hooghe and D. Stolle (eds.), *Generating Social Capital: Civil Society and Institutions in a Comparative Perspective*. New York: Palgrave Macmillan, pp. 19–42.

Svallfors, Stefan (2013), "Government Quality, Egalitarianism, and Attitudes to Taxes and Social Spending: A European Comparison", *European Political Science Review* **5** (3), 363–380.

Svendsen, Gert T., and Gunnar L. H. Svendsen (2009), *Handbook of Social Capital: The Troika of Sociology, Political Science and Economics*. Cheltenham, UK and Northampton, MA, USA: Edward Elgar Publishing.

Tabellini, G. (2010), "Culture and Institutions: Economic Development in the Regions of Europe", *Journal of the European Economic Association* **8** (4), 677–716.

Uslaner, Eric M. (2002), *The Moral Foundation of Trust*. New York: Cambridge University Press.

Uslaner, Eric M. (2008), *Corruption, Inequality, and the Rule of Law: The Bulging Pocket Makes the Easy Life*. Cambridge: Cambridge University Press.

Uslaner, Eric M. (2012), *Segregation and Mistrust: Diversity, Isolation, and Social Cohesion*. Cambridge: Cambridge University Press.

Villoria, Manuel, Gregg G. Van Ryan, and Cecilia F. Lavena (2013), "Social and Political Consequences of Administrative Corruption: A Study of Public Perceptions in Spain", *Public Administration Review* **73** (1), 85–94.

Wollebæck, Dag, and Per Selle (2003), "Participation and Social Capital Formation: Norway in a Comparative Perspective", *Scandinavian Political Studies* **26** (1), 67–91.

You, Jong-sun (2012), "Social Trust: Fairness Matters More than Homogeneity", *Political Psychology* **33** (5), 701–721.

APPENDIX

Table 10.A1 *Summary statistics*

Variable	Obs	Mean	Std. Dev.	Min	Max	Source
TRUST	212	0.43	0.191	0.06	0.81	Charron et al. (2015)
EQI (2010)	189	0.12	0.942	−2.44	1.75	Charron et al. (2013)
noneuborn	183	5.64	5.400	0.00	30.06	Eurostat
lognonEUbrn	182	0.97	1.630	−3.91	3.40	Eurostat (author created)
civicindex	111	0.06	0.051	0.00	0.25	European Value Survey, (author created)
STlifeex	189	0.00	1.000	−2.53	1.39	Eurostat (author created)
povrisk	181	16.17	6.713	4.90	38.40	Eurostat
loggdp	189	9.89	0.627	7.95	11.01	Eurostat
LogPopDens	189	2.50	1.647	−0.02	8.49	Eurostat
autonomous	212	0.08	0.279	0.00	1.00	author coded
capitalreg~n	212	0.11	0.318	0.00	1.00	author coded

Table 10.A2 *Robustness checks*

	Alteration	QoG measure	beta	s.e.	ci_low	ci_high	n
1	prr only	EQI10	0.032	0.013	0.0065	0.057	125
2	alt civ part (turnout)	EQI10	0.027	0.013	0.0001	0.052	122
3	alt civ part (party comp.)	EQI10	0.031	0.015	0.0002	0.062	91
4	alt diversity (A & Z)	EQI10	0.042	0.022	−0.001	0.086	91
5	none	life_exp	0.030	0.011	0.0062	0.052	181
6	prr only	life_exp	0.040	0.017	0.002	0.068	125
7	remove outliers	EQI10	0.028	0.007	0.011	0.04	170
8	remove outliers	life_exp	0.027	0.009	0.008	0.045	170
9	pop. Weights*	EQI10	0.018	0.008	0.0002	0.035	181
10	pop. Weights*	life_exp	0.028	0.011	0.005	0.05	181
11	gini weights*	EQI10	0.025	0.009	0.0064	0.043	181
12	gini weights*	life_exp	0.033	0.015	0.0036	0.063	181
13	no non-sig pairwise diff.*	EQI10	0.026	0.009	0.0063	0.044	131
14	no non-sig pairwise diff.	life_exp	0.028	0.014	0.0004	0.056	131
15	no non-sig pairwise diff.	EQI10	0.027	0.011	0.004	0.050	131

Note: "Prr" is "politically relevant regions." "Alt" implies alternative measures from Table 10.A1. * Model was run with OLS estimation and country fixed effects. All other models use a hierarchical specification with the regions nested in countries. "Ci_low" and "ci_high" are the low and high estimates for the estimated coefficient for the QoG variable calculated from the standard error.

Index